Endorsements for *Regulating the Psyc*

If you've ever asked: 'Why doesn't the psycho-e.
this book will answer your questions. Denis Po
and dynamically informed. It also possesses the (
practice today: clarity, logic, and a rigorous pas
vocational fires rekindled.
Christopher J. Coulson, MAHPP, psychotherapist and counsellor, one-time delegate
to the UKCP

I am very grateful for this intelligent, passionate, well researched, and carefully documented
book which underlines the dangers of a fear-based state regulated approach to evaluating
clinical practice and preventing abuse. As an American, coming from a culture that is
dominated with this approach but full of abuse, I have hitherto been impressed with the
comparatively high level of integrity of the practitioners of the UK. The higher fear level
does not eliminate abuse, but has instead begun to restrict our creativity, breadth of
approaches and ability to heal.
Dina Glouberman, co-founder Skyros Holidays, and international imagework trainer

Denis Postle has kept his finger on the pulse of the psychotherapy regulation saga in the
UK for going on 20 years and this comprehensive collection of his writings on the matter
is a detailed guide to the convoluted twists and turns of a misguided project. Writing in
an engaging and accessible style, he brings wit and insight to bear on an obscure business
and exposes its true nature for those willing to see it.
Richard Mowbray, The Open Centre, author of *The Case Against Psychotherapy*
Registration: A Conservation Issue for the Human Potential Movement

What kind of relationship ought counsellors and psychotherapists to have with the
organisations that represent them? Codes of ethics and practice are noticeably silent in
this regard. For the last ten years Denis Postle has hosted a website dedicated to scrutinising
the dynamics of professionalisation. He has collated the material that has come his way,
examined it, probed it and asked questions of it. In doing so he has performed an
invaluable service for both his colleagues and the public at large. This collection provides
startling evidence of muddle and incompetence, of a blatant disregard of evidence and
research, and of the active search for power, status and money at the expense of integrity
and good practice. All counsellors and psychotherapists who want to know what has
been—and is being—done in their name should study it carefully.
Arthur Musgrave, IPN, and BACP accredited counsellor and supervisor

Denis Postle has struggled for a lifetime to demonstrate, in his conduct and his writing,
there is nothing remotely unusual about the best kind of counselling. Decency, respect for
others and kindness are what are required. Meanwhile, the ever growing professional
world of counselling seeks respect (and good pay packets) through appeals for
accountability, complicated practitioner guidelines and their Holy Grail—registration.
If you value a humane approach to counselling others, read as much Postle as you can.
If you seek a counsellor, ask yourself a simple question after your first meeting—'Do I
feel a little better about life now?' If the answer is 'Yes', you might go again. If the answer
is in the negative and you happen to have a friend or two, talk to them instead. Denis
Postle's message is that the self interest inherent in the so-called professionalism of

counselling should make us very wary indeed of people who don't even include decency and kindness amongst their qualifications.
Craig Newnes, Director of Psychological Therapies, editor, writer, past Chair BPS Psychotherapy Section

In the light of the responsibilities thrust upon us by our historical times and those traditions entrusted to our keeping there is an unequivocal urgency for a cacophony of voices seeking to stem the seemingly unstaunchable push for the professionalisation and the regulation of the psychotherapies. One of these seeking to crank up the volume is Postle in order to excite the reader in other directions, in other forms of thinking, always sensitive to the invisibility of ideology and the issues of power. His provocation amply situates itself within the field of Derrida's favourite word: resistance.
Chris Oakley, The Site for Contemporary Psychoanalysis

Postle presents passionate arguments for diversity of practice and against attempts to shut us up.
Ian Parker, Professor of Psychology, Psychoanalyst, Manchester Psychoanalytic Matrix

Every therapeutic practitioner in Britain should by now be thinking through the issue of State Regulation, and Denis Postle's book is essential reading in this process. Combining a stunning overview of the field with passionate exploration into the arguments, it not only clarifies the subject but also provides a crucial counterbalance to conservative views. If you haven't yet read 'Regulating the Psychological Therapies', you haven't yet seen the whole picture on State Regulation.
Sue Quilliam, agony aunt, relationship psychologist, broadcaster, author

Denis Postle is the Searchlight of psychopractices. His passionate arguments against State regulation of Psychotherapy must be read and debated.
Simona Revelli, Psychoanalyst

This book contains information and arguments which I think deserve careful consideration by all practitioners in the field and it would in my opinion be folly to ignore them.
John Rowan

I find myself totally aligned with the spirit of Denis Postle's collection of lively, iconoclastic writing about compulsory government regulation of psychotherapies. It sets out a clear warning to anyone interested in using psychological interventions to help people. Psychotherapy is, as he shows, at such a primitive stage of development, with no clear theoretical agreement as to purpose and methodology, that regulation is likely to inhibit new thinking and perhaps crush innovation and creativity entirely.
Ivan Tyrrell, Principal of MindFields College

Regulating the Psychological Therapies

From Taxonomy to Taxidermy

DENIS POSTLE

PCCS Books
Ross-on-Wye

This collection first published in 2007

PCCS BOOKS
2 Cropper Row
Alton Road
ROSS-ON-WYE
HR9 5LA
UK
Tel +44 (0)1989 763 900
contact@pccs-books.co.uk
www.pccs-books.co.uk

**Regulating the Psychological Therapies:
From Taxonomy to Taxidermy**

British Library Cataloguing in Publication Data.
A catalogue record for this book is available from the British Library.

ISBN 978 1 898 05994 3

Cover design and cover photo by Denis Postle

Printed by Cromwell Press, Trowbridge, UK

CONTENTS

WEBLINKS PAGE
All the web addresses referred to in the text can be accessed from this Internet page:

<http://ipnosis.postle.net/rpt.htm>

GLOSSARY

AHPP: Association of Humanistic Psychology Practitioners
BAC: British Association of Counsellors (1977 – 2000)
BACP: British Association of Counsellors and Psychotherapists
BCP:British Confederation of Psychotherapists
BMC: British Medical Council
BPC: British Psychoanalytic Council
BPS: British Psychological Society
CBT: Cognitive Behavioural Therapy
CHRE: Council for Healthcare Regulatory Excellence
CI: Cooperative Inquiry
COSCA: Counselling and Psychotherapy in Scotland
CSPA and S: Continuing Self and Peer Assessment and Scrutiny
DoH: Department of Health
ENTO: Employment National Training Organisation
GMC: General Medical Council
HPC: Health Professions Council
HPRG: Human Potential Resource Group, University of Surrey
ICO: Independent Complaints Company
IDHP: Institute for the Development of Human Potential
IPN: Independent Practitioners' Network
NICE: National Institute for Clinical Excellence
NOS: National Occupational Standards
NVQ: National Vocational Qualification
PFDL: Practitioner Full-Disclosure List
QAA: Quality Assurance Agency for Higher Education
SAAFA: Sufficient Accessible Adult Functional Autonomy
SEMTA: Science, Engineering, Manufacturing Technologies Alliance
SfH: Skills for Health
SR: State or statutory regulation
TAXONOMY: the practice and science of classification ... taxonomies are frequently hierarchical in structure, commonly displaying parent—child relationships. *(Wikipedia)*
UKCP: United Kingdom Council for Psychotherapy
UKRC: United Kingdom Register of Counsellors
UKSCP: United Kingdom Standing Conference on Psychotherapy (1981–85)

FOREWORD

This collection of pages, covering the period from 1990 until the present time, constitutes a fascinating archive for those who in years to come will be concerned to write the history of counselling and psychotherapy in Britain. They bear graphic witness to a cultural shift among the therapists, from an enthusiastic commitment to the flourishing of human potential to a consumerist mentality motivated by the desire for status and professional advancement. It chronicles the end of the pioneers, the arrival of the legalists and the march of those intent on professionalisation.

Denis Postle has been the ever-observant and relentlessly confronting watchdog of the changing scene throughout this period. This self-appointed protector of the client experience has viewed with increasing scepticism the emergence of the powerful therapy associations—most notably UKCP, BACP and BPS—and the seemingly irresistible movement towards the statutory regulation of counsellors and psychotherapists. With logical persistence and unquenchable fervour he has consistently exposed the spuriousness of the argument advanced for state control of the talking therapies. He has sniffed out the power-mongers, stripped the polite language of its veneer to reveal the aggressive vested interests of many practitioners and barged into the discourse conducted in government offices. His articles and editorials do not make for comfortable reading and it is clearly his intention in compiling this book to aggravate the discomfort so that it reaches the point where, at the eleventh hour, rational, compassionate and fair-minded people will awaken from their trance-like state. For Postle, the many sleep-walkers are the victims of the oft-cited mantra which endlessly repeats that 'state regulation is inevitable'.

In the growing confidence of the Independent Practitioners' Network, Postle sees glimmers of light. It is his hope—and mine—that readers of this, at times, coruscating analysis of the current scene will not only awake out of sleep but, in the words of the ancient Advent Collect, 'put on the armour of light'. That armour will be needed, there can be no doubt.

Brian Thorne
Norwich: Advent 2006

PREFACE

Start a huge, foolish project, like Noah.
Rumi

In the last 16 years, there has been a growing threat to my freedom as a practitioner to meet manifestations of the human condition in clients with whatever care seemed necessary, with whatever could be got to work between us. The threat—from pressure to buy into a catalogue of risk-averse, fear-inducing, professional policing of counselling and psychotherapy—has seemed increasingly intolerable.

Was I suffering from Oppositional Defiant Disorder (DSM-IV-TR, 2000)? Or was I, owing to training in the alchemy of group life, picking up evidence of the colonisation, expropriation and more recently the beginnings of state regulation of key sectors of the field of psychopractice? And didn't these moves, driven quite openly by the motors of status and economic benefit, not only fail to protect the client's *experience* but threaten to damage it in significant ways? The more I realised this was indeed what the evidence pointed to, the more, in Petruska Clarkson's memorable phrase, I became unwilling to 'bystand it' (Clarkson, 1996).

As years of regulation watching have turned into decades, resisting, interrupting and confronting* the institutional incongruities of the regulation of counselling, psychotherapy and more recently psychoanalysis, have more and more become a role that found me, rather than one I sought.

I have lately come to see the scenario that is confronted in these texts as more generic than I did initially, more referring to, or reflective of other recurring historical contests about what might constitute human nature. Is institutional warfare, dog-eat-dog competition and bullying inescapably, inevitably, human? Even as it seems, for *therapists*? Alongside the necessary local detail, I hope you'll see that the texts are also about the archetypal cultural junctions between nomads and settlers, autonomy and control-freakery, self-generating cultures and audit/surveillance cultures, and above all the power of love and the love of power.

It might seem a bit of an inflation to identify with Noah, but long ago I tended to see the professionalising of UK psychopractice as a flood tide coming in (or—see Chapter 2—as an encroaching glacier). If I were to push the metaphor with Noah further, I'd see the Independent Practitioners' Network [IPN] as a necessary vessel for surviving the regulatory flood.

IPN provides a lived experience of the ecologically essential shift towards organisations that feature 'power-with' cooperation, negotiation, collaboration

---

* The unsolicited drawing of attention to behaviour of which people seem unaware

and working from love, and that say farewell to hierarchical, dominance-based 'power-over', coercive forms of 'democracy'.

I have chosen to add short introductory paragraphs to the articles and internet pages that I hope will ease the reader through some of the context that might otherwise be missing. Where I felt I disagreed with my historic self, rather than preserve the original, I have usually opted to add the current take.

Acknowledgements

I am indebted to many people for support and critique; my wife Barbara continues to be a partner in the task of learning to live from love that underlies the critique of the love of power that follows. A decade of conversation, critique, collaboration and feedback from Richard House has both energised and shaped what you will find here; he and I were founder members of the *Leonard Piper* Independent Practitioners' Network group, with Tony Donaghy, Irene Galant, Jutta Gassner, Guy Gladstone, Juliet Lamont, Annie Spencer and Maggie Taraz. It has been a privilege over the last 12 years to explore with them working from love and co-creating an institution of civic accountability that honours and protects the experience of our clients. It grounds everything that I have to say here.

That grounding also owes a lot to John Heron and Jill Anderson from whom I learned much that I needed to know about both love and power—not least the notion of 'confrontation' as a way of challenging oppression. My son Bruno has been endlessly patient in the task of making and maintaining the internet resources that have enabled me to reach out beyond IPN to other practitioner constituencies.

Protecting the experience of the people who have shared their wishes, woes and trust with me as clients has energised and sustained my engagement with professionalisation. Their diversity and uniqueness have constantly challenged me to get out of the straight and narrow of what therapy is supposed to be into living with the unfolding nuances of where they actually were.

I am indebted to Barbara Somers for the notion of 'facilitate the power of love—confront the love of power' which is at the heart of what you'll find here; and also to the late Ian Gordon Brown for generously threading through my supervision details of the regulatory process through which, as it seemed to me, he was selling the soul of the training organisation he had founded.

Lastly, a word about the shifting cast of actors occupying roles in the mainstream accrediting institutions that feature in many of the articles and papers that follow. With the exception of individuals such as Heward Wilkinson, there has been an apparently systematic failure by these bodies to do more than pay lip service to the ongoing critique first, of registration, and more recently of the state regulation of the psychological therapies of which this book is a part. The longer this *totschweigen*, ignoring to death, has gone on, the more I have felt licensed to become a public lightning conductor for some of the anger, disappointment and frustration that this ethical cleansing has evoked in people around me. While it has been my intention to always be addressing the institutional role and distinguishing it from the person wearing it, I have felt free to find feisty phrasing for those frequent occasions when—to rephrase Richard Mowbray (and Danny Kaye)—the 'the king was in the altogether, the altogether, he was altogether as naked as the day that he was born'.

References

Clarkson, P (1996) *The Bystander (An End to Innocence in Human Relationships?)* London:Whurr/Wiley.

DSM-IV-TR (2000) *Diagnostic and Statistical Manual of Mental Disorders*, Fourth Edition, Text Revision American Psychiatric Association.

Oppositional Defiant Disorder: <http://www.emedicine.com/ped/topic2791.htm><http://www.behavenet.com/capsules/disorders/odd.htm>

Rumi (1998) We are Three. *The Mathnaw, Vol VI* (pp. 831–845) Zia-al-Quaran. <http://www.rumi.org.uk/poems.html>

INTRODUCTION

Protecting the
Client *Experience*

Historical and Cultural Background

In the UK in the fourth quarter of the last century there was a rich ecology of self-directed and open-ended inquiry into a variety of aspects of the human condition, mostly but not always in groups. People signed up for courses or therapy out of some felt need in their lives; personal, spiritual and political development were often interwoven, and the key criterion for value was did it work; did it enhance life tasks such as survival, recovery or flourishing?

This array of development opportunities, rooted in self-direction and promoting self-direction, had the rich, profuse diversity of a meadow or a prairie. The Human Potential Resource Group 'HPRG' at the University of Surrey, for example, had around 80 courses a year run along these lines. Few carried qualifications. Deep, personal work in the course communities sometimes led to people becoming a practitioner; often, even commonly, it did not.

Around the beginning of the 1990s colleagues and I noticed a subtle mutation—a shift from open-ended, self-directed development, valid in itself, to a more consumerist attitude, with questions like, 'What do I get at the end of the course?' In effect, 'what is the product I am buying?'

This observable shift, the origins of which I do not pretend to understand, subsequently deepened and appears to have affected the whole field of psychopractice. Spending on personal development came to be seen as an 'investment' that had to 'pay off' in terms of work, employment, or career development and, not least, as a vehicle for escaping from aversive, high-stress jobs.

This not-so-subtle cultural shift from personal development for its own sake, to an emphasis on personal development as instrumental vocational development, was accompanied by NVQ and other audit and surveillance cultures. During the 90s they appear to have shaped and in turn been shaped by the professionalisation agendas of the United Kingdom Council for Psychotherapy [UKCP] and later the British Association of Counselling and Psychotherapy [BACP] and related groups such as the British Psychological Society [BPS].

These organisations were major providers of qualification-based vocational trainings or, as in the case of BACP, of the accreditation of an explosive growth in counselling training. The BACP/UKCP Initial Mapping Project (Aldridge and Pollard, 2005) identified 570 psychotherapy and counselling practitioner-training courses. If they each graduate around 10 students a year, this puts the number of new counselling and psychotherapy practitioners currently coming into the field as more than 5000 a year.

From Vocation (Calling) to Profession (Job)

I have often had a sense that training as a counsellor had become a way of sidestepping some supposed stigma of admitting to 'being a person who needed therapy' and that many—even too many—personal development needs were becoming displaced into training to provide paid psychotherapeutic help for other people. A not-too-inaccurate caricature would suggest that the territory of personal development is increasingly populated by people for many of whom it isn't a vocation—a calling founded in the first instance on a deep confrontation with their own formative narratives—but a job.

For such people protecting their investment, enhancing their status and job security (finding work) and moving, via qualifications, towards belonging to a 'profession' like a lawyer or doctor, is an understandably high priority.

Why does this shift in orientation matter? It matters because this is psychotherapy and counselling we are talking about: the exploration of the deepest reaches of the human condition. How do we fully honour this privileged role, the task in each session of enjoying the client's uniqueness, and the drama of our joint indwelling of the unfolding present moment? In my experience, both as practitioner and client, a climate of open-ended, self-directed inquiry with an experienced guide remains the most fruitful approach. While this may be only one of many possible psychotherapeutic 'regimes of truth' (House, 2003), is it not essential that whatever form of psychopractice we engage in, it actively seeks to extend and sustain a rich ecology of meaning about what it may signify to be human, rather than a restricted one?

Professionalised psychopractice—as a colleague describes it, medicalised, marketised, academicised, and bureaucratised psychotherapy and counselling, along with their psychoanalytic variants—embraces restriction, rationalising it as the price to be paid for the privileges that come from being higher up in the social and political pecking order. How can such professionalised practice avoid shaping working alliances with clients by employer-led, job-description-driven, cost-effective, risk-averse, technical priorities? As the DoH's *Next Steps* agenda for capturing psychotherapy and counselling makes clear, the latter approach is what Skills for Health expects to find (Lyall, 2006). And, because there is evidence (see Chapter 25) that some training organisations will eagerly seek to accommodate such a vision, this is also what the DoH taxonomy enterprise will tend to create.

As professionalisation driven by the mainstream accrediting organisations expanded its grasp in the last ten years or so, I began to see psychopractice as an ecologically rich prairie where a group of 'ranchers' had fenced off sectors of the territory, claiming possession and exclusive access—and, to push the metaphor only a little too far, seeking state endorsement of the right to exploit this asset they are attempting to steal from the rest of us.

Monocultural Therapy

As time has gone on, this vision of psychotherapy and counselling professionalisation has deepened and settled. The ranchers of psychotherapy and counselling professionalisation built bigger and better fences and have gone on to deform the ecology of the psychopractice prairie by claiming privilege for certain crops, while dismissing the rest as weeds to be eliminated (see Chapter 4). Worse, the government, entranced by targets and efficiency, has installed as exemplars narrowly specialised psychopractice crops, monocultures of the mind such as Cognitive Behavioural Therapy [CBT]. Curiously, the NICE evidence-based fanfare for CBT (weblinks page), and its denigration of most other ways of helping people who appear to be depressed and feeling very afraid, sits in stark contrast to the lack of any significant DoH evidence base that the level of harm due to around 20 million annual therapy contact hours merits state regulation.

The psychopractice market is being rigged. That is what professionalisation means.

What shifts this from being a subject for irony or humour, why it matters, is the prospect, earnestly lobbied for by the ranchers of professionalisation, of having their set of monocultures of the mind, and the fences they have built around them on the psychopractice prairie, endorsed by the state as *the* global expertise on the human condition. And, not outside the limits of possibility, to eventually make it a criminal offence for non-members of their monocultures to engage with people in deep human-condition work.

Murmurs of Dissent

Richard Mowbray's book *The Case Against Psychotherapy Registration* (Mowbray, 1995) provided a significant impetus for the task confronting this malign evolution of UK psychopolitics that has preoccupied me for a decade and a half. With the arrival of the internet, I developed G.O.R.I.L.L.A., a website (weblinks page) that provided a focus for the confrontation of the professionalisation culture and which continues as an archive of texts from this debate.

The emergence of the Independent Practitioners' Network, an exemplary contradiction of the notion that psychopractice framed and administered by the state is necessary, inevitable, or good for the client experience, has been very formative for me. It has provided grounded practice and theory of how to combine civic responsibility with the challenge and support that client/practitioner accountability requires. There have been other initiatives, such as the *Letting the Heart Sing—The Mind Gymnasium*, a compendious CD-ROM contribution to client education, and *livingfromlove.org*, an ongoing experiential inquiry into the power of love and the love of power. These together with participation in IPN have, I hope, provided a sufficiently potent antidote to the shadow side of resistance. As John Heron puts it in this cautionary note to co-counselling teachers:

> … we need to teach social action in terms of creating social alternatives, of creating the new society rather than opposing the old. If we put all our energy into opposing the rigidity and oppression of the old society, our radical identity becomes parasitic on what it opposes; we are defined by the evil we condemn; we feed off the energy of what we resist; we slip into the distressed place of compulsive rebel, re-enacting the child's ineffective rebellion against overwhelming odds. So we need to teach the value of drawing energy from a positive future, bringing a new

society, a self-generating culture into being, one that is continually innovative in shaping every aspect of social life.

Having written and published several articles that appear in the earlier part of this book, I found the resource to hand to establish *ipnosis.org*, a website for the IPN (weblinks page), that has provided a continuing platform for non-mainstream therapy news and opinion. Many of the Opinion/Editorial texts that follow have been published there.

But back to the bigger picture.

Cultures of Domination and Incongruity

In one of his two books (Scott, 1992; Scott, 1998) that should be read by everyone in the professionalisation culture, James C. Scott details the ubiquity of dominant and subordinate discourses. The dominant discourse tells stories to its constituents that reinforce the legitimacy of their domination, while marginalising, sidelining, ignoring or demeaning dissenting voices. And of course sometimes crushing or silencing them.

The stories of the people who find themselves on the receiving end of this dominance—a subordinate discourse, as Scott outlines—tend to be preoccupied with surviving the dominant culture, i.e. avoiding or recovering from the damage it causes; and, on occasion, engaging in active resistance. The subordinate culture learns that reasoning with the dominant culture doesn't work, i.e. having a conversation with this culture without showing that you defer to it or belong to it, tends to be a dialogue of the deaf.

What can inhabitants of the psychopractice subordinate culture—the 'weeds', as a former UKCP chair described us—do? One important action, of which IPN's 'best practice accountability' is an example, is to 'make the thing we want'. This matters because it is important to avoid antagonising the dominance culture. Putting this into practice, as IPN does, provides an empirical base for validating assertions about accountability that contradict the dominant discourse on such matters.

Secondly, subordinate cultures can develop strategies designed to break or interrupt the trance-inductions of the dominant culture and the corresponding powerlessness of the spellbound subordinate culture. For *Ipnosis* this has meant on the one hand 'confrontation', and on the other finding an appropriate 'voice', while holding, I trust successfully, a loving relationship with the persons being confronted.

What does this mean in practice? Confrontation doesn't imply fighting, as might be supposed; it entails an unsolicited pointing out that someone doesn't seem to notice that when they do X, I and others feel Y; that a consequence of their behaviour is Z; and would they please consider stopping, changing, or moderating it, or otherwise take account of our feedback?

For example, when professionalisers say 'register now before it is too late', I and others feel coerced and oppressed; we see this is as using fear of exclusion to force us into a regulated relationship. When they say 'state regulation is inevitable',

I see this as a trance-induction intended to suppress choice and discrimination. The incongruence of such approaches (this is psychopractice, after all) undermines the credibility of the institution, leading to a request to stop or change this behaviour.

When speaking about the behaviour of the dominant professionalising culture, 'voice' has meant finding a low-bullshit directness that interrupts the polite reasonableness and genteel brutality of the dominance narratives, coupled with a technical ability—due to owning the means of internet production—to broadcast over the heads of the mainstream accrediting institutions: past them, to their constituents.

The dominant discourse of psychotherapy professionalisation has tended to find all of this irritatingly counter-cultural. Curiously, as might be expected of psychopractitioners, they don't seem to see this 'resistance' as something to be worked through jointly, that might tell them something they need to know, but as a token of some functional pathology in the dissenters.

The ignoring to death of dissenting voices—voices that have comprehensively spelled out the extent to which professionalisation and the pursuit of state regulation of counselling and psychotherapy, while claiming to 'protect the client', will damage the client's *experience*—is a key characteristic of the period that this book chronicles.

Therapy on the Brink?

As this book goes to press, the mainstream accrediting organisations look to be on the point of getting their wish for state regulation, i.e. state endorsement of their unmandated, top-down colonisation of psychopractice, but very unhappily not in the form they wished for. The sight, close up, of what state power actually entails has evoked considerable panic and despair—even the overnight construction of a psychoshantytown, the Psychological Professions Council. As I believe this chronicle will show, all this has been blatantly obvious to anyone who cared to pay attention to the profound ethical incongruity between the loving, caring help of client–practitioner working alliances and the fear-inducing cultures of domination, rippling with ungrounded ethical righteousness (and good intentions) that the mainstream accrediting bodies seem to have become.

Repetition

One last word: this is a compilation of articles triggered by, or responding to, local contingencies, reports, consultation documents, a Bill in the House of Lords, or other more local irritations. Because these events tend to have a fractal* relationship with each other, the text may at times seem unduly repetitive. I make no apology for this; quite often, I suspect, when a Mistake as big as the social insanity of state

---

* Branching patterns that arise in Nature from the conflict between random and constraining forces.

regulation of psychopractice is being promoted by sections of its participants, the key arguments that contradict their error may be few. I hope that their repetition will have the effect of making any choices you face around psychopractice regulation well informed, courageous and above all concerned with protecting the client's *experience*.

References

Aldridge, S and Pollard, J (2005) Interim report to Department of Health on Initial Mapping Project for Psychotherapy and Counselling:7

G.O.R.I.L.L.A archive (1995) <http://g.o.r.i.l.l.a.postle.net>

Heron, J (1995) Original theory of co-counselling & the paradigm shift <http://ipnosis.postle.net/pages/heronnewpara.htm>

House, R (2003) *Therapy beyond Modernity: Deconstructing and Transcending Profession-Centred Therapy*. London:Karnac

Lyall, M (2006) Interview in *Therapy Today*, December

Mowbray, R (1995) *The Case Against Psychotherapy Registration: A Conservation Issue for the Human Potential Movement*. London: Trans Marginal Press

Scott, J (1992) *Domination and the Arts of Resistance: Hidden Transcripts*. New Haven: Yale University Press

Scott, J (1998) *Seeing Like a State: How Certain Schemes to Improve the Human Condition Have Failed*. New Haven:Yale University Press

Part I

Waking Up to the Shadow of Professionalisation

Background: At the time Jill Anderson and I co-wrote this article, I had been working as a therapist for five years; at the University of Surrey we were leading a variety of personal and professional development courses that were open to the public, and co-facilitating a two year part-time facilitation training also at the University of Surrey, accredited by the Institute for the Development of Human Potential [IDHP].

CHAPTER ONE

Stealing the Flame

... professions ... tend by definition to be monopolists of knowledge and through that knowledge power. (Sir Peter Imbert, Metropolitan Police Commissioner)

In the last ten years we have been busy composting a mix of new learning, study and the accumulated experience of the previous two decades. For each of us these have now become a fertile soil in which working lives as group facilitator, counsellor and psychotherapist are growing. Parallel with this, it seems that several decades of the life and work of other practitioners in the field of personal development are beginning to crystallise into proposals which seek to establish psychotherapy as a profession.

As we look at our own work and hear of these developments, both political and personal questions are raised for us. First the political ones.

If the active empowerment of psychotherapy clients is the first priority for all of us, how can the pursuit of professional issues of credibility, respectability and security of employment avoid pushing this into second place? Isn't the professionalisation of psychotherapy denying one of the lessons of its own history, that the trapping of expertise in professions leads to defensive monopolies that legislate against innovation and change? For us this has been one of the fundamental realisations to come out of the personal development tradition that embraces psychotherapy.

Are not the handful of key people at the centre of the present moves towards professionalisation in effect erecting a wall around a section of the personal development tradition and attempting to take possession of it? To change the metaphor, through locking up and making claims of privileged possession of psychotherapy expertise aren't they 'stealing the flame' that belongs to everyone? And even if they succeed in this dubious enterprise, how can they ensure that their professional 'light' at the centre does not cast a shadow that perpetuates mystification, deference and ignorance in those outside the professional domain? Isn't this what the medical profession so obviously does and is trying to modify?

Many of the people and organisations who are active in the present moves to professionalisation seem to be economically committed to psychotherapy training. Is this really going to ensure that ethical and practice standards are upheld across an unfolding career? Is this really a reliable basis from which actively to pursue the wider empowerment of potential clients? If protecting clients' interests is really at the centre of the moves to create a psychotherapy 'profession', wouldn't

This article first appeared in *Self and Society*, 18:1, January 1990

an association using a 'business', 'trade' model, along the lines of those in other service industries, actually be more appropriate?

For instance, the kind of do-it-yourself plumbing, building, heating and electrical skills that are commonplace in this country used to be non-existent in Switzerland, because there, those professions had the legal power to refuse to supply or deal with anyone who wasn't a member. How do we avoid similar restrictions if psychotherapy becomes a profession? For example, co-counselling or re-evaluation counselling are DIY approaches to psychotherapy; they actively demystify and make openly and cheaply available much of the core knowledge from psychology about human functioning and the related strategies of personal development and transformation. Where in the designs for the new psychotherapy profession do they sit? Are they represented at all? If not, why not?

The second layer of questions is more personal.

In the new scheme of things, would we personally be acceptable as psychotherapists—for example as members of AHPP, the most obvious organisation that we would seek to join? As things stand, the answer is 'no'.

According to the AHPP guidelines, study at a recognised psychotherapy training centre and long periods in personal psychotherapy both appear to be overriding requirements. We have neither, but our core experience of many years of ad hoc training, rooted in the practice and teaching of co-counselling, provides the basis for what we regard as our considerable competence as counsellors and psychotherapists.

Should we just accept this professional demarcation? We could always take up the easy option of becoming an AHPP member as a group facilitator, for which we have reason to believe we would be acceptable. But suppose we did that: wouldn't it be grossly anomalous? As a group facilitator we would then be 'licensed' to work with individuals in a group setting, over a period of months or years, on any material or topic and to any depth that seemed jointly feasible; but we would not be 'licensed' to work with the same people on the same material on a one-to-one basis over the same period. How could we join an institution that insisted on this kind of incongruity?

The AHPP full membership process asks for an 'honest self-assessment statement' and on the basis of this text, operates as a gatekeeper who utters a 'yes' or 'no'. How come AHPP seems to have no appreciation of the essential contribution of peer assessment to an accreditation process? To unilaterally set criteria for acceptance that require us to be responsible and self-directing in our work with clients, and that deny our capacity to evaluate our own competence, seems fundamentally contradictory and oppressive. It smacks of an unresolved clinging to an autocratic, 'medical', 'treatment', model for personal transformation that has yet to come to terms with the challenge of the 'education' model for personal development, i.e. that psychotherapy is intrinsically a branch of general education. All of this has suggested to us that a whole range of other people would be likely to be sitting on equivalent anomalies, exclusions or doubts. Are you one of them, we wonder? If so, what do we do about it?

Obviously as individuals we can be actively vigilant about attempts to professionalise psychotherapy. We can give reminders about the political value of making psychotherapy more widely available through co-counselling or its equivalents. We can also devise and diffuse an exemplary way of providing a valid form of self, and peer, accreditation as practitioners—some process that will provide an appropriate level of ethical rigour, while honouring the diversity of routes into the effective practice of psychotherapy and how an individual's competence sits within the broader field of personal development. How might this look?

What we would like the AHPP guidelines for practitioners to say is something like this: 'Yes, we affirm your capacity to constantly monitor and appraise your professional competence and development and to take personal responsibility for the ethical, financial and organisational issues which arise in your work as a practitioner.

'In support of this, we require you to engage in a full peer- and self-assessment process over, say, 6 – 12 months, following a declared/published, but evolving, set of criteria. At the end of this process you arrive at an agreed self-accreditation for a stated period of perhaps three years. This will set out what you are competent to do and what you are excluding from your work as a psychotherapist; which areas of knowledge, experience or pathology require attention; and any plan of action needed to implement these. This document, along with the peer amendments and requirements, is to be lodged with AHPP and available for inspection'.

We would be interested to hear from anyone who feels aligned with either these views or these proposals. We plan to institute a version of the accreditation process outlined above and we would be willing to support others in doing the same.

Background: The six years following publication of 'Stealing the Flame' (Chapter 1) saw the United Kingdom Standing Conference on Psychotherapy [UKSCP] mutate, in 1992, into the United Kingdom Council for Psychotherapy [UKCP]. In the first of several assertions of prior virtue, the psychoanalytic UKSCP partners, having failed in their attempt to insist on forming a controlling 'Security Council', left UKCP to form the British Confederation of Psychotherapists [BCP]. Perhaps because I had some non-trivial experience of the internal dynamics of accrediting organisations, and had been a training member of one of them, the incongruity of these psycho-therapy organisations' aggressive and imperial behaviour left me appalled. What was going on?

CHAPTER TWO

Glacier Reaches Edge of Town

I thought I had given up resisting the psychotherapy regulation glacier, in favour of making the thing I want to have (the Independent Therapists' Network); but clearly I haven't quite, because last month the UKCP published its register of psychotherapists. This, followed by the September issue of *Self & Society*—with John Rowan's open letter to Richard Mowbray, the (curiously short) Emmy van Deurzen-Smith interview, and Petruska Clarkson's ad for her services—all combined to fan the dormant embers of my concerns into flame.

First, the Emmy van Deurzen-Smith interview. '[Psychotherapy] can now be scrutinised like any other profession': yes, but suppose many of us, not being proprietors of training schools but being familiar with the hidden agendas of existing professions, want it to remain an occupation, not a profession? '... obliged to work to specific and agreed standards': yes, but you didn't ask me to join with you to set those standards, so why should I join you in the obligations? '. . . the need for all those with an interest in psychotherapy to broker relationships involving power; inevitably there has been a tendency for a hierarchy to form.' Inevitably? Really? Here is a psychotherapist who appears to accept dominance as 'natural'. Isn't it one of the fundamental tasks of psychotherapy to challenge such unaware assumptions—for instance, in the 'specific and agreed standards' to which they work, and in the organisations they set up?

The formation of UKCP has always seemed to me about the seizure of power in our field. It is intrinsically about promoting the dominance of trainers. I want to ask Emmy van Deurzen-Smith how UKCP will ensure that this 'naturalness' of dominance is not reproduced down the line, up to, and including, the client – therapist interaction. 'There is more choice for the public ... with the increasing emphasis on improving training and ethical practice, the clientele will be better served.' This is disinformation. As Richard Mowbray (1995) has convincingly shown, there is no evidence that clients will be better served by UKCP-registered practitioners. UKCP is an attempt to structure and regulate a market. It is primarily in the interests of the training schools and the multi-tiered therapist/supervisor/trainee businesses that they sustain.

What Emmy van Deurzen-Smith says reinforces my view of UKCP as economically driven 'ethical cleansing', dressed up as care for clients. It needs to be strenuously resisted and if possible derailed, in the interests of clients.

Next, John Rowan's 'Open Letter to Richard Mowbray'. John begins by raising questions about Richard Mowbray's alternatives to the present set-up. Then, by

This article first appeared in *Self and Society*, 23: 6, January 1996 way of discussing the level of commitment that good practice requires, he outlines two modes of working with people. The first is psychotherapy: this requires 'commitment through holidays', 'weekly meetings for months or years', 'competence with transference'; *'observes strict boundaries'* [my emphasis]; practitioners have 'supervision', a 'therapist support group', 'ethical codes' and 'fuller and deeper resources and better and longer training'. He goes on to assert that psychotherapy is more demanding than the second working mode, personal growth, which he sees as 'short term commitment', 'one-off workshops', 'self-taught or perhaps apprenticed practitioners *who don't know about transference'* [my emphasis] and are likely to lack 'supervision', 'therapy' or an 'ethical code'. This won't do; it's a spurious polarity.

In my 'humanologist' practice, I sometimes work with people once or more than once a week. I often work with people once a fortnight, or once a month. With numerous people, I have been holding continuity of their client issues for as long as six or seven years. With some people it is primal work; with some it is assertiveness; with others, managing the delights and struggles of coupledom; with still others, it is transpersonal work. I am in supervision and always have been. I am also in open-ended 'therapy'. I embrace both ends of John's polarities and so do many other people I count as colleagues. John's listing of the attributes of 'psychotherapy' also suggests that the 'work' is the therapist's project, rather than that of the client. People have to come every week, or more than once a week, or it is not serious work. How can clients hold their own against a therapist in such a framework? How can they gain significant ownership of their own development?

And transference: does John really believe that people like me, or Juliana Brown, or Nick Totton, don't know about, or work with, transference? Of course it's ubiquitous, but is it really in the client's best interest to psychologise everything that they present as transference/countertransference/resistance, while their interpersonal skills, or bodily armouring, or the politics of their lives remain safely off-stage? I have long suspected that the practitioners who favour this approach inhabit one of the deepest shadow areas in our field.

And then there is 'self-taught', which is one of John's indicators of the limitations of the personal-growth approach. How can we avoid the implication that the only learning that counts is 'other-taught'? That the core ability needed to work effectively with clients is academic, the capacity to sit still and be talked at, and to absorb, digest and re-present expertise? By contrast, independent, self-directed learning is fundamentally suspect. And if it is suspect for the practitioner, will it not also be suspect for clients?

No, this won't do either. I don't know, but I'd guess that John himself, as with others of his generation is as 'self-taught' as I am. I want to point him to his copy of John Heron's 1979 Assessment Revisited:

> For any domain of enquiry there is a source point when its originators flourished through self-directed learning and enquiry and through self- and peer-assessment ... these or their successors become the original unilateral academic assessors; they assess themselves as competent to assess others. And they assess others as relatively incompetent to be self- and peer-assessing and self-directing in learning and discovery ... If I am among the first to establish knowledge in some field, I

can use that knowledge to establish a power base in the social order ... If I can get others, through their hunger for power, to collude with my unjust discrimination towards them ... then I have established a new profession, a body of experts who sustain their power and perpetuate the injustice through the myth of maintaining excellence. The founding treason is that the founders, through this professional dominion, betray their own origins in self-directed learning, self- and peer-assessment.

My awareness of what AHPP/UKCP are up to dates from around 1990. Against my deepest inclinations, which were then uninformed by the recent debate, I did try to gain representation, to have at least a voice at the table. I decided to join AHPP. I prepared all the material that AHPP required, detailed my training and experience and so on.

My application was a de facto self-assessment that the eclectic array of self-directed studies of facilitation that I had built up, based on self- and peer-assessment, meant that I was a competent practitioner. It amounted, as I recall, to 2000 hours of training/experiential learning, which built on one of the best self-directed educations in creativity available this century (at the Royal College of Art) and my two decades as a broadcast film-maker.

I remain convinced that this adequately supported my competence as a facilitator of both group and one-to-one work, in both the long and short terms. I also believe that this bundle is at least as good as the outcome of a 'recognised', three-year, part-time psychotherapy course.

My then supervisor, perhaps anticipating the outcome of my application, suggested that I tune it up by sending it to someone on the AHPP board who might point out omissions or discrepancies. So I sent it to John Rowan, with a note outlining my situation. His response was to say that the application would not be accepted because I had not done a recognised training, and that, 'Anyway, AHPP has no category for polymaths.' He went on to say that when I had licked my wounds, perhaps I'd consider applying to the group leader section.

My self- (and peer-) assessment of my capacities figured nowhere in the AHPP consideration of competence, only a 'recognised training' did. When I had cooled down and made a few other enquiries, I realised that a movement was afoot in our field to create a psychotherapy profession. People were saying that 'clients had to be protected' and that professionalisation was the way to do it. In setting the goalposts where they did, AHPP, among others, were policing the boundaries of the new profession.

In other areas of commerce and trade, people openly attempt to 'structure the market': they limit entry to it through raising the price of entry and they form trade associations to manipulate prices and suppliers; but they don't call it creating a profession, and they don't usually pretend that it is primarily in the interests of their clients.

One of John's criteria for psychotherapy as opposed to personal growth is that psychotherapy requires 'strict boundaries'. Do all AHPP/UKCP registered people strictly maintain the boundary to undertake no groupwork without deep and proper training? Are you all scrupulous about that? Or, as I suspect, do not many UKCP/AHPP registered people feel entitled to run groups with little or no groupwork training?

As I understand it, a 'strict boundary' in UKCP/AHPP terms would mean 'no groupwork without a recognised training in groupwork' for the level of work you were doing. Is this a part of the ethical framework of AHPP and UKCP? I do not recall seeing it. And if such groupwork is all right without training, how does this serve the best interests of clients?

I feel that John's piece points to a lack of awareness (or a denial) in UKCP/AHPP, of a fundamental contradiction in the regulatory glacier. It is this: if a practitioner is to be trusted to behave responsibly, effectively and ethically in interactions with clients, and to manage their own development down the years, how come the same therapist is not capable, with peer support, of assessing this capacity for themselves? And if they aren't to be trusted, what regulatory regime could conceivably fill that space?

In my view, a process which asserts the prior and fundamental value of an ability to self-assess competence in a peer context is for our field the most appropriate and rigorous way of identifying people who are not yet ready—or never will be ready—to self-manage themselves in an ethical way.

Of course if you own or run a training school, such an approach is harder to market. The authority of top-down expertise is easier to sell, especially to the public, because it is congruent with the prevailing fundamentalist worldview: that dominance expressed through hierarchy is 'natural' and 'normal'.

No doubt much of the inner life of UKCP/AHPP is locally manifested through elegant expressions of 'power-with' between caring people, but the overarching agenda is clearly 'power-over'. And with bedfellows as dedicated to dominance as are psychiatry and the British Psychological Society (look out for their parliamentary bill to capture the word 'psychologist') who can doubt that the rich meadowland of our field is in danger of losing the argument with the bulldozer?

That brings me to Petruska Clarkson's advertisement. Here is an example of the bulldozer in action. 'PhD', 'MA', 'Associate Fellow of the British Psychological Society', 'Consultant Chartered Clinical and Counselling Psychologist', 'Accredited Supervisor', 'UKCP-registered practising Psychotherapist', 'Accredited Organisational Consultant': this is how Dr Clarkson lists the reasons why we should value her. Is this really the way forward for our field, a model for the rest of us to emulate? Or to shift metaphor, isn't this a node of the national regulation grid inviting us to plug into her power and influence and expertise?

The tone of what I have said may seem sharp, or harsh, or hurtful, or intemperate; but I feel that I have looked on for long enough in despairing passivity while one of the most precious developments of the second half of the twentieth century is bricked up to starve—and some of the people doing the bricking are from my own family. That hurts.

If you agree with these assertions, what can be done? I think: create or support good pieces of resistance to the idea that a psychotherapy trade association is in the best interests of clients (Richard Mowbray's book is exemplary); create forms of practitioner/client support that do not unconsciously reproduce the deepest and most problematic dynamics of the society we inhabit (the Independent Therapists Network [IPN] is well on the way to being 'good-enough' at this task);

and finally, actively educate existing and potential clients in how to manage their interactions with practitioners. This is a neglected area, urgently awaiting new initiatives.

Endnote

In acknowledgement of Petruska Clarkson's suicide in 2006 and in honour of the confrontations with the UKCP that she mounted several years after the above piece was written, and to which I lent minor support, I include a short section from her 40-page *Open Letter to the UKCP* of 9 November 2000 which richly evokes the price that such institutional challenges can entail.

> … your whole world changes. Hundreds of people who had always demonstrated their personal and professional trust of you *over decades* suddenly start treating you with suspicion. Unexpected 'communication' difficulties arise (e.g. with publishers) in situations where there had been easy and happy working relationships in the past. It strangely and suddenly becomes extremely difficult, if not impossible to resolve disagreements—even to talk about them—in the way one had done in the past. People whom you had nurtured, helped, *loved*, suddenly 'become afraid' of you. Friends don't return your calls any more. Students, clients and supervisees very suddenly terminate working with you for what sound like obscure and surprising reasons—after years of appreciating your services. *And* they won't talk about it …
> … The rich and varied relational world of a lifetime disappears overnight. You desperately try to find out what is going on. People won't talk to you. You write letters. People refuse to reply. You try to get help by following the ethics and complaints procedures. No way. They call you mad …
> … Your mouth feels like it is being systematically broken into your skull by one of those torture implements with which they used to kill people by inserting them into the vagina or anus. You can't sleep. You spend the nights crying. When you do sleep, you have horrible nightmares of helplessly running away from an angry mob and being slowly burnt at the stake. You've *got* to keep working all hours because all your reasonable expectations of an income based on decades of professional dedication CRASH for no apparent reason. You just can't keep up. Any mistake or misunderstanding turns into a relentless catastrophe. You wonder what's wrong with you. You feel completely disoriented. Your heart breaks.

References

Mowbray, R (1995) *The Case Against Psychotherapy Registration: A Conservation Issue for the Human Potential Movement.* London: Trans Marginal Press
Self & Society (1995) 22:5

Background: The Norwich Collective hosted two conferences about psychotherapy registration in Cambridge in 1991 and 1992 that raised many practitioners' awareness of the dangers of psychotherapy professionalisation, and 1994 saw the founding of the Independent Practitioners' Network [IPN]. This first web page is from the G.O.R.I.L.L.A. website that I developed a couple of years later. It was a first tentative attempt at reaching out via the internet to air the disquiet many of us felt about the glaciation, incongruities and bullying in the psychopractice field and to see who else shared our concerns.

CHAPTER THREE

Resisting Psychotherapy Registration

Why am I and many of my colleagues adamantly opposed to *statutory* registration of psychotherapists?

I agree that 'some' standards are appropriate for psychopractitioners; the question is, *whose* standards?

That question is answered as much through attending to 'power' and 'congruence' and 'client population' as it is about 'high standards of practitioner competence'. These matters in their turn seem highly dependent on the model of human nature that underlies a practitioner's orientation.

Many—perhaps most—clients for psychotherapy have Sufficient Accessible Adult Functional Autonomy [SAAFA] (Mowbray,1995); i.e. they travel to appointments and perhaps pay fees. I would assert that the power relations between the practitioner and such clients should be only of the 'power-with' variety—that is to say, the practitioner has an explicit contract with the client to 'facilitate' his/her declared agenda/s. Only so far as a client has no, or negligible, SAAFA would any variety of 'power-over' relations be appropriate, i.e. in the realm of 24-hour institutional care.

If this assertion of 'power-with' facilitation is accepted for the client–practitioner contract, i.e. that this is a fundamental value, then holding congruence would seem to demand that representative organisations of psychopractitioners also have 'power-with' relations, both internally and externally. And if not, why not?

Now to jump on for a moment, the issue of power seems to me to be hugely affected by the model of human nature that is implicit in any particular form of psychopractice. Two (at least) divergent models are abroad at the moment. One, the broadly psychodynamic/ psychoanalytic one, characterises human nature as a thin veneer of civility over a chaotic mass of destructive and sexual instinctive impulses. (See also Chapters 6 and 15.) In other words control and containment and regulation are essential because everyone, including practitioners, would otherwise be likely to run amok.

In my view, this model of human nature naturalises 'power-over' relations expressed through hierarchical structures. The psychoanalytic community's cascades of training/supervisory deference, and its assumption that interpretations be given *to* clients, seem to exemplify this perspective.

Another model of human nature, the broadly humanistic/human potential movement one, sees human beings as intrinsically OK, except insofar as their

This article first appeared in G.O.R.I.L.L.A. as Editorial #1, 21 November 1996 unfolding potential has been damaged, interfered with, or distorted. In this view of human nature, there is no fundamental destructive instinctual impulse to be contained or regulated. Practitioners who subscribe to it prefer 'power-with' structures, with a great deal of emphasis on diversity of practitioner style and self-reflexive regulation. Hierarchies of experience and talent tend to be respected; those of status or seniority or position tend to be viewed sceptically.

Now back to 'congruence' and the 'professionalisation' of psychopractice. A person who follows the psychoanalytic model of human nature will be likely to be very concerned with containment, regulation and control and setting high standards, because of their presumption that without them instinctual chaos will reign. It seems to me that the UKCP's approach to professionalisation has been captured by this perspective on human nature. It looks and feels like a 'power-over' structure and this is certified for me by its pursuit of statutory registration which epitomises 'power-over', i.e. 'getting the state to police the boundaries of the profession'. And four out of the six UKCP officers are, I believe, from the psychodynamic sections.

However, about half of the UKCP's constituents are in the HIPS section. Their literature, course brochures, etc. are full of statements pointing to the humanistic model of human nature; yet the UKCP structure they inhabit is committed to 'power-over' ways of moving in the world and, through legislation, of an increasing alignment with state power. So for me, HIPS participants like AHPP—let alone the transpersonal ones such as the Pyschosynthesis Trust, Karuna, and the Institute for Transpersonal Studies, which also have an explicitly humanistic focus—are a long way down the road to treason to their origins. Why? Because of the level of 'values incongruence' implicit in their support for the 'power-over' *statutory* registration of psychotherapists, while training people in 'power-with' modes of psychopractice. Small wonder there is a lot of anguish among humanistic practitioners these days.

Making the thing we want

Together with some dozens of other humanistic practitioners who hold the issue of 'congruence' between psychopractice and psycho-organisation to be inalienable, I am a participant in the Independent Practitioners' Network [IPN]. IPN consists of a network of small groups with a minimum of five and maximum of ten practitioners, each of whom takes collective responsibility for the quality of practice of the others in the group. Each group must be linked to two other groups, who are charged with verifying the quality of the process through which a group is able as we say 'to stand by' the quality of work of our fellow members. There is no national 'quality control' beyond the requirement that each member group circulate its statement of ethical commitments to the whole network.

This is an extremely demanding and exemplary example of extending to social organisation what has been learned about power in groupwork these last decades. It promises to work very well and I certainly believe it is 'good enough'.

If you want to follow up on any of this, you might in the first instance get hold of Richard Mowbray's book *The Case against Psychotherapy Registration* (Mowbray, 1995) which comprehensively demolishes the logical and values foundation for UKCP and so is tending to be ignored or derided. I suppose that if you are a supertanker under way at 15 knots, it takes a long time to change direction!

Reference

Mowbray, R (1995) *The Case Against Psychotherapy Registration: A Conservation Issue for the Human Potential Movement.* London: Trans Marginal Press

Background: Readers may need reminding that in 1997 the hot psychopractice regulation issue was *registration*. Following UKCP's publication of their practitioner register in the autumn of 1996, they and BAC shamelessly invoked fear in their constituencies of being excluded, of being unable to practise. These invocations were at odds with practitioners' core values of trust and personal integrity, seemed intrinsically discriminatory and, as in the views I tried to confront in this article, seemed lacking in the sensibility you might expect from a leading figure in an organisation claiming to occupy ethical high ground.

CHAPTER FOUR

How Does the Garden Grow?

A vigorous opponent of (psychopractice) registration, Denis Postle challenges Emmy van Deurzen's view of counselling as a garden that needs pruning and weeding.

As the market for psychopractice in the UK changes, it is putting many practitioners in a tight corner. How do I register? Can I register? Do I want to register? It has produced a jostling for dominance by the pro-register faction of such incongruity that the creative juices of some practitioners like myself have been stimulated into putting together a viable alternative: The Independent Practitioners' Network. [IPN]. And it has spawned one particular metaphor—gardening—that I'd like to explore here.

In a recent talk to a conference at St George's Hospital entitled 'Registration: what it will mean to you, the counsellor', Professor Emmy van Deurzen, a former chair of UKCP, had a lot to say about counselling and registration that seems to me highly dubious. I am quoting her talk here in some detail because it furnishes a good example of the worldview that has energised the development of alternative ways of being accountable.

In the opening of her presentation, she adopted the curious professorial/parental device of telling the audience what they think:

> You know what registration is about in practical terms. You have been told how the United Kingdom Register of Counsellors is going to work. You know the facts and you still have the fantasies. Sometimes you think that being registered would guarantee your professional status and make you feel a whole lot better about yourself. At other times you think that all this registration business will just make the distinctions between people more artificial and more definitive. You fear that you might be really penalised if you cannot obtain registration, or that registration will just make everybody less interested in what they do as the profession becomes bureaucratised and systematised, perverting and distorting its original purpose.

And in an interview about UKCP last year, Professor van Deurzen spoke of the inevitability of hierarchies forming. Yet is the institutionalised dominance that counselling and psychotherapy registers represent really inevitable? Or the only choice? Isn't it, at the very least, open to question?

One of the feminist tradition's sweetest gifts has been its challenge to the 'naturalness' and 'inevitability' of male dominance and therefore dominance in general, since the theorising about dominance had hitherto been in the hands of—

This article first appeared in *Counselling News*, June 1997

surprise, surprise—mostly men. And isn't this, as I would suppose, a perspective that belongs in any self-respecting counselling or psychotherapy training?

If so, how can it be, as I find myself repeatedly asking, that some of the leading register builders seem entirely at ease with the way that their institutions seek to dominate the market for their services? Take, for example, statutory registration. Speaking about statutory regulation and the EU, Professor van Deurzen remarked: 'There is a long road ahead—but this road will eventually lead to potential statutory registration of counsellors and psychotherapists.'

But how can this stance, this institutional agenda that implicitly means engaging the state to help police the boundaries of a profession of counselling and psychotherapy, possibly be congruent with the work of counsellors and psychotherapists who espouse an empowering posture in their practice? Is it not the case that many, if not most, clients come with difficulties that are at root to do with power, with the playing out of agendas of dominance and subjection?

Since I believe that most psychopractitioners do indeed try to work, and even live, from this 'power-with' ethical stance, it seems reasonable to expect that the organisations that represent them should also do so. How are clients well served by having a dominance-free practice coupled to a dominance-laden institutional structure?

Professor van Deurzen certainly seemed to feel entitled to tell us what's good for us. In her talk she went on to say that, when counselling and psychotherapy were small-scale and scarce, she was happy with self-monitoring: 'Of course this freedom was sometimes abused, but there is no doubt that the advantages of creativity and diversity that it engendered on balance outweighed the negative factors.'

Yet now this had mysteriously changed.

> The situation that has now evolved with the rapid expansion of this sector has required us to check this unbridled freedom and diversity. We have needed to mitigate the creativity and individuality with quality control and accountability.

The question for me and, I guess, for many readers of *Counselling News* is—who are the 'We'?

Are they the 'We' of the BAC, feeling understandably a little congested after the indefensible tabloid attacks of the BBC's *Watchdog* programme? Or are they the 'We' of the UKCP?

When I looked into how UKCP is structured I found that it is comprehensively influenced by its psychodynamic/psycho-analytic member organisations, who comprise more than half the total membership and who contribute many of the principal officers.

Also, psychiatrists now form half the executive committee of the governing board of the UKCP, and one of this inner ring is the Chair of the Registration Board. Is that the kind of 'We' that you, the reader—as a counsellor—would find acceptable? As numerous complaints about inaccessibility and lack of democracy attest, some surfacing even in the UKCP's journal, it is manifestly not an organisation that represents its membership.

Contrary to its claims to be the core of a united profession of psychotherapy, UKCP is actually a trade association, composed primarily of training organisations, that is trying to structure the market for its services. In hastening—I fancy slowly— to put up a register of counsellors, this is the company that BAC and UKCR invites you to join.

And so on to horticultural metaphors. Professor van Deurzen asserted in the conclusion of her talk that:

> When a garden has been very fertile and has been left to itself for a long period of time it is overgrown. Sprawling plants obscure each other's light and deprive each other of nutrients. It is then necessary to cut the plants back, quite drastically and carefully select the ones that one wishes to encourage and make room for, at the same time as uprooting those plants considered to be weeds.

Again, this seems to me riddled with presumptions that domination and control are natural and inevitable. There is the presumption that the field of UK psychopractice is a garden and not, for example, a meadow.

As Professor Yi-Fu Tuan has pointed out, gardening is one of the areas, along with pet-keeping, (Tuan, 1984) where dominance commonly finds expression: 'It is then necessary to cut the plants back ... '

Again, who is the 'it'? Who decides? Who is it who claims to know what to cut back and what to select, and which are weeds to be uprooted? On what criteria? Professor van Deurzen is undoubtedly aware of the dangers in what she's suggesting. Such pruning ...

> ... if it is done haphazardly and too aggressively, the result can be a sparse, unattractive environment in which little growth can be observed for a long time to come. However in these times of rapid growth ... the pruning of registration and standard setting is a welcome and entirely necessary phenomenon ... as far as I am concerned: it was high time that we began to disentangle this overgrown field, for it had turned into a jungle, where some weird and wonderful creatures were sometimes doing untold damage.

Here the word 'jungle' is used to represent a state of appalling and threatening disorder, populated with damaging creatures. But jungle also means rainforest; far and away the richest ecological structure on this planet and one on which the whole of its climate and possibly its future depends. And one indeed populated with weird and wonderful creatures, such as the gorilla, which along with the jungle, has also been notoriously abused as a carrier of negative projection, yet in reality is a gentle, vegetarian creature.

For me, Professor van Deurzen's talk provides a narrowed, inadequate and fundamentally unreliable perspective from which to claim to know who in counselling or psychotherapy is a weed and who is not. I thought it worth spelling out, at length, some of these incongruities and the questions that are thereby raised, because in many ways they represent the factors of disinformation and hubris that have done so much to generate the climate of fear and uncertainty that registration evokes in many psychopractitioners.

However, confronting the inadequacies of existing organisations, particularly their tendency to mirror societal norms around the distribution of power, implicitly raises another question. What kind of institution would properly represent the ethics and values of counsellors, psychotherapists and facilitators? After at least five years of informal debate and ad hoc conferences, I and others found one answer to this question—the formation, in November 1994, of the Independent Practitioners Network. IPN has long since moved out of its initially reactive posture and is, week by week, becoming a settled, ethically sound and organisationally congruent way of holding practitioner accountability.

It is based on a desire for an institutional structure that does not unawarely reproduce the societal norms of dominance and hierarchical, top-down control. (The first screen of the UKCP's website [in 1997] features a large colour picture of the Houses of Parliament.) IPN's solution is a network of groups of practitioners, a minimum of five and a maximum of ten in number, who get to know each other well enough personally and professionally to be able to 'stand by each other's work'. Implied in this is an extensive and intensive process of both support and challenge. The task entails that the group members share with the rest of the group details of their practice, its limits, their ethical commitment, and also that they disclose enough about their personal lives to enable the other group members to confidently support their competence. I have found this a delicate, challenging, onerous but very rewarding process.

Overall, the network consists of an array of relatively autonomous groups connected together via link groups. There is no central bureaucracy; there are no offices or indeed officers. Practical initiatives that need to be taken or responded to from time to time are carried out by subgroups who form to take responsibility for that task and dissolve afterwards. The network meets at national gatherings about every three months or so, to look at current concerns and to help participants and member groups consolidate their work. These, and other regional gatherings, are open to all practitioners.

As of early 1997, IPN has two hundred participants: 30 groups quite evenly distributed across the country in various stages of formation, and four full member groups. As in any group there are differentials of influence and skill, but none of seniority or positional power and no-one is empowered to speak for the network.

Articles such as this one are initiatives from individual participants. However, such initiatives from within the network are welcomed and supported and this has led, among other things, to an independent newsletter, extensive publicity material and a website. IPN does not actively recruit (at least up to now). It has been growing steadily through accumulation, as individuals whose practitioner needs it meets join with each other, form groups and get to know each other, or decide they already constitute a group and reach out to meet other such groups.

IPN seems to suit people who are inclined to be self-directing and willing to engage in cooperatively devising ways of getting their professional needs met. It's inexpensive but, at least initially, can be time-consuming because of the commitment to face-to-face 'encounter' and relationship with one's fellow practitioners.

For most people IPN will not replace supervision, though some IPN groups were initially co-supervision groups. IPN opens up access to a national array of practitioners who take themselves, their clients and their accountability very seriously; who enjoy peer relations with other similarly inclined practitioners; and who find unrepresentative, bureaucratic institutions quite incompatible with the fundamental values on which their practice is based.

To put it another way: are you looking for a congruent way of taking charge of your own process of being accountable, for delivering an ethically sound counselling to your clients, and do you have the capacity to negotiate and sustain these standards with other practitioners? After all, isn't that the kind of capacity that clients can reasonably expect of competent counsellors? If so, then IPN could work well for you.

Reference

Tuan, Yi-Fu (1984) *Dominance and Affection*. London: Yale University Press

Background: This is the first of several editorial fragments written to accompany additions to the G.O.R.I.L.L.A. archive. You can find internet links on the weblinks page.

Readers may not be aware that in 1998 the deep divisions between the sharply diverse strands of UK psychopractice—psychology, counselling, psychoanalysis and psychotherapy—were such that they even excited mainstream media interest. Anne Casement, chair of UKCP, had a tough time defending her organisation on the Radio 4 *Today* programme in April 1998, when the interviewer pressed her about the major disagreements in the field that were preventing the government from regulating 'the industry', as she called it.

However, with hindsight, my optimism in this G.O.R.I.L.L.A. fragment about the benignly irreconcilable diversity of psychopractice proved to be misplaced. Fear-driven audit/surveillance cultures still seemed embryonic in 1998 but subsequently, accelerated perhaps by the events of 9/11 in the US and the succeeding 'war on terror', their embrace began to play a significant role in homogenising psychopractice.

CHAPTER FIVE

Psychopractice for a Post-modern Era?

Events in the field of UK psychopractice move on. I get the sense, from leakages here and there and with feedback from my colleagues House and Totton's *Implausible Professions* book, that the argument about statutory regulation of psychotherapy has been won. Divisions between the diverse worldviews which make up UK psychopractice are (happily) so deep that statutory regulation is probably off the menu.

However ...

... if there was a tabloid feeding frenzy due to some off-the-wall practitioner behaviour, then this might still superglue the hard hats and the government together in statutory collusion.

Let's keep paying attention to the eyes in the backs of our heads.

Meanwhile, open, transparent, best-practice client/practitioner accountability is available and thriving, in the form of IPN, the Independent Practitioners' Network.

******

Via 'managed care', the US health insurance industry is inexorably turning the cottage industry of psychotherapy into a production line delivering standardised treatments.

Take a look at 'Emancipatory therapeutic practice in a turbulent transmodern era: a work of retrieval', a long but very cogent and internationally relevant article about this downward spiral by Maureen O'Hara from last summer's *Journal of Humanistic Psychology*, (Vol. 37 No. 3, 1997, pp. 7 – 33) (weblink page).

> When parallel but incommensurate logical, moral, and ethical systems collide, as they increasingly do within the mental health community, ensuing disagreements frequently become divisive, interminable and shrill (Macintyre, 1981). The strain this puts on any community is enormous. In the absence of any universally respected final authority—science, God, Truth—if disagreements are to be resolved at all, it is frequently through the exercise of force—coercive or brute by the stronger over the weaker.
>
> Dawes ... suggests that outpatient psychotherapy plays an educational or spiritual rather than therapeutic function in people's lives. He calls for the complete deregulation of outpatient psychotherapy and suggests that because it is not medicine, it be marketed on a caveat emptor basis like any other personal service or product. He argues that professional licenses should be required only

This article first appeared in G.O.R.I.L.L.A. as Editorial #2 28 February 1998 by those therapists who work in institutional settings such as hospitals, prisons, and residential treatment programs, where inmates are relatively powerless and so need some kind of organized protection from abuse of psychiatric power.

Therapeutic psychology and its spin-offs, clinical social work, marriage and family therapy, psychiatric nursing, and organizational behavior, are disintegrating as academic disciplines and as fields of professional practice. The field of psychology and the individuals who inhabit it are in the midst of theoretical, epistemological, methodological, and ethical meltdown. Pluralism in graduate school training, discussions about licensing and credentialing, variations in clinical theory and practice, debates about the status of psychological knowledge as science and as evidence in courts of law, shifting definitions of ethical and unethical behavior, and proliferation of antitherapist consumer protection laws are just some of the ways the postmodern crisis is already affecting the field. And it will get worse.

Strongly recommended.

Reference

MacIntyre, A (1981) *After Virtue: A Study in Moral Therapy.* London: Duckworth

Background: In a previous life, so to speak, I was a documentary film-maker, and in 1997 I decided to research the issues around psychopractice accountability, credentialing, accreditation etc, as though I was making a film. After much generous dialogue with the then editor, Heward Wilkinson, the fruits of this inquiry appeared in Volume 2, No.3 of the *International Journal of Psychotherapy*.

Viewed from today's perspective this article, researched in 1997 and published in 1998, reflects the divisions among the proponents of psychotherapy regulation psychopractice at the time. The pressure exerted by a BCP ultimatum prohibiting dual membership affected several UKCP psychoanalytic organisations and was symptomatic of the couch wars of the time. The BPS and the BAC, as it then was, are off-stage in this account.

CHAPTER SIX

The Alchemists' Nightmare:
Gold into lead
—the annexation of psychotherapy in the UK

Abstract

To psychopractitioners not affiliated to UK psychotherapy training schools or accrediting bodies, the debate about professionalisation of psychotherapy in the UK has seemed one-sided and unsound and the institutional outcomes oppressive and damaging.

Is the attempted professionalisation of psychotherapy in the UK a rational, aware process—one that supports the needs of clients? Or is it an incoming tide of collective collusion in which a trade association consisting primarily of training schools and accrediting bodies seeks to colonise and dominate the field of psychopractice?

Why should local UK developments in psychotherapy merit attention from practitioners in other countries and cultures? Apart from psychiatry and clinical psychology, psychopractice in the UK has hitherto been relatively unstructured. Creativity, innovation, diversity of practice and access to varied levels of training have flourished. Perhaps as a result of this, in the last twenty years psychological knowledge has permeated quite widely into UK society. Men in tears are not uncommon on TV and 'stressed out' is a common non-medical term for feeling 'very upset' that usefully side-steps psychiatric categories. I sometimes have the sense that every third person I meet is 'training to be a counsellor'.

Despite (or perhaps because of) this diffusion of psychological knowledge into the UK population, some strands within UK psychopractice want to restrict the spread and application of psychological expertise to psychotherapists registered as 'competent' and 'ethically sound' within the tight boundaries of a 'psychotherapy profession'. This conversion of UK psychopractice from a meadow into a formal walled garden raises a number of questions that I believe are widely relevant.

Whose interests does psychotherapy professionalisation ultimately serve? Is it 'inevitable', or does it mirror an over-determined concern with 'security' in UK society? Does it really represent an urgently needed protection for clients? How can psychotherapy continue to serve clients if it becomes absorbed into the infrastructure of society? What drives the desire for a psychotherapy profession?

Such questions stimulate answers that can range from despair, through resignation, to arguing that registration is a 'least evil'. Another response has been territorial rivalry with, as I understand, five competing psychotherapy registers

This article first appeared in 1998 in the *International Journal of Psychotherapy*, 2: 3

belonging to the British Confederation of Psychotherapists [BCP], British Psychological Society [BPS], United Kingdom Register of Counsellors [UKRC], United Kingdom Council for Psychotherapy [UKCP], and the Tavistock and Portman NHS Trust, the largest trainer and employer of psychotherapists in the UK public sector.

I don't suppose that what I have to say here will please those people who have set sail for this registration sunset. It arises from my almost wholly negative experience of the consequences of 'professionalisation'. This has included; dismay at the migration of several long-standing clients when their training schools insisted they have an 'approved', 'registered' therapist; consternation at the unfolding story of a school founded by my supervisor as, when faced with the option of joining UKCP, it appeared to compromise its values and alienate some of its supporters; anger at the experience of a highly innovative, but non-registered colleague being isolated and marginalised in her community by a UKCP training school, despite having run training and shared supervision with its founders and most of its staff; distaste at the dissembling of senior humanistic psychology practitioners over statutory support for psychotherapy registration; disappointment at the poor reception of Richard Mowbray's scholarly book (Mowbray, 1995) on the registration issues and the way it seems to have been side-lined or ignored.

This discomfort converted what had been a nagging concern over the last eight years into a commitment to researching and enquiring into the professionalisation of UK psychotherapy. The more I investigated, the more settled I became in the view that it amounts to an attempted annexation of the previously open space of UK psycho-territory. I also formed the opinion that the level of damage and harm that professionalisation will inflict amounts to the conversion of the gold of the previous open psychopractice into the lead of a bureaucratised, uncreative psychotherapy. In the last two years I have moved from feeling troubled about this creation of a 'profession', based as I see it on considerations of commercial advantage, professional competitiveness and political defensiveness, into active resistance and the creation of alternative forms of accountability.

As the text has moved towards publication, I have been encouraged to convert the initial angry rhetoric into a more direct confrontation that nonetheless acknowledges the passion of those adherents of registration who see it as beneficial. However, if the tone of this text still seems here and there overly strident or disagreeable, then keep in mind that this is written by one of the dispossessed.

I begin by saying something about how the professionalisation of psychotherapy has affected myself and others and what we have done about it. I attempt to extract from our alternative approach to accountability, some criteria for a form of organisation to help clients and therapists hold accountability of their work that is congruent with primary practitioner values.

I follow that with a series of arguments against UK psychotherapy registration. I begin with the Argument from Equivalence—if statutory regulation of psychotherapy is on the way, what other activities might similarly be regulated? I follow that with the Argument from Human Nature—ideas about what is human and natural often provide hidden foundations beneath the institutional and legal brickwork of psychopractice institutions. The Argument from Incongruity points to a mismatch between practitioner and organisational power relations in the

UKCP. The Argument from Ecology raises concerns about the threat that psychotherapy registration poses to psychopractice diversity and innovation. The Argument from Creative Style lends further support, from a broader perspective, to the notion that the UKCP's annexation of psychotherapy represents a consolidation of vested interests and the marginalising of dissent.

I conclude with a section that responds to some of the criticism that the article has attracted and anticipates other objections.

The view from outside the 'registers'

I suppose that within UKCP, BPS and BCP there has been debate and disagreement about the value of a register of psychotherapists and whether it should have statutory support. If so, these conversations have excluded UK psychopractitioners unaffiliated to psychotherapy training or accrediting bodies, and the deliberations have rarely percolated beyond the boundaries of these organisations. Yet there are many psychopractitioners whose practice overlaps with the as yet poorly defined territory of 'psychotherapy' that the UKCP claims, and who reject the premise of a register for psychotherapists and especially any register that seeks statutory status. Their voices are beginning to be heard.

The Cambridge Conferences in the early 90's led indirectly to the founding, in 1994, of the Independent Practitioners Network [IPN] (Totton 1994, 1995), which offers an alternative form of practitioner accountability. There has also been, within some sections of the Human Potential Movement, a continuing and spirited challenge to the professionalisation of psychotherapy (Heron, 1992; Kalisch,1990; Mowbray and Brown, 1990; Postle, 1994; Wasdell 1992; House 1995,1996,1997); one substantial book (Mowbray, 1995); and at least one other (House and Totton 1997).

So yards of critique from the outside— but very little response to it from inside the UKCP, the largest of the registrars.

Accountability to clients and peers

The following arguments might seem to indicate a desire for an unregulated market in psychotherapy, and indeed I think it would have been a better option for clients than professionalisation, especially if it were to follow the US, Canadian or Australian examples (Mowbray, 1995). However, my scepticism about 'regulation' (who regulates the regulators?) does not mean that I am not in favour of some kind of accountability. The question is, what form should it take?

As Richard Mowbray has cogently argued (Mowbray, 1995), there was nothing wrong with the status quo (certainly so far as the human potential field is concerned). He quotes Schutz, one of the pioneers of the human potential movement, as outlining a 'Full Disclosure provision' whereby:

All persons offering services aimed at enhancing the human condition (in whatever way) would be required to provide potential customers with a full disclosure of all information relevant to the competence of the professional. Such information would include the practitioner's education, training, philosophy, fees, membership in professional organisations, awards and anything else the professional feels is relevant. (Shultz, 1979: 156)

Mowbray follows this by noting that: 'The role of law in a full-disclosure system would be to determine the veracity and completeness of the information and to police lying and deceit, rather than to decide who is competent and thereby usurping the customer's choice.' However, a full-disclosure provision is a possible enhancement, not a necessary remedy.

In a market that may be close to saturation, due to oversupply of trainee practitioners amid very turbulent economic conditions, the formation of trade associations to protect training interests was perhaps inevitable. It has led to a quality of status-seeking professionalisation that I believe merits the title of this article. With professionalisation in place, improving the status quo through 'full disclosure', however desirable, would also support the insidious assumption that something was wrong in the first place. It no longer seems to be an option, not least because doing it unilaterally would be akin to cycling on the M25, though not (as yet) similarly illegal.

So if neither UKCP nor its cohorts are acceptable—and for me they aren't—what would I argue for?

It took me some time during the early years of this decade to extricate myself from the culture of fear that UKCP both reflects and propagates. Once out of it, I recovered the right to decide how, and through what agency, I might choose to extend how I already took responsibility for the wider implications of my work as a psychotherapist, counsellor and facilitator of one-to-one development with clients.

A full account of the outcome of these enquiries is beyond the scope of this article. I will confine myself to outlining what has shaped my preference for a no-hierarchy, low-bureaucracy approach to taking account of my client's interests and, alongside those, caring for myself.

Self- and peer-assessment

Through my work in affective education with the Institute for the Development of Human Potential [IDHP] and the Human Potential Resource Group [HPRG] at the University of Surrey, I gained considerable experience of self- and peer-assessment of practitioner competence, both as a participant and as a trainer. I came to value it highly.

At the core of this process is a developed practitioner capacity for generating a detailed assessment of their areas of competence, their deficiencies and vulnerabilities, and their plans for managing or resolving these. A group of peers who know the assessee personally and who have experience of their work scrutinise this assessment. The peer-review phase of the process thoroughly explores the 'fit' of the assessment—how accurately it matches the perceptions of the assessors, and any issues that the group have with the assessee or with their work. Lastly, after considerable discussion and exploration, the assessment may be accepted, perhaps with voluntary, or non-negotiable, caveats.

Coupled with this experience of peer assessment, I was also practising and teaching facilitation in a variety of settings where group dynamics and the distribution and deployment of power were recurring topics. For example, I co-facilitated two 2-year part-time Facilitation Styles trainings at the University of Surrey, and I initiated and participated in a number of cooperative inquiries (Heron, 1996). Out of this emerged a high value for an intrapersonal, 'power-from-within'orientation (Starhawk, 1990) in my own and client's development, and a correspondingly high value for interpersonal, 'power-with' cooperation (Starhawk, 1990) in both organisational and developmental work—plus a theoretical understanding of the necessary conditions for the flourishing of cooperation. (Postle, 1989).

Independent Practitioners' Network

Towards the end of 1994, a proposal from Nick Totton matched these preferences. Following a highly aversive experience of UKCP's procedures, he picked up an idea from his partner, Em Edmondson, for a network of independent therapists. The proposal called for:

Self- and peer-accreditation
The unit of membership will be a *group* of at least five practitioners who *know and stand by each other's work*. In joining a group, they take responsibility for the other members of that group: for sorting out any complaints or problems around their work—or failing that, for jointly being removed from membership of the network.

No hierarchy, low bureaucracy
There will be no distinction of more or less qualified or 'registered' members, since we recognise that therapeutic ability is not based on hours of training or numbers of essays written. Nor will we be scrutinising each others qualifications … nor will there be a central code of practice.

Open definitions
The network will not try to define terms like 'therapy' or to distinguish between different styles of work, since we see a richly pluralistic and multiskilled ecology as the ideal. (Totton and Edmondson, 1994)

This proposal led to a crowded meeting at the Open Centre in November 1994 and the formation of what later became the Independent Practitioners' Network [IPN]. In the two years since then, IPN has gathered several hundred supporters spread widely across the UK. Many are presently in member groups in various states of formation.

Since the initial proposal was first published, the structure has been confirmed as a network of autonomous member groups, each linked to other groups, with no central administration and with no individual membership, but accessible in principle to any psychopractitioner who can meet the network criteria. The defining task of an IPN group is to get to know each other well enough personally and professionally *to be able to stand by each other's work*. This entails a lengthy process of support, enquiry and challenge.

Refinement has led to, among other things, two mandatory requirements. One is that to be able to declare itself a Member, each group must have active links to at least two other IPN groups that are prepared to validate the process through which the group reached their agreement to stand by each other's work. The second is that member groups publish to the network the names of their members, together with a statement of their ethical commitment.

IPN has evolved with numerous centres of influence, but no centre of control. In its pursuit of 'power-from-within' for ourselves and our clients, it continues to sustain itself exclusively via 'power-with' social relations, with varying levels of elegance and certainty.

For someone like myself whose practice spans facilitation, psychotherapy, counselling, and coaching, I find that, as a model of accountability and validation IPN is amply 'good enough'.

Some criteria for practitioner accountability

IPN is an elegant social innovation. It is ripe both for expansion in the UK and for reproduction in countries that have similar issues of practitioner accountability and the distribution of power. If you wanted to replicate IPN in your community what would be the core learnings about an adequate way of holding the client/practitioner relationship that would be relevant? After consulting with other IPN members, I came up with the following list:

- Responsibility for competence and accountability is vested in the practitioner, with external support and challenge, rather than centralised 'policing'.

- The basis for being able to stand by a practitioner's work is extended and ongoing face-to-face contact and knowledge of their client's work and life circumstances.

- The accountability culture is small-scale, local and self-generating.

- The national organisation grows out of the local ones; it is practitioner-driven rather than bureaucracy-driven.

- The wide diversity of models and means that constitute effective psychopractice is acknowledged.

- The power relations in the organisational structure are congruent with the psychopractice of member groups and individual practitioners.

- The organisational structure is horizontal rather than vertical, with the decision-making process being based on a 'pluralistic consensus' model rather than one of centralised representative 'democracy'.

- The organisational structure is the minimum needed to hold to its original intentions.

- The attitude to accountability/quality control seeks to eliminate 'defective practice' through core process design rather than post facto detection of defective practice and the rejection of practitioners.

- Client access to an individual practitioner's group colleagues is open, direct and immediate.

- The organisation gives constant attention to how it manages the distribution of power.

- There is a constitution that sets out the conditions for 'participation', which is open to any practitioner, and 'Membership', which is open to any group of practitioners who satisfy the network criteria.

- Client–practitioner disputes are framed in terms of 'conflict resolution' rather than 'complaints procedures'.

Is there a downside? What might be IPN's limitations? As with any effective community, participation in IPN takes a considerable commitment of time, energy and attention. As with any truly cooperative venture, it requires developed emotional competence (Heron, 1992; Postle, 1993) and a level of affective education that is not necessarily commensurate with psychotherapy competence (and even less with 'post-graduate' status). Participation also seems to require a measure of developed self-direction and practitioner autonomy. It is a very demanding option and these requirements may set a limit to its growth.

A consequence of the network structure we have adopted is that no-one is entitled to speak for the network; there is no 'official' IPN policy. Some might consider this a disadvantage. However, IPN tends to support individual initiatives and there are well-attended national 'gatherings' every three months or so at which policy issues are debated and decisions taken.

From the perspective of where I stand as a practitioner and in the light that IPN sheds on psychotherapy 'professionalisation', I develop at length, in the sections that follow, five arguments against current registration approaches to accountability of the UK mainstream accrediting bodies.

The Argument from Equivalence

'The self-regulation of UK media-workers, presently administered by the UK Media Consortium [UKMC], received a boost today when the Heritage Minister outlined legislation to confer statutory status on the UKMC's voluntary registration scheme'. Voluntary registration has already begun to install far-reaching regulation of journalists, TV producers and directors, photographers and advertising executives.

'The Minister welcomed the UKMC initiative, noting that it built on the success of the statutory register of psychotherapists'. She claimed that readers and viewers welcomed the government backing for measures "to protect them from the inaccuracy and intrusiveness of a minority of maverick journalists, intrusive photographers and the trance-inducing quality of some broadcasting".

'The minister added that while the requirements for media-worker registration were stringent, they were also fair, and aimed to balance diversity of editorial opinion with protection of the public.

'The government believes that, as the media-worker register comes into full operation, it will guarantee that all content provided for public consumption is factually accurate, ethically sound, and has been obtained without intrusion into privacy, and that comment is fair and objective.

'The new legal prerequisite for media-worker registration includes the satisfactory completion of a four-year postgraduate training, including 900 hours of supervised practice, adherence to strictly administered codes of ethics, complaints procedures and working practices, breach of which may result in being 'struck off' the media-workers register. Media observers note that these new requirements have already created an explosion in the demand for training as everyone in the field realises the economic consequences of being unregistered.

'A further announcement is expected soon from the Heritage think tank that is looking into the possibility of extending statutory registration to artists, painters, sculptors, musicians, singers and composers ...'

Need I go on?

In comparison to the global culture-setting capacity of TV, newspapers, magazines and advertising, the effect on national life of psychotherapists is peripheral. Yet there is no conceivable way that, say, journalists in the UK would accept a statutory register with equivalent limitations on access to the media.

Would not restricting the production of films, or journalism, or fashion photography to a list of accredited practitioners amount to an oppressive constriction on freedom of speech and action? Is not a similar course of action in attempting to regulate psychotherapy, especially if it involves statutory enforcement, similarly oppressive and limiting? Many psychopractitioners outside (and some inside) the UKCP think so.

I have suggested that it amounts to 'a stealing of the flame' (Chapter 1), asking how a professional 'light' at the centre of UKCP or other 'professional' bodies can avoid casting a 'shadow' that perpetuates deference and ignorance outside the registration domain (Postle, 1989). Kalisch described UKSCP, the forerunner of UKCP, in terms of 'dependencies being created, empires built and nests lavishly lined'—to be followed in their wake by restrictive practices, closed shops, protection and collusion' (Kalisch, 1990). Heron has pointed out that, 'The political argument for professionalisation, based on legally accredited competence in handling transference, is a rationalisation of a deep-seated transference phenomenon.' He sees this as a paradox: 'One can scarcely have much confidence in psychotherapists whose need to have their management of transference government approved is itself a sign of unresolved transference material' (Heron, 1990). Wasdell sees individuals primarily involved professionally in one-to-one relationships as at the mercy of unconscious, irrational and often destructive forces being acted out at the corporate dynamic level of psychotherapy, counsellor and analysts' organisations. He couples this with the proposal that the aggregate dynamics of the profession as a whole mirrors the most common societal defence-maintenance processes. He sees the psychodynamics of the psychotherapy profession as collusional counter-transference that maintains the pathology of the social system (Wasdell, 1992).

This line of argument can of course be deconstructed as a 'tyranny of the unconscious', in which anything disagreeable—in this instance, to those of us who are dispossessed—is ascribed to pathology on the part of those of whom we disapprove. No doubt the reverse could, and will, be argued. However the extent of scepticism about the psychotherapy registration process is considerable—and publicly accessible, too (Postle, 1997), in contrast to the negligible public defence, or justification of it.

In what other ways does psychotherapy 'registration' pose a serious threat to freedom of speech and action?

Self-directed learning

People in the UK commonly assemble for themselves a career in art, journalism, writing, film, theatre or music through self-directed experiential learning. This may take the form of ad hoc training, casual and short-term employment, supplementary courses, coaching, mentoring, apprenticeship and supervision. This often chaotic and uncertain cultural milieu has contributed, in recent decades, to an internationally renowned flourishing of creativity in the UK. I want that to continue to include psychopractice.

Many people are inclined, for reason of life experience, inclination and, as I will show below, creative style, to also take a strongly self-directed line in assembling for themselves the elements of psychopractice competence. I see no reason to suppose that this is an exclusively UK phenomenon. 'Registration' as now constituted presents, and is intended to present, an almost insurmountable obstacle to this.

I think that before groups of psychotherapists are entitled to ring-fence their view of psychotherapy via registers, they need to show conclusively that this informal, self-directed mode of entry to psychopractice is damaging to clients (rather than damaging to a 'profession' of psychotherapy). In the absence of such a demonstration, registration, and particularly the pursuit of statutory registration, is oppressive and unbecoming in an occupation devoted to relationship. So far as other colleagues and I who take an interest in these matters are aware, no such defence of registration exists.

Support for this view recently emerged from an unexpected quarter. Anne

Richardson, Senior Policy Advisor at the UK Department of Health, outlined factors that, in the view of the Department, decisively militate against statutory regulation of psychotherapy. After reminding her BCP conference audience 'that there is no agreement here in the UK, or it would appear in Europe, about what exactly does or should constitute the activity of psychotherapists', she went on to say:

> There are no plans to regulate what after all we have to call an *activity*, rather than a *title*. I mean psychotherapy is something that people *do*. It's something doctors, psychologists, nurses, social workers, lay psychotherapists, do. Lots of different people practise this activity. Many … most … some … with training, some without training … with different kinds of training. Psychotherapy is an activity, not a job title … It's important to say it would be extremely difficult to regulate by statute something which is an activity like that. Could you imagine trying to write a law? It would be impossible.
>
> Another thing that militates against [statutory regulation] is the increasing evidence of the effectiveness of a variety of approaches which some people wouldn't call psychotherapy. Some sorts of stress management … you might not call psychotherapy … some forms of psycho-educational approaches … you might not call psychotherapy but others would do. And there is good evidence for the effectiveness of some of these approaches with mental illness groups. So if you were to regulate or legislate, you might stop that, prevent that diversity, and that would be unwelcome.

However improbable statutory regulation looks from the admirably well-informed perspective of the UK Department of Health, the glacial political strength of the 'psycho-security' that psychotherapy and counselling registration purport to offer may yet dictate otherwise. Evidence of a unified profession looks like a minimum pre-condition for the notion ever to be taken seriously.

Certainly the adoption of an industry-wide standard which requires that 'everyone get themselves bar-coded', as a psychiatrist I know recently described it, will strongly support the marketing of psychotherapy services. And of course, the UKCP's seventy-three bodies, a diverse and formidable array principally of training interests, with 3500 names in one register-text, can be claimed to support the idea that a 'profession' of psychotherapy does exist.

However, from the wider perspective of psychopractice, the 'unified profession' will shortly embrace five competing 'registers': BPS, Tavistock, BCP, UKCP and the UKCR, with very divergent criteria for membership. Of these registrars, UKCP is the largest and has by far the best-established public face, which is why I tend to focus on it in this text.

But is UKCP a wonderful federal expression of diversity, or is it more a territorial non-aggression pact between at least two , fundamentally contradictory worldviews?

The Argument from Human Nature

Some years ago, in a previous life so to speak, I made a film about Human Nature with Robert M. Young, a historian of biology and the human sciences and presently a psychoanalytic psychotherapist and Professor of Psychotherapy and Psychoanalytic Studies at the University of Sheffield. The film 'Behaving Ourselves' (Postle and Young, 1982) looked at the way models of human nature influenced such human activities as scientific research, animal experimentation and genocide.

I remember being shocked to discover that my perspective on human nature, informed then and now by Humanistic Psychology theory and practice, was fundamentally different from that of Bob Young, who favoured psychoanalysis.

From my Humanistic Psychology perspective I saw human beings as being born fundamentally OK. We have innate capacities for giving and receiving love, understanding and being understood, choosing and being chosen, but are vulnerable to primal wounding, deficits of care and nourishment and distorted learning (Heron, 1992; Postle, 1989).

Bob Young's psychoanalytic perspective emphasised Freud's view that:

> People are innately aggressive. 'Man is a wolf to other men' and hence must be tamed by institutions (Gay, 1988, p. 541).

> The constitutional inclination to aggression is the greatest hindrance or impediment to civilisation. (*S.E.* 21, pp. 129, 142) (Young, 1992)

And as he says in recent writings, 'this is a dour doctrine':

> Life *consists of—is—*a struggle between love and destructiveness. Civilisation *consists* of renunciation ... [Freud] says elsewhere that 'love and necessity are the parents of civilization' (p. 101). We live our lives in a space between the two great meta-instincts, and the main forces at work are rapacious sexual and destructive instincts, guilt, renunciation and sublimation. (Young, 1992)

> ... Social institutions are many things for Freud, but above all they are dams against murder, rape, and incest. (Gay, 1988, p. 547)

In another recent article, Young presents a cogent image of what this means for the psychoanalytic perspective on human nature:

> I want to spend a moment on the image of a veneer. I chose it to emphasise the delicacy, vulnerability and beauty of the more moral, generous and creative dimensions of human nature. A veneer is usually thin, made of a precious material, applied to cover a baser, less presentable one to make it more attractive. A typical example is a thin layer of a precious wood, glued on top of a coarser one. It is easily damaged and needs maintenance, usually cleaning and polishing. We use cloths, mats and other items to prevent it being burned, stained, or scratched. A moment's carelessness can seriously damage it. Characterising human decency as a veneer implies that I see it as an imposed surface phenomenon. (Young, 1992)

He goes on to say that he personally supports the Kleinian approach to our 'nasty' side: 'the idea that destructiveness was as strong as erotic impulses at the basis of our most primitive natures'.

This image of civility in human nature as a thin and fragile veneer covering a substratum of rage, aggression and sexual rapacity helped me a lot. I began to understand why the coming together of psychopractitioners to form a psychotherapy profession as UKCP and other bodies could be perceived by some people as desirable and inevitable, and by others and myself as oppressive and incongruous. In other words, whether you thought it a good thing or not depended, at least in part, on what model of human nature you subscribed to as a psychopractitioner.

If you believe that people are innately good, but become damaged and so think and behave in distressed ways, then your institutions are likely to favour relatively open, negotiable boundaries, trust, self-direction, and self-reflexive regulation. For example, many of the people who have joined the Independent Practitioners' Network have a high level of expectation that they can be trusted to take responsibility for their psychopractice with external *reference*, but without prescriptive, external controls and certainly without legal ones. In this universe people may make mistakes, or unwittingly act out hurts, or behave in inadequate or inappropriate ways, but not because they are 'naturally' aggressive or sexually rapacious.

By contrast, if you are committed to a belief that people are innately aggressive, with hard-wired instinctual desires to damage, punish and act out sexual desires, and that unless this tendency to 'emotional disorder' is very highly contained, chaos will result, you will expect that *all* practitioners are *quite capable* of behaving badly. The only way to minimise this is to create a container with tight boundaries, lots of control and sanctions, preferably legal, against bad behaviour. Statutory registration would then look like a virtue, because it adds the power of the courts to police these boundaries.

The more I looked, the more evidence there was to support my intuition that the psychoanalytic view of human nature seemed to be having a profound influence over the professionalisation of psychotherapy. For example, as some of the following material shows, many psychoanalytic practitioners see the UKCP as impossibly liberal and wishy-washy about training and standards. Even so, UKCP office holders are strongly weighted towards psychodynamic/psychoanalytic practice. More on that anon.

I find it difficult to believe that the twenty-five or so organisations of the UKCP Humanistic and Integrative Section [HIPS] subscribe to the psychoanalytic view of human nature set out earlier. For example, one of its members says in a current brochure that:

> There are certain situations and personal capacities towards which we are all more or less consciously attracted: for instance, the ability to have good relationships with others, to enjoy good health, to make free and conscious decisions, to use our mind to its maximum potential, to enjoy all that is beautiful, to be competent in our work and calm even in moments of crisis, to be open to serenity and joy, and finally the ability to love ... Psychosynthesis is a unified conception of human development ... (Psychosynthesis Trust, 1996)

In another recent article, Young argues that:

> If you have a developmental psychology, you have a theory of human nature ... I take the view that if you have a psychology, that's equivalent to having a theory of human nature, however much latitude for the role of different experiences

and different developmental pathways there may be within the particular theory you espouse. (Young, 1995)

And this view is supported by a former chair of UKCP:

> ... the study of psychotherapy is about understanding human nature in all its complexity. (Deurzen-Smith, 1996)

The hints of a model of human nature in the *Psychosynthesis* brochure, its 'unified conception of human development', sound a long way from the psychoanalytic model of human nature:

> Neither Freud nor Klein, nor for that matter Karl Menninger ... believed in innocence. All believed that destructiveness was inherent in human nature. On this account, there is no innocence to be lost. Instead, we are initially given to destructiveness, and our task is to become civilised and to remain so as much as we can.
> ... the struggle between Eros and Death, between the instinct of life and the instinct of destruction, as it works itself out in the human species. This struggle is what all life essentially consists of ... (Freud, 1930, p. 122; Young 1995)

But insofar as UKCP and their like-minded partners are installing a collection of trade-restrictive practices, ring-fencing their psycho-territories and gearing up for a politically timely move to statutory registration, they do seem to be behaving collectively as though they subscribe to a view of a human nature that *has* to be contained and controlled.

For instance, I was left wondering why so many people in the Association of Humanistic Psychology Practitioners [AHPP] and in the rest of the HIPS section of UKCP, whom I would suppose shared my perspective on what is 'human' and 'natural', could be so committed to a form of organisation that appears to be so incongruent with their core beliefs.

The UKCP trade association comprises some 75 member organisations. It is, as Diana Whitmore says in a recent *Self and Society* article, an 'organisation of organisations'. On the ground this amounts to about 3500 UKCP-registered psychotherapists. Overlapping with this are about 2000 psychoanalysts, perhaps half of them with dual membership of UKCP and BCP. Then there are the two outsider groupings, The Institute of Psycho-Analysis and the Independent Practitioners' Network, with about 200 each (and though they seemed out of the picture at the time there were also the BACP and the BPS).

Looking at these totals I realised for the first time what a large proportion of the total the psychoanalytic tendency occupies, about half of UKCP; or if we count the 'psychodynamic' organisations as essentially psychoanalytic in their values, more than half. Furthermore, psychoanalysis is by far the oldest and most established of the psychopractices with an extensive international array of trainings and a very extensive body of theory. It has also, I understand, deep roots in the NHS and a lot of influence through occupying many of the senior consultancy posts, with the patronage that flows from positional power. One such person is the current chair of the UKCP.

As I researched this section of 'The Alchemists' Nightmare', I came across another of Bob Young's papers that went some way to explaining how the structural style of UKCP may have come into being. In a long and intricately written paper on the psychodynamics of psychoanalytic organisations, he details the shenanigans that resulted in the departure of the psychoanalysts (as distinct from the psychoanalytical psychotherapists) from the UKCP. I believe that these events are the tip of an iceberg. They show how a psychoanalytic perspective on human nature is likely to have had a considerable and lasting influence on the UKCP's organisational style. While the analysts may have left, they have been present throughout the UKCP's formative period.

Before we come to his narrative, here are some remarks from Bob Young about the culture of British psychoanalysis, including psychoanalytic psychotherapy.

> ... people are mixtures ... they behave well in some contexts, less well in others, badly in others. In psychoanalytic organisations, as Kenneth Eisold has helpfully shown, dissent is not tolerated. There seems to be no space for genuine and open political debate and uncertainty. A situation has been developing in this subculture for some years which has, in my opinion, reached a level which seems to me to pose serious problems under the general heading: 'Physician, heal thyself!' (Young, 1996)

In a talk given to a US audience, he narrates some of the difficulties that the formation of the UKCP posed for the psychoanalysts.

> The problem which soon became apparent was whether or not the IPA psychoanalysts, i.e., The British Psychoanalytical Society, would get into bed, first with the Jungians and then with the psychoanalytic psychotherapists ... there were reasons for optimism until the psychoanalysts said that the price of their staying in [the UKCP] was that their representatives should have a veto over the decisions of the council—not the section, mind you, but the council of the whole organization. No kidding. They claimed to be senior to all other psychotherapeutic practitioners and referred to the device they advocated as 'the Security Council model', after the body in the UN where any one of five countries has a veto and the Security Council can in some circumstances overrule General Assembly decisions. There are about three hundred members of the Institute of Psychoanalysis practising in Britain out of a total of about 2500 reputable and recognisably psychodynamic psychotherapists. (The current chairman tells me that there are about 3400 on the register at present.)

He goes on to describe the turning point.

> A person who was not a psychoanalyst but worked closely with them was not elected to a key committee [of the UKCP], and the whole house of cards fell down. The representatives of the psychoanalysts and their allies decided that they 'had had enough'. A new and rival organization had been a building in the wings, and it was inaugurated. Only certain psychotherapy organizations were invited to join it ... The analysts withdrew, and the positions of several organizations close to them became very unstable because of divided loyalties. Practically all other psychoanalytic psychotherapy organizations which joined the newly created British Confederation of Psychotherapists (BCP) remained in the UKCP, as well. It now has ten member organizations, with a lot of overlapping

membership, e.g., analysts who work at the Tavistock Clinic or people who work there and are also members of the Association of Child Psychotherapists or any of the above who are members of the Association of Psychoanalytic Psychotherapists in the National Health Service. (Young, 1996)

So far as I am aware, this dual membership of the breakaway Confederation and the UKCP is still in place.

These events lead me to infer that there was, and probably remains, an understandable desire in the rest of UKCP to adjust its standards and/or values to accommodate the analysts, or at least to find some compromise that would keep them on board or help them return to the fold. Candidates for this would seem likely to include longer courses, more frequent therapy, more supervision, consolidation of the move towards postgraduate entry and an expansion of theory at the expense of experiential work, which some students are reporting.

An internal memorandum to all registrants of the psychoanalytic/psychodynamic Sections of UKCP lists seven reasons why they should not leave. The text ends on an anxious note, urging the reader not to 'stand idly by whilst our profession becomes split even further' (Tantam, 1996)

Even to someone such as Bob Young inside the psychoanalytic tradition, the actions of the analysts were off the scale in their arrogance. He continues:

> Attempts to designate a group of highly qualified psychoanalytic (or religious or political) practitioners as superior by virtue of having particular qualifications and then place them over the rest of the profession is a breathtaking usurpation. For them to object to people not allowing that they constitute a 'Security Council', and then to set up a breakaway organisation whose main structural features are keeping organisations out which don't kow-tow to them and declaring all other practitioners of an inferior caste (or perhaps even charlatans) is clearly and simply a power play and should be transcended. That is, we must find a way of going beyond the present situation. However, in order to achieve this healthy iconoclasm, we have to unscramble the self-infantilisation and deference of the organisations whose members have allowed it to happen. That may be harder. Mandarinates trade on the low self-esteem of ordinary people, even and especially ordinary people who express their ordinariness in being good and non-self-idealising psychotherapists, priests or politicians. (Young, 1996)

I believe that many of the people whose names the UKCP register carries within its pages are also 'ordinary people who express their ordinariness in being good and non-self-idealising psychotherapists'. But I rather suspect that as UKCP has evolved, the infinite easygoingness of the humanistic/integrative culture has led them into a loss of political will, a failure of nerve and/or courage in relations with the psychoanalytic tradition.

Unscrambling the 'self-infantilisation and deference of the organisations whose members have allowed it to happen', of which this article is an example, is a task that seems also relevant for the HIPS section of UKCP. As Mowbray so cogently puts it, 'involving a removal of as many heads as possible from the sand before eager register builders add the cement' (Mowbray 1995)

If this feels unduly critical in tone, I want to say that a considerable tension that is hard to hold—between wanting to tolerate diversity of belief and practice and a determination to resist what I experience as oppression—has shaped this writing. That some people wish to have a registration-based type of organisation I can live with, though I regard it as ill advised. However, I refuse to be over run by a psychotherapy trade association/trainers club that seeks to determine who in the field of psychopractice are cultivars and who are weeds, or, to shift metaphor a little, who seem intent on making a daisy-free lawn out of the UK psycho-meadow.

The UKCP style may seem decent and civilised and innocuous, but it bears a resemblance to the arrogance of the analysts in believing that they should constitute the 'security council' of psychopractice, that they have a corner on quality in a way that no-one else has. Is not the UKCP a self-declared 'security council' that embodies 'power-over' domination in exactly the same way as the United Nations version does? Evidence of its agendas (van Deurzen-Smith 1996; Tantam 1996) easily sustains this parallel.

I'm tempted to leave this argument here, but in case you don't yet find it compelling, Bob Young goes on to outline some of the qualities of the organisations that *eventually* couldn't stomach the plurality of UKCP but with which about half of the current UKCP membership nonetheless share a bed—and were there from the early Rugby Conference days. I give the quote at length because this is a rare insight: whistle-blowing done at some risk to the author, as he outlines elsewhere in his text.

> What I want to say about the other organisations which broke away [from the UKCP] is contentious, but the simple truth as far as I have been able to discern it. For the most part they kow-tow to the Institute of Psychoanalysis. This is not true of the Jungians, but it is of the others. In particular—and I suggest that this is crucial—they insist that (with vanishingly rare exceptions)the people who are allowed to be training therapists in their psychotherapy trainings should be psychoanalysts. The same is true, although not quite to the same extent, of who can supervise and who gets asked to lecture and run seminars.. Who can say how much we are looking at insistence on quality versus the maintenance of a patronage network and the hegemony of one organisation over a number of others?

Young goes to detail how, in this 'caste system', the analysts dominate psycho-analytic psychotherapy.

> The analysts analyse and supervise the psychotherapists. They decide if and when they are ready to see training patients and eventually to qualify. They do or don't make referrals of patients to them. They do or don't appoint them to positions as honorary therapists in the hospitals where the analysts control practically all the consultant posts in psychotherapy ... As the analysts put it at a recent British conference on the relationship between psychoanalysis and psychotherapy (and as it was put by another in an internal memorandum describing their proposed programme in psychoanalytic studies), they represent 'the gold standard'; the therapists are alloys and baser metals—copper, as I recall one saying. (Young, 1996)

The BCP is quite shameless about its 'seniority'. In their website screens (BCP, 1997) they outline the reasons why they separated from the forerunner of the UKCP, an umbrella body that was catholic in it membership and where, in order to recognise difference of titles and function, member institutions were divided into separate sections.

The momentum by which this was achieved made it difficult for the older more established institutions ... to have their seniority recognised within the structure of UKSCP. (It is difficult to represent with sufficient force the problem this presented. It was as if the United Nations had no permanent members of the Security Council, only nations elected to it from the General Assembly in which each nation had a single vote.) The institutions of the UKSCP were not equal in their contribution to the field nor in public esteem. Current and historically based realities of that kind could not be accommodated within the constitutional structure of the UKSCP ... and this was a decisive factor which led to the establishment of the BCP as a separate body. (BCP, 1997)

To what extent, after reading this, you feel that the IPA, the BCP and UKCP amount to a 'gold standard' in the field of psychopractice in this country I suppose depends on what model of human nature you subscribe to.

The point I seek to make here is not to denigrate the practice of psychoanalysis, undoubtedly one of the flowers in the meadow of psychopractice. Nor do I intend to demean the objectives of the BCP in pursuing the highest standards of training and practice, or their assertion that 'a proper self-definition and self-discipline by institutions intent upon self-regulation protects the public'(BCP 1997). I want to keep our attention on how psychopractice organises itself: to reiterate that Young's storytelling points to a set of values that have been at the heart of the UKCP since its earliest days, that remains current in about half the member organisations and that have decisively shaped the attitude and structure of those organisations.

As with persons, UKCP's history is formative of its present behaviour. It sets the perspectives that can be entertained, lays down the comfort zones of what can be tolerated, and determines what can be embraced and what is anathema. I believe that the attitudes to power and human nature that Bob Young has so well delineated have been formative in UKCP's history to such an extent that allegiances, alliances and administrative and constitutional style have been decisively skewed towards those long in place in psychoanalysis, and not least those in medicine. As Christopher Coulson, until recently Association of Humanistic Psychology Practitioners [AHPP] representative to UKCP, has commented in reviewing this article:

... the skewing ... is not just towards an analytic mode, but towards the medical model and particularly the NHS medical model. The chair, general secretary and head of the registration board are all doctors. (Coulson personal communication)

For our present purposes, what matters about this bias is how it affects the ways in which an organisation handles the distribution of power. One choice is to merely reproduce the societal norm of hierarchical dominance, as UKCP appears to. Here is Coulson again:

The fear culture/battle for market dominance thrives within the UKCP. Pure training organisations are beginning to challenge accrediting organisations ... to query whether they are competent to judge therapist competence. The implicit claim is that only training organisations are fit to accredit practitioners and therefore presumably to re-accredit at intervals. Goodbye, independent accreditors. Hello, total control by the industry. (Coulson personal communication)

This choice of how to handle the distribution of power appears to match the values of UKCP's psychoanalytic/psychodynamic registrants. But how can it be acceptable to Humanistic and Integrative practitioners?

The Argument from Incongruity

The structure of UKCP appears to be federal as regards training schools and institutions but it is not representative, accessible or accountable, either to clients, or to those of us outside its range. Nor apparently even to registrants, who have been told in the UKCP house journal that, even though motions from the Executive and Governing Board had been rejected at an annual conference, and the way through from local organisation to Section was far from clear, 'There is no need, however, to camp out in trees. *Twice a year (at least)* [my italics] you can speak to all fellow registrants in these pages' (UKCP, 1996).

Yet through its 'register', UKCP purports to be a body that uniquely represents the whole spectrum of psychotherapies in the United Kingdom and to embody ways of holding and discharging core ethical and occupational responsibilities among practitioners, trainers, trainees and clients.

How has this been done? Through a searching, open exploration of the views of existing practitioners inside *and outside* training schools and accrediting bodies? No; a variety of influences—for example, a defensive preoccupation with hostile attacks from the media and elsewhere—(House, 1996), the need to consolidate training businesses in a near-saturated market and the desire to build a profession with equivalent status to science and medicine—has led to what is effectively the formation of a trade association of psychotherapy training schools and accrediting bodies. It is a formulation that has subsequently been partially acknowledged (Tantam, 1996).

Among committed supporters of UKCP, and also in the BPS and BCP, there is concern about the 'status' of the psychotherapy 'profession'—its status relative to psychotherapy in other countries, but especially Europe and, not least, its scientific status.

In the first paragraph under the banner heading 'Scientific Program', the announcement of the First European Conference on Group and Psychoanalysis comments that the conference will encompass ...

 ... the group phenomenon that in all European countries the situation for long-term psychotherapy is problematical, especially in the public sector.

This scientific enterprise would try to answer the question:

 How can we guarantee a future and space in the public sector and society for our way of helping patients?

This journal (IJP) has carried some indications of other aspects of the urge to redefine psychotherapy as an independent scientific discipline. The 'Strasbourg Declaration' of the European Association for Psychotherapy declares that:

> 2. Training in psychotherapy takes place at an advanced, qualified and scientific level (EAP, 1996)

The UKCP person who looks after European matters is on record as believing that: 'We have to transform what used to be a craft or an art, based on moral or religious principles, into a scientifically based, accountable, professional expertise' (van Deurzen-Smith, 1996). There is also a desire to be seen as a profession with equivalent status to medicine, because 'only after the profession [of medicine] had been organised and proper qualifications put in place ... funds became available for more research ...' (van Deurzen-Smith 1996)

Not surprisingly, there have been doubts. One line of argument, which I support, says that because psychotherapy has no autonomous theory-base independent of general psychology and anthropology, it must therefore have an inherent diversity. Following on from this, since no position regarding psychic causality can define the nature of the field, the connectedness of psychotherapies can usefully be expressed only in terms of commonalities of praxis. What kind of organisation does this point to? A trade association? But not, surely, a 'profession'?

Christopher Hauke concluded a conference introduction to the UKCP Analytical Psychology section by noting that 'a psychological perspective that acknowledges diversity and multiplicity in the psyche also questions the need for either synthesis or hierarchy as the means for resolving the apparent fragmentation of psychotherapy' (Dinwoodie, 1996).

However, the UKCP mirrors other political institutions, in the UK and elsewhere, in seemingly being rooted in an uncritical acceptance of 'power-over' dominance as natural and inevitable:

> Power-over comes from the consciousness I have termed estrangement ... It is the consciousness modelled on the God who stands outside the world, outside nature, who must be appeased, placated, feared and above all, obeyed. (p. 9)

> The language of power-over is the language of law, of rules, of abstract, generalised formulations enforced on the concrete realities of particular circumstances ... in the worldview of power-over ... value must be earned or granted ... in the secular world, the worth we acquire is constantly rated against that of others ... we internalise a primal insecurity about our own right to be, which drives us to compete for tokens of pseudo-value ... Power-over motivates through fear. Its systems instill fear and then offer a hope of relief in return for compliance and obedience. (p. 14)

> Power-over shapes every institution of our society. (Starhawk, 1990 p. 9))

'Power-over' shows up in the structural form of the UKCP. Emmy van Deurzen-Smith, a previous UKCP Chair, admitted in an interview (Jones, 1992) that as people elbowed for position, 'inevitably a hierarchy will form'. David Kalisch describes it thus:

UKCP is a dominator hierarchy seeking to borrow power from another dominator hierarchy in order to impose its dominance ... [He continues] It is not possible to canvas for pluralism and diversity *whilst voting for statutory registration* [my italics]. (Kalisch, 1996)

That UKCP could get itself into the position of claiming to do both speaks to me of a deep lack of awareness of how ubiquitous 'power-over' dominance is.

In my view, despite the no doubt honest and genuinely felt motivations of many of its supporters, UKCP exists, at least in part, to express colonial/imperial ambitions. It is imperious in manner, as witness Pokorny's dismissive comments about Mowbray's comprehensive and scholarly book, *The Case Against Psychotherapy Registration* (Mowbray, 1995).

> ... we are offered a strange collection of analogies, dogmatic statements, and opinions, embedded in a number of facts ... All these are arranged in such a way as to be almost unrecognisable ... this book, far from being embarrassing for the UKCP, is nothing other than a collection of opinions and fragmented facts which are stitched together in a particularly idiosyncratic manner and thus purport to be evidence. (*The Therapist*, 1996)

A letter to *The Guardian* was open about UKCP's agenda to colonise and dominate the field of psychotherapy. 'While Sigmund, Karl and Melanie indeed simply "set up shop in their back bedroom", Tom Dick and Harriet will discover that since 1989, Jo Public is highly unlikely to come to them unless they are registered with the UK Council for Psychotherapy' (Oakley, 1995). The writer was apparently unaware of the irony of publicly declaring as a virtue the exclusion of present equivalents to innovators such as Freud and Klein!

Recent supporters of UKCP in the press have claimed that statutory registration is a 'political red herring' (Tricia Scott, 1996), yet an internal memorandum to registrants of the analytic and psychodynamic sections who might be considering leaving claims the pursuit of statutory registration as one of the seven reasons for staying in the UKCP. 'The Council continues to work to achieve statutory regulation of the profession' (Tantam, 1996). What else does statutory registration of psychotherapists mean in practice, if not engaging the sanction of state law enforcement to police the boundaries of a psychotherapy 'profession'? Even without legislation, is it not also true that a 'voluntary' register plus time equals a 'de facto' 'statutory' register?

Whether awarely or not, power is expressed through UKCP as 'power-over', across the council/others boundary; that is to say, between the council and unregistered practitioners (and also between the council and registered practitioners insofar as it holds the sanction of removal from the register for misconduct)—also, as I recently witnessed, between the UKCP and other competing organisations. Speaking about European umbrella organisations at a recent BCP conference on registration (BCP, 1997), Anne Casement, representing UKCP, even felt licensed to (erroneously) claim 'that in this instance, UKCP, for the United Kingdom, is the body that actually regulates anything to do with psychotherapy here'.

But power relations between persons are not inevitably of the power-over variety. The last several decades have seen the emergence of efforts, at least in the

Anglo-Saxon culture, to install (some would say re-install) ways of relating to each other—both interpersonally and through institutions—that do not unwittingly reproduce 'power-over' consciousness. I'm thinking of the wide range of self-help communities and initiatives such as the ParentLink Network, Alcoholics Anonymous, Hearing Voices Network, United Kingdom Advocacy Network [UKAN] and co-counselling and reciprocal counselling. Because there are also 'power-from-within' and 'power with'.

> Power-from-within ... sees the world itself as a living being made up of dynamic aspects, a world where one thing shape-shifts into another, where there are no solid separations and no simple causes and effects. In such a world, all things have inherent value ... We do not have to earn value. Immanent value cannot be rated or compared. No one, nothing can have more of it than another. It is language in action, which speaks in the body and to all the senses in ways that can never be completely conveyed in words.
>
> Power-with sees the world as a pattern of relationships, but its interest is in how that pattern can be shaped, moulded, shifted. It values beings, forces and people according to how they affect others and according to a history based on experience. It can recognise inherent worth, but can also rate and compare, valuing some more highly than others. (Starhawk, 1990, p. 15)

In the co-creation of a psychotherapeutic encounter, are not ethically sound relationships between practitioner and client of the 'power-with' variety? Are they not aimed at awakening 'power-from-within' in the client?

Yet the organisation that seeks to regulate psychotherapy 'expects that the importance of the register will increase until there will come a time when members of the public, or healthcare providers, will only engage the services of registered psychotherapists' (Tantam, 1996), i.e. a time when the register monopolises the market for psychotherapy.

To me, as a competent, ethical, but non-registered psychotherapist, this determination to dominate the market for psychotherapy looks fundamentally incongruent, particularly for the HIPS member—as though a herd of gentle, cooperative psychotherapists had taken flight through fear, whether of exclusion, or unemployment, or 'Europe', into delegating to willing bureaucratic hierarchs the building of an elaborate 'security' system. To protect clients? Or to protect themselves?

A recent international report (Travis, 1997) shows that England and Wales are the most security-conscious countries in the industrialised world. These countries top the international league for home-security devices, with more than three-quarters of homes boasting an alarm, or special door locks, or grilles on windows or doors. What if this style of home security, and the enthusiastic embrace of 'psychotherapysecurity' in the form of registration, were related? What if they both signal the absorption into our unconscious of some of the key prevailing values (and effects) of the continuing marketisation and globalisation of UK national politics?

There is a high probability that practitioners whose speciality is one-to-one work will be unaware of the collusive group psychodynamics of their organisations (Wasdell, 1992) and it follows that such groups would be likely to have an unnecessarily restricted range of options when seeking a structure for their organisation. It is perhaps unsurprising that they would unwittingly reproduce the underlying, unconscious norms about power of the society around them, i.e. dominance expressed through stratified hierarchical bureaucracy, supported by forms of voting that are likely to privilege majorities. (Pokorny and Fanning, 1996).

Yet is it not so that many, if not all, clients who come for therapy have some difficulty with exactly these power relations? Not least the degree to which domination (and submission) continues to seem 'natural' or 'second nature'? Do not many of these clients, in their struggles to find a way out of, say, a victim orientation, look to the therapist for a model of how relationships can be? One that demonstrates, as they co-create the therapeutic relationship, a lived capacity for 'power-with', i.e., cooperation, authenticity, negotiation, clarity of boundaries, etc.? My experience of living and working in Belgium has demonstrated that this is not exclusively a UK or Anglo-Saxon problem.

For me this is a fundamental element of ethical psychopractice. If you think so too, yet you are also a UKCP- registered psychotherapist, or working towards registration, how do you justify the incongruence between aligning yourself with an institution that embodies 'power-over' relations while running your own practice in 'power-with' mode, aimed at awakening 'power-from-within' in your clients? And if you are able to justify it, perhaps economically, how do you avoid this incongruence contaminating relations with your clients?

Since the unaware acting out of dominance appears to be a fundamental flaw in how the UKCP is constituted, I thought it worthwhile to take step back and examine how such an outlook may affect the services to clients that psychotherapy exists to deliver.

The Argument from Ecology

While we in the UK have yet to reach the medicalised, insurance-driven 'managed care' of the US, I am convinced that the incoming tide of professionalisation in the UK will seriously diminish diversity and innovation in psychotherapy.

For example, UKCP-registered psychotherapists 'are required to refrain from any behaviour that may be detrimental to the profession, to colleagues or trainees …' and they 'are required to take action … with regard to the behaviour of a colleague which may be detrimental to the profession, to colleagues, or to trainees' (Mowbray, 1995). As Mowbray asks: 'Who decides what is detrimental? The profession, of course.' This is exactly the kind of circular collusive dynamic that will create 'no go' areas in psychotherapy content and practice.

Furthermore, the present Chair of UKCP is on record as hoping that psychotherapy:

> registration will weed out unpromising, ineffective, or downright harmful innovations at a much earlier stage. (Tantam, 1996)

Notice the phrase 'weed out'. But psychotherapy registration is not some informal evolutionary process; a register *creates* weeds. Indeed, for it to make sense, it *has to create* weeds to justify the high cost of the education of cultivars.

This is a cultural and political decision: the conscious creation of privilege. I believe that it damages the interests, both of the psychotherapy client population and of psychotherapists in general. The former are likely to be denied sufficient choice to find a good match for their issues. And the latter, becoming locked into a culture where hierarchical bureaucratic control dominates quality assurance, will gradually drift towards a 'play safe', 'low risk', 'defensive' style of practice. This is especially likely if this control is focused through cascades of supervisory deference (Young, 1996) or a desire to end the 'balkanisation' of therapy (Savage, 1996). As Kalisch has suggested, at the heart of the bureaucratisation that UKCP represents is a desire that the wildness, iconoclasm and potential dangerousness of creative thought and imagination be tamed, anaesthetised and rendered anaemic in order to be safe for human consumption (Kalisch, 1990).

Perhaps anyone who feels that psychotherapy registration does not compromise creativity would outline how they would propose setting up from scratch a new psychotherapy training school and gaining UKCP recognition for it.

Diversity matters, and those who move to damage it generate confrontation and resistance, 'Society is like an amoeba: it moves from the margins, not from the centre. Cut off from its margins it can only sclerotise and shrivel, become ever less responsive to change' (George Monbiot, 1996): I return to these matters later in some detail in the next section.

But before that, in seeking to understand the ecology of psychopractice, I recommend to you the eloquent testimony of Vandana Shiva, in *Monocultures of the Mind*, a book about what happens when diversity is damaged or undermined. (Shiva, 1993). Shiva is writing about the destruction of forests in India but her observations seem to me to apply very well to the UKCP's annexation of psychotherapy.

The UKCP may argue that within its structure there is a wide diversity of practice. Local flavours there certainly are, but if we take an ecological perspective of the emergence of the UKCP as a public body, several factors combine to make it 'monoculture of the mind'. These factors include:

- the requirement that entry and training be at postgraduate level (UKCP, 1993);
- the belief that outside the remit of the UKCP and its participant organisations there is no tradition of psychotherapy of comparable value (Tantam, 1996);
- the conviction that welding together the disparate sects of psychotherapy into a profession that has the same sort of status as science or medicine is an intrinsically worthy project;
- the belief that the public needs to be protected from psychotherapists (Tantam, 1996);
- the belief that the public can be protected from charlatans by the existence of adequate training standards, codes of practice and complaints procedures (van Deurzen-Smith, 1996).

Shiva writes, 'Monocultures first inhabit the mind.' Then, as monocultures take root, they have a characteristic relation to the world around them.

... monocultures of the mind generate models of production which destroy diversity and legitimise that destruction as progress, growth and improvement ... [this leads to] impoverished systems both qualitatively and quantitatively. They are also highly unstable and non-sustainable systems not because they produce more, but because they control more. The expansion of monocultures has more to do with politics and power than with enriching and enhancing systems.

Monocultures identify themselves through their attitude to the distribution of power: 'Uniformity goes hand in hand with centralisation, while diversity demands de-centered control.' Resisting monocultures she argues, requires active protection of, and promotion of, diversity. 'Diversity as a way of thought and a way of life is what is needed to go beyond the impoverished monocultures of the mind.'

Shiva's ecological overview points to another characteristic of monocultures: the inflation of one local practice into global dominance so that, for example, a local tradition, British public school education, becomes the means by which a whole continent is subjugated—India in the nineteenth and early twentieth centuries.

Power is also built into the perspective which views the dominant system not as a globalised local tradition, but as a universal tradition inherently superior to local systems.

What has been a local tradition is inflated into global dominance. So that 'scientific psychology', 'psychotherapy', and perhaps soon 'counselling' are elevated from being local varieties of psychopractice to being the globally dominant.

What people who overvalue control in human affairs miss is that the universal will emerge anyway and that the ethical, technical and theoretical corsets of UKCP will frustrate this evolution. As Shiva reminds us:

The universal would spread in openness. The globalising local spreads by violence and misrepresentation. The first level of violence unleashed on local systems of knowledge is not to see them as knowledge.

Knowledge (or practice and experience) that does not fit the criteria of the dominant 'universal' definition of 'psychotherapist' is declared inadequate, wrong or dangerous. A person claiming to practise psychotherapy outside the umbrella of the UKCP is then potentially a 'charlatan'.

The public needs ... to be protected from charlatans by the existence of adequate training standards, codes of practice and complaints procedures ... we were also disadvantaged by the fact that anybody could set up as a therapist and in some cases practise erratically and irresponsibly, tarnishing our reputation. (van Deurzen-Smith, 1996)

As Shiva goes on:

When local knowledge does appear in the field of the globalising vision, it is made to disappear by denying it the status of a systematic knowledge, and assigning it the adjectives 'primitive' and 'unscientific'.

An example is the separation of weeds and cultivars. Shiva has this to say about weed-making:

> Declaring a locally useful species a weed is another aspect of the politics of disappearance by which the space of local knowledge shrinks out of existence. The one-dimensional field of vision of the dominant system perceives only one value, based on the market, and it generates practices which aim at maximising that value.

After I had drafted this text I came upon a couple of descriptions of psychotherapy as a garden:

> ... unfortunately everything in a garden is not lovely. Some plants are poisonous. Others become vectors for pests and viruses. Trees are not ideal for every situation, but neither are ground-cover plants. Bulbs will mature and flower in a year, but shrubs will take much longer. Some nurseries undercut others by producing poor stock cheaply ... and so on. I am sure you can see how this metaphor applies to psychotherapy, and how it could be made to apply further. (Tantam, 1996)

Gardening, along with pet keeping, is one of the most ubiquitous pointers to underlying attitudes of domination (Tuan, 1984). The gardening metaphors as employed imply above all a 'gardener', a 'controller': applied to psychotherapy, the assumption of an intrinsic right to dominate. Exactly the point I seek to make here.

Shiva goes on to further delineate how colonisers who succeed in inflating their local knowledge into universal dominance consolidate their gains.

> By elevating itself above society and other knowledge systems and by simultaneously excluding other knowledge systems from the domain of reliable and systematic knowledge, the dominant system creates its exclusive monopoly.

Attempting to inflate psychotherapy, a local tradition, to that of a dominant universal, a process that will necessarily marginalise the alternatives, requires concealment. An ambitious 'dominant universal' such as UKCP requires a public face, a serviceable political fascia of 'public accountability' and 'ethical responsibility', and 'public protection' in support of its attempt at creating a monopoly. Behind this, it can conceal its inaccessibility to 'outsiders' and, most significantly, clients, because individual participation is impossible. Once more, Shiva has a useful perspective on the process: 'Paradoxically, it is the knowledge systems which are considered most open, that are, in reality closed to scrutiny and evaluation.'

Sadly, this is what tends to be typical of existing dominant professions such as law, medicine and science, and now it seems that psychotherapists, through some strands of opinion within UKCP, along with BPS and BCP, are intent on helping create their own customised stronghold.

Part of the difficulty of confronting psychotherapy professionalisation is finding adequate ways of grasping it whole, of avoiding being entranced by the apparent solidity and reasonableness of it as an institution, or unduly privileging the perspective of the beholder. Examining the models of human nature that are explicitly—or as seems to be the case, implicitly—informing professionalisation is one way of doing it; the ecology of the field is another; the power relations yet another. In addition, there is the historical, legislative and ethical case against psychotherapy professionalisation and the experience of licensing in other countries such as the US, Canada and Australia that Mowbray has assembled (Mowbray, 1995).

What else could provide an adequate, if necessarily local way of looking at the phenomena of psychotherapy professionalisation as a whole? Considerable anxiety certainly seems to be associated with it, and because of this I was tempted to explore in depth the view of deep structures of group cohesion put forward by Kellerman. He points to the way that 'the accumulated or collective anxiety or tension of members (that) constitutes the substance which is converted into cohesion energy'(Kellerman 1979). He identifies three kinds of group: intra-punitive, extra-punitive, and impunitive. Intra-punitive groups tend to look inward, rather than attend to personal behaviour and moral and ethical responsibilities. The members of such groups concern themselves with personal sin and its expiation. Extra-punitive groups tend to solve problems through scapegoating. They cast difficulties in the shape of some out-group that must be dealt with severely. In the extra-punitive group, intra-group relations are inherently hierarchical and antagonistic. This is because the group contains an authoritarian structure that justifies its existence by seeking scapegoats or victims onto whom dissatisfactions are placed. By contrast, impunitive groups are those in which members tend to examine their motives, feelings and learning process. They will also generally not insist that any one member unconditionally follow collective instructions or persuasion; they are not inherently hostile towards members who disagree, or towards other groups.

IPN would appear to be constituted formally as an impunitive group, while UKCP and the psychoanalytic communities that Bob Young describes appear to have at least some of the characteristics of extra-punitive groups.

Though this and Wasdell's lengthy and detailed perspectives on the psychodynamics of professionalisation (Wasdell, 1992) that I have mentioned earlier are tempting, I found myself drawn to another way of looking at professionalisation.

The Argument from Creative Style

The UKCP, an umbrella structure for psychotherapy training and accrediting organisations, claims to honour diversity. However, there are other dimensions to diversity apart from models of human functioning and therapeutic practice and some of them have a significant effect on organisational structure and behaviour. One of them is 'creative style'. I argue here that the UKCP's diversity of practice favours a consensus of creative styles and unawarely devalues and/or restricts access to practitioners who favour certain other varieties of creative style.

Adaption/Innovation Theory [A/I Theory] (Kirton, 1989), widely used in Europe, the Far East and the US, is one of the fruits of occupational psychology. It provides a very useful perspective on how creative styles differ, as do the effects thereof. The theory says nothing about the *amount* or *level* of creativity as such; it focuses solely on the *style* of creativity, i.e. how we approach any task that involves creativity. I believe A/I Theory sheds light on the registration of psychotherapists in the UK, particularly on who might welcome or resist registration, and why.

Nomads and settlers

Kirton asserts that there is a spectrum of creative styles that range from very *adaptive* to very *innovative* in a normal distribution (Kirton, 1989; Postle, 1991). People whose creative style is very *adaptive* prefer settled, clearly defined boundaries. They prefer to remain within an agreed consensus and tend to perceive change as useful only insofar as it is expressed as an evolutionary improvement of existing conditions.

> *The Adaptor*
> —Seeks solutions to problems in tried and understood ways
> —Liable to make goals of means
> —Is an authority within given structures
> —Challenges rules rarely, cautiously, when assured of strong support
> —Tends to high self-doubt. Reacts to criticisms by closer outward conformity.
> Vulnerable to social pressure and authority; compliant. (Kirton, 1989)

People whose creative style is very *innovative* have little respect for boundaries. They tend to range across them, freely entering and leaving settled communities or interest groups. They tend to be impatient with improvement and prefer mould-breaking change.

> *The Innovator*
> —Queries problem's concomitant assumptions: manipulates problems
> —Seen as unsound, impractical; often shocks his opposite
> —In pursuit of goals treats accepted means with little regard
> —Tends to take control in unstructured situations
> —Often challenges rules, has little respect for past custom
> —Appears to have low self-doubt when generating ideas, not needing consensus
> to maintain certitude in face of opposition. (Kirton, 1989)

Just as people with average-sized feet have a lot of choice in shoes, so people around the middle of the range of creative styles have a lot of choice in people with whom they can happily associate. However, because they form a majority they may tend to feel that their perception of creative style is 'normal' and that other creative styles are 'deviant', 'irrational' or even 'pathological'.

A/I Theory makes two other useful suggestions about creative style. Firstly, through 'coping' behaviour anyone can learn to function across the range of creative styles; but adopting a style far away from our preferred one is stressful, and eventually we tend to revert to the 'home' style. Secondly, any of the range of creative styles is intrinsically valuable. As a corollary to this, A/I Theory demonstrates how much of a gross distortion is the white, Western cultural norm that equates creativity only with innovation. A concomitant distortion is the perception that adaptivity is not creative at all.

If we bring A/I Theory to bear on the phenomenon of psychotherapy registration in the UK, what does it show us?

The first thing that comes to mind is that there is likely to be a large consensus to which most people belong, and other much smaller groupings or a number of individuals for whom this 'herding together' is anathema, or brings grave difficulties.

If we look at the range of British psychotherapy practitioners we see the Independent Practitioners' Network, a grouping that prefers a no-hierarchy network structure consisting of self-regulating cells of practitioners. There is also the British Confederation of Psychotherapists who have left UKCP and are trying to detach other organisations from it (Tantam, 1996). They appear to prefer formal, settled groupings with strongly and clearly defined boundaries and appear to be intolerant of dissent (Young, 1996).

And then there is the UKCP, which claims to represent the 'profession' of psychotherapy. It takes the form of a flattened hierarchy, with several thousand 'registrants' connected to 77 or so training and accrediting bodies. Each of these has representation in the governing body and executive council, and all meet annually to discuss/ratify ongoing business. The UKCP decision-making model was recently described as 'consociational democracy' (Pokorny and Fanning, 1996).

From the perspective of creative style, the IPN grouping looks strikingly 'innovative'. The psychoanalytic grouping looks 'adaptive'. And the UKCP appears to represent the varieties of creative style in between them.

The invention of charlatans

Well, you may say, that's all right then: the majority have voted with their feet and formed a weighty consensus that occupies the middle ground. And yes, there is a certain statistical inevitability about that. The difficulty comes from the equally likely myopic tendency of practitioners in this consensus to see outsiders with differing creative styles as anathema or problematic—or worse, as quacks or charlatans.

Practitioners with a highly *adaptive* creative style will tend to see significantly more innovative practitioners (a majority of the population) as unreliable, casual about quality, and disrespectful of seniority and settled boundaries. They will also be likely to be dismissive of practitioners with a more innovative creative style, seeing them as undisciplined and anarchic, and their practice as superficial. This accords well with my face-to-face contact with BCP members.

Practitioners with an *innovative* creative style will tend to see significantly more adaptive practitioners (again a majority of the population) as collusive, complacent and bureaucratic, and to perceive highly adaptive practitioners as rigid and pedantic, and their practice as ineffective or irrelevant. This is a view commonly expressed within IPN.

Practitioners with creative styles that occupy the central two-thirds of the spectrum will also tend to identify the one-third of practitioners outside their central consensus as either unreliable and anarchic, or alternatively complacent and pedantic. However, unlike highly adaptive or highly innovative practitioners who are likely to feel marginalised, the practitioners who occupy this central consensus will, through sheer weight of numbers, be inclined to hold a position of tolerance of *their* diversity while imposing *their* view of good practice as *the* view that matters.

This is because, for any variety of creative style towards the centre of the spectrum, there are large numbers of others whose style is adjacent, if not identical. Hence agreement is likely to be easier to reach, even though the divergence of creative style across this central majority is still likely to be considerable and a source of great tension.

I am not suggesting that these are tight categories; obviously there are innovative psychoanalysts and adaptive human potential practitioners. But the centres of gravity of these groups are likely to be distributed in the way I have outlined. I would suspect that a similar distribution would appear in other countries.

Why should this perspective on organisation and creative style in the field of psychotherapy matter?

UKCP, the occupiers of the middle ground, while claiming to honour diversity, have erected a boundary fence around those kinds and levels of psychopractice that the central consensus majority of creative styles agree constitute 'psychotherapy'. From this perspective, in espousing regulation of psychotherapy, they attempt to institutionalise their consensus creative style.

Once erected, this boundary—symbolised and enacted initially through registration, with the promise of eventual legal sanctions—is likely to give many practitioners within it a deep sense of security and 'rightness'. For others inside the boundary, but not so near the middle of the range of creative styles, it is likely to generate serious tension. Not enough to mean they can't live with it, but enough to mean they constantly feel sceptical, unenthusiastic, uncomfortable, compromised, or are simply silent about their doubts and discomfort.

For practitioners outside this consensus of creative style, there seem to be two kinds of reaction. In those practitioners like myself who are strongly innovative in creative style, the central consensus of UKCP evokes anger at the attempted annexation of a sector of the field and anxiety at the likely economic effects of this action, coupled with a determination to create a form of organisation congruent with my values and to resist any attempt to show that 'psychotherapy', as represented by UKCP or its cohorts, is a united profession.

In my quest to understand the phenomenon of psychotherapy registration, the lens of creative styles has brought into focus another important element. I began to suspect that the majority consensus of creative styles is not symmetrical, i.e. not evenly distributed around the mean. The central consensus is skewed, and I believe it is skewed towards the adaptive style. Since I first drafted this section I have discovered what appears to be evidence in support of this, and of discomfort about it within UKCP.

One registrant has compared the internal dynamics of the UKCP to the ecumenical movement within the Church (Savage, 1996) He equates the Freudian/ Jungian Analytic wing with the Orthodox/Catholic tradition within the Church, and then goes on to note that the Church's ecumenical governing board has five Orthodox/Catholic officers out of six. Of its four members representing the main body of 'churchgoers', all four are Orthodox/Catholic. He ends this ecclesiastical survey by noting that, 'Of an Ecumenical Governing Board totalling twenty-one souls, no fewer than thirteen would belong to the Orthodox/Catholic persuasion. So long as this state of affairs prevails, it is difficult to accept that decisions made are not coloured by the perceptions or prejudices of the dominant group.'

If you accept my premise that the centre of gravity of the psychoanalytic wing of psychotherapy has an adaptive creative style then here is evidence of a major bias within UKCP towards that style and towards psychoanalytic/ psychodynamic agendas.

Savage concludes: 'When I once asked why the Analytic wing of UKCP had three sections to everyone else's one, I was told *"for historic and pragmatic reasons"*. To paraphrase the old Irish joke about the response of a local to a stranger seeking directions, *"If you are looking for democracy, I wouldn't start from here"* '. (Savage, 1996)

Should this seem exceptional, the facing page of the same publication featured a more coded and incomplete article about decision making in the UKCP (Pokorny and Fanning, 1996). It observed that 'the greatest danger to us is that we become led by a majority faction who can overrule any awkward minority interests and call the process unity'. After a quite detailed discussion of the dangers of adopting a proposed model of decision making that was 'explicitly based on a model of national government', the article went on to conclude that the health of the Sections is our safeguard against any system that can trample on minorities. And that 'One of the biggest fears at the Rugby Psychotherapy Conference was that one form of therapy would predominate'. We think this danger has reappeared.' Decoded, this appears to refer to the weight that the psychoanalytic tendency has within UKCP.

How curious that this anxiety about a threat to in-house democracy is coupled with a failure to notice that in promoting a profession with statutory boundaries (rather than a trade association that recommended its members), the UKCP enacts exactly the same kind of oppression on those of us who don't share the consensus creative style.

To summarise: there are four points I want to make. Firstly, that from the perspective of creative style, the UKCP does not represent the full spread of psychotherapy practice in the UK. Secondly, that the consensus of styles that it does represent is likely to be skewed towards adaptivity in creative style and towards the psychoanalytic/psychodynamic and, as a reviewer has reminded me, the NHS/medical model of practice. Thirdly that this, coupled with the dominance of the central consensus, results in an oppressive devaluing and marginalising of practitioners who are strongly innovative in creative style. Fourthly, there is a certain symmetry in the way the organisational situation has unfolded. The 'adaptive' analysts have rejected the UKCP consensus on the grounds of unrecognised 'seniority' and inadequate training standards and the 'innovative' Independent Practitioners' Network rejects the consensus on the basis of values incongruence.

I want to reiterate that what is at issue here is the preservation and valuing of diversity. It is not a trivial matter. So far as it strongly pursues its present course of mimicking other institutions such as law and medicine, and creating a 'profession' with or without state enforcement of its boundaries, the UKCP has the capacity to undermine, deform or even destroy the territory outside its orbit.

During the recent recession there appears to have been a decisive shift in the UK's collapsing labour market towards overvaluing paper qualifications. This tends to mean that individual, self-directed, experiential learning (which appeals to people with a highly innovative style) is correspondingly devalued. So that anyone who wants to develop as a psychopractitioner tends to see the writing on the wall—no paper qualification, no work. Joining the dominant consensus means moving away from ad hoc education, no matter how deep or valuable, and joining an 'accredited' or 'recognised' course.

This brings with it dangers for the consensus too, As Kirton has pointed out very convincingly (Kirton, 1989), over time the consensus centre tends to shed its innovators as too obstreperous or too divisive, or the innovators quit as they become fed up with the demands for deference. The organisation then drifts towards greater adaptivity, bureaucracy and stasis.

As many organisations (and nations) have found to their cost, when the consensus creative style feeds back on itself in this way, innovation and renewal become more and more threatening, until maintaining the existing boundaries starts to dominate the life of the organisation. The former East German Republic and the former USSR, along with countless businesses, are examples of this in action.

Both highly adaptive and highly innovative psychopractice seems likely to continue, either underground within the registered consensus, or in exile. Though it is likely to remain marginal and under-resourced, that may be better both personally and for clients than the alternatives: extinction or souldeath.

Critique

As this article has gone the rounds of colleagues, it has accumulated a variety of feedback and criticism. While some of this has shaped revisions, I want to take the opportunity both to respond to some of the critical comment and to anticipate other likely objections.

By suggesting that UKCP, and in particular the HIPS section, are in the pockets of the totalitarian pessimism of psychoanalysis, you define the field in terms of one portion of it. Doesn't this amount to a totalitarianism of content which is what you oppose from the dogmatic psychoanalysts? It is important to be scrupulously fair in these matters. I doubt that there is a 'scrupulous fairness' that is not shaped by ideology. Nonetheless, my intention in deploying Kirton's adaption/innovation model was precisely to contradict an overly myopic, single-lens view of the field of psychopractice that unduly privileged the educational—humanistic—psychology perspective that I bring to it.

From my 'nomadic' perspective, UKCP represents a massive privileging of psychoanalytic pessimism and the medical model. To name this is not to argue for a reverse privileging of a 'nomadic', i.e. 'innovator' approach to accountability that, for example, the human potential movement represents, but for the *maintenance of a valid space for it* in the psycho-prairie.

Isn't your devotion to opposing psychotherapy regulation and resistance to hierarchical authority a displacement of some unresolved personal material, perhaps some compulsive outsiderist complex?

Projective identification is the glass in the lens of perception. The best any of us can do is recognise this and be diligent in personal therapy and collegial consultation around engaging issues. However, where there is a challenge to institutional power, I am also watchful for dissent of the kind I have assembled here being dismissed as pathology. As I mentioned earlier, I am inclined to deconstruct such a line of criticism as a 'tyranny of the unconscious'.

Your reduction of the issues to an ideological clash between models of human nature is not only a displacement of the really important issues that are to fight for in the political context, but also reinforces the impotence of those who think as you do because it gives no alternative long-term political pathway.

The issue for me is not that someone should subscribe to a particular model of human nature, but that they are aware of how it shapes political institutions such as psychotherapy registration.

There are no innocent bystanders in this matter. To have a model of human development is to have a model of human nature. Models of human nature that seem inclined to naturalise dominance as medicine and psychoanalysis profess to, will lead to institutions that install dominance, hierarchical control, gatekeeping and the policing of professional boundaries.

I don't see that creating an alternative form of accountability, as in IPN, that is congruent with the model of human nature that underlies much of humanistic and human potential psychopractice, in any way reinforces my impotence. Does not such a suggestion presume a discourse of dominance and subjection? IPN's clusters of emotionally competent practitioners are developing a discourse of cooperation, mutuality, 'power-with' and 'power-from-within', in a network based on affinity and shared values. Is this not a political act of considerable social and political potency?

The article is unfair. You don't honour the passion of those practitioners within UKCP who seek to establish institutions that support tolerance and diversity.

I think that this is again to misunderstand the article's origin as an expression of the politics of the dispossessed—'nomads' faced with 'settlers' who have fenced off a very large section of the communal psycho-prairie and are denying access to it (without discussion) to those who previously ranged freely across it. I and many other colleagues find ourselves with our livelihood damaged, our probity demeaned, and described as charlatans. By whom? People, some of whom we know well, who own and staff a collection of training schools and accrediting bodies. These are persons who have decided with such confident certainty that they are in possession of the truth about 'standards' in a psychotherapy they as yet decline to define, that they even seek statutory support for their position.

Opposing this kind of unaware dominance, as I and others intend to do, is likely, as Shiva points out, to attract devaluation of the form of discourse employed to resist it. Like too 'polemical', 'petulant', 'bad faith', 'insufficiently rigorous' and especially, 'unfair'

But who is being unfair to whom here? Why should I overly honour the passion of someone who is oppressing and harming me? Should victims of oppression be denied the right to make loud sounds?

You don't give anything like enough attention to the influence of the medical model and the National Health Service.
I think that this is undoubtedly correct. The BCP, which [at this time still had] a substantial overlapping membership with UKCP, is very transparent about its medical alignment, claiming accountability to an advisory board made up of representatives of mental health professions. This includes the Royal College of General Practitioners, the Royal College of Nurses, and the Royal College of Psychiatrists (BCP,1997).

As the biggest employer in Europe, the NHS is a massive embodiment of the medical model of human functioning. It is easy to imagine that for those who toil within, or even adjacent to it, relations with the medical model and its values dominate most conversations about pay, status and conditions of employment. Psychotherapy registration and the creation of a matching 'profession' would clearly enhance a career path within the NHS. I imagine it already has for many people. I would find this socio-economic agenda easier to accept if registration was not being sold to the public and practitioners by UKCP and others as a necessary protection for clients from malpractice.

The article takes insufficient account of the difficulties that training schools have in setting and maintaining standards.
While I have seen at very close quarters the distortions that entry to UKCP imposes on accrediting bodies (sign up or fade away), it hasn't been part of my intention to take account of training issues except insofar as I argue that the institutional *modelling* of standards comes first, and that is where I have given my attention.

You should try to straddle the divide, not sharpen it; this is a cut-throat situation, loaded with Machiavellian realities and sooner or later we will all have to get into the same tub. We have to work for the best we can get, which means getting access to the levers of political influence and you can't do that from an ideal position.
I can accept that this 'pragmatic' approach to UK psycho-politics represents a commonly held view from inside the registration approach to accountability. I find it very unappealing.

I don't see that I am 'sharpening the divide' but I am staking a claim for the conservation of a valuable tradition. Just because some psychotherapists have created a politics of psychotherapy that is a 'cut-throat situation, loaded with Machiavellian realities', it doesn't mean I have to join them in their folly. I also don't see that we need to eventually get into the same tub. We *were* in the same tub until unilateral action delineated a privileged space for the agendas of psychotherapy training.

'Working for the best we can get', as I hope I have shown, depends on the core values that define our starting points. An uncritical acceptance of dominance/

subjection in psychotherapy institutions may provide a starting point that facilitates 'access to the levers of political influence', but in whose interests? And 'you can't (get access to the levers of political influence) from an ideal position'. No? Nelson Mandela did.

References

Brown, J and Mowbray, R (1990) Whither the Human Potential Movement. *Self and Society* 18:4 [Reprinted in Mowbray (1995) pp. 223–7]
Chamberlain, T (1996) *The Psychotherapist*, 6, 2
Dinwoodie, J (1996) *The Psychotherapist*, 6, 8
Eisold, K (1994) The Intolerance of Diversity in Psychoanalytic Institutes. *International Journal of Psychoanalysis*, 75, 785–800
European Association for Psychotherapy, The Strasbourg Declaration (1996) *International Journal of Psychotherapy*
Freud, S (1953) *The Standard Edition of the Complete Psychological Works of Sigmund Freud, 24.* London:Hogarth Press
Gay, P (1988) *Freud: a Life for Our Time.* London: Norton
Heron, J (1990) The Politics of Transference. *Self and Society*, 18:1
Heron, J (1992) *Feeling and Personhood: Psychology in Another Key.* London: Sage
Heron, J (1996) *Co-operative Inquiry: Research into the Human Condition.* London: Sage
House, R (1992) A Tale of Two Conferences: organisational form and accreditation ethos. *Self and Society*, 20:4 (pp.35–7)
House, R (1995) Registration Is Dead! ... Long Live Registration?—a sympathetic review article. *Clinical Psychology Forum*, December (pp.43–4)
House, R (1995) The Dynamics of Power: Why Mowbray is right about professionalisation. *Counselling News*, 20 (pp.24–5)
House, R (1996) Audit-Mindedness in counselling: some underlying dynamics. *British Journal of Guidance and Counselling*, 24:2 (pp.277–283)
House, R (1996) In the wake of '*Watchdog*' ... Whither professionalisation now? *Counselling*, 7:2 (pp. 115–16)
House, R (1997) From Professionalisation Towards A Post-Therapy Era. *Self and Society* 25:2 (pp.31–5)
House, R and Totton, N (1997) *Implausible Professions: Arguments for Pluralism and Self-Regulation in Psychotherapy and Counselling.* Ross-on-Wye: PCCS Books
Jones, D (1992) Interview with Emmy van Deurzen-Smith, *Self and Society*, 23:4
Kalisch, D (1990) Professionalisation—A Rebel View. *Self and Society*, 18:1
Kalisch, D (1996) Letter in *Self and Society*, 24:2, 38
Kellerman, Gruner and Stratton (1979) The Deep Structures of Group Cohesion. *Social Cohesion.* New York
Kirton, M. J (ed) (1989) *Adaptors and Innovators: Styles of Creativity and Problem-Solving.* Oxford: Routledge
Monbiot, G (1996) Campaigners Become Enemies of the State. *The Guardian*, 29 August
Mowbray, R (1995) *The Case Against Psychotherapy Registration: A Conservation Issue for the Human Potential Movement.* London: Trans Marginal Press
Oakley, H (1995) Letter. *The Guardian* 23 November
Pokorny, M (1996) *The Therapist*, 3:4 (pp. 46–47)
Pokorny, M and Fanning, A (1996) *The Psychotherapist.* 6:13
Postle, D (1982) *Behaving Ourselves.* C4/Central Television London

Postle, D (1989,2003) *Synergy: creativity in interpersonal relation*, Wentworth Learning Resources <http://www.mindgymnasium.com/TheMindGymnasium/MGDownloadSections/Conflict.pdf>

Postle, D (1989) *Learning and Unlearning.* Wentworth Learning Resources <http://g.o.r.i.l.l.a.postle.net/hpvoices/hpvoices.htm>

Postle, D (1989) *The Mind Gymnasium.* London:Macmillan

Postle, D (1991,2003) *Bringing About Change.* Wentworth Learning Resources <http://www.mind-gymnasium.com/TheMindGymnasium/MGDownloadSections/BringAboutChange.pdf>

Postle, D (1993) Putting the Heart Back into Learning, in (ed.) D Boud, C Cohen and D Walker, *Using Experience for Learning.* Milton Keynes:Open University Press

Postle, D (1994) The Glacier Reaches Edge of Town. *Self and Society* 23:6 (January 1996)

Postle, D (1996) (ed) G.O.R.I.L.L.A. world wide web psychotherapy professionalisation archive Wentworth Learning Resources.<http://g.o.r.i.l.l.a.postle.net/confrontUKPP/carppp.htm>

Postle, D (1996) *A Client's Guide to Psychotherapy.* Wentworth Learning Resources <http://g.o.r.i.l.l.a.postle.net/clientcorner/cliegide.htm>

Postle, D and Anderson, J (1989) Stealing the Flame. *Self and Society* 18:1

Pyschosynthesis Trust (1996) Brochure

Richards, A. *Psychotherapy Registration A view from the Department of Health.* Paper given at the British Confederation of Psychotherapists Conference: Regulation of Psychotherapy in Europe 7 June 1997

Savage, P (1996) *The Psychotherapist*, 6:12

Schutz, W (1979) *Profound Simplicity.* Joy Press USA

Scott, T (1996) *Human Potential Magazine.* Autumn 1996

Shiva, V (1993) *Monocultures of the Mind: Perspectives on Biodiversity and Biotechnology.* London: Zed Books

Starhawk (1990) *Truth or Dare: Encounters with Power, Authority, and Mystery.* (pp. 9,15–16) San Francisco: Harper

Tantam, D (1996) *International Journal of Psychotherapy,* 1:1 97–100

Tantam, D (1996) Letter. *Self and Society,* 24:2, 41

Tantam, D (1996) UKCP internal memorandum. 7 August

Therapist, The (1996) Editorial, 3:4, 3

Totton, N (1995) *Independent Practitioners' Network [IPN].* (1996)

Totton, N and Edmondson, E (1994) Proposal. *Independent Therapists' Network*

Travis, A (1997) Survey Gives Lie to Howard's Boast. *The Guardian* 27 May

Tuan, Yi-Fu (1984) *Dominance and Affection: The Making of Pets.* New Haven: Yale University Press

UKCP (1993) Training Requirements

van Deurzen-Smith, E (1996) *International Journal of Psychotherapy,* 1:1, 15, 17, 19

van Deurzen-Smith, E (1996) *Registration—What it Will Mean to You the Counsellor.* Fifth St George's Counselling in Primary Care Conference, 12 June

Wasdell, D (1992) In the Shadow of Accreditation, *Self and Society*

Young, R (1992) Guilt and the Veneer of Civilisation, in *Psychoanalytic Week,* The New Bulgarian University, Sofia. <http://human-nature.com/rmyoung/papers/paper11.html>

Young, R (1994) *Character and Morality.* <http://human-nature.com/rmyoung/papers/paper10.html>

Young, R (1995) *Human Nature.* <http://human-nature.com/rmyoung/papers/

    paper12.html>

Young, R (1995) *Good and Evil, Character and Morality.* <http://human-nature.com/
    rmyoung/papers/paper10.html>

Young, R (1996) *Psychodynamics of Psychoanalytic Organisations.* <http://human-
    nature.com/rmyoung/papers/paper53.html>

Background: By 1998 the G.O.R.I.L.L.A. website had mutated into an archive, *Confronting UK Psychopractice Professionalisation,* and a variety of texts under the title *Human Potential Voices,* all of which are still available (weblink page). From time to time I ventured an editorial to air current concerns and introduce new items on the site. In the third of these, I began to try to find a voice that matched the unfolding regulatory situation.

CHAPTER SEVEN

The Rush to Professionalise:
Hidden agendas

As the years grind on in the world of UK psychopractice, and despite the best Machiavellian efforts of the UKCP, the field continues to look healthily split. The BCP's March 1999 deadline to psychoanalytic organisations presently within UKCP, to exit or be excommunicated, looks set to ensure that three more psychoanalytic groups will leave. To make life easier for those of the psychoanalytic tendency who remain, a new grouping within (or adjacent to) UKCP is being put together.

At one level we might guess this involves deep sadness for some of the practitioners caught up in the reshuffle; at another it is an example of the continuing elbow work between UKCP and BCP et al for dominance in the field.

*****

There are two (at least) undeclared hidden agendas behind the rush to professionalisation in the UK. One is the explosive growth of counselling courses that have flooded the market with practitioners ... 'How do we ring-fence our work so as to keep these newcomers out?' ... and secondly, deeper and more corrosive, 'how do we break the stranglehold that psychoanalysis has on lucrative work within the NHS?'

For too many people inside mainstream psychotherapy, a few days' teaching and a full book of client work seems to feed a complacency that blinds them to the incongruity between their empowering client work and domineering professionalisation.

Perhaps it was ever thus. When a Profession is made King, a Court populated by courtiers, chamberlains and commissionaires is created. These courtiers administer access, deal with transgressions and pursue the Court's business, which, as in other Courts down the centuries, is primarily to stay in business. A Court, if it is not identical with the State, will seek a deal with the State to legitimate its dominance. Such a deal seeks to privilege the superior value of the cultivars inside the palace gardens (well-bred) and the weeds outside (mongrelish).

Is this over the top? I don't think so. The court of professional psychotherapy propagates fear, controls through fear (it's cheaper and needs fewer resources than actual conflict). And it controls through defining what are or are not acceptable forms of discourse: that is to say, it supports the development of etiquette, more or less formal agreements about protocol, what can or cannot be done in what circumstances.

This article first appeared in G.O.R.I.L.L.A. as Editorial #3, October 1998

Etiquette is about recognition; it seems to re-emerge whenever there is a lot of anxiety about being able to recognise who is really a Lady or a Gentleman, i.e. how to tell whether or not you are a proper Psychotherapist. One of the Courtiers recently published a book that outlines the UKCP etiquette on grievances and complaints within psychotherapy. It seems to me a text written from, and intended to propagate, fear. If you take an interest in these matters you might like to read my forthcoming review (Chapter 8).

Background: Whether consciously or not, in the 90s of the last century, some officers of the UK's mainstream accrediting bodies often attempted to gain or consolidate support for their colonisation of the territory of UK psychopractice through what I have come more recently to see as trance inductions. One of these, which we will come to again, is that 'regulation is inevitable'; another is that regulation provides a place of safety for practitioners and protects clients from being abused by them. Common to all of these is the political strategy of promoting fear.

CHAPTER EIGHT

Review of *Complaints and Grievances in Psychotherapy* by Fiona Palmer Barnes

This is a book about quality assurance: how to manage complaints and grievances. Why did I feel so sceptical of the procedures that it outlines? Mainly because the model of quality assurance put forward is retrospective—make a bad mistake, be found out, get struck off. In other words, identify rejects and throw them in the waste bin for rework or scrap. For a book that makes much of 'up-to-date understanding of good practice', I find it curious that Fiona Palmer Barnes propagates with such certainty a quality-assurance stance that has elsewhere been discredited.

In manufacturing industry, up-to-date, best-practice quality-assurance uses methods that monitor production. Before the work is about to go out of specification, some intervention is made to return it to the specified quality, so that the probability of making rejects is reduced to close to zero (See Conclusion). The psychopractice accountability of the Independent Practitioners' Network [IPN], based on linked small groups of practitioners who get to 'know and stand by each other's work', is an example of this second approach to quality assurance. The text does not refer to it. Because of these and other considerations, I didn't warm to the book much.

It classifies, categorises and catalogues, and a medicalised approach to psychopractice is regarded as intrinsically virtuous. Early on the author announces that she will use 'the term "patient" because it is the most usual way for analysts and psychotherapists to speak of those who are our clients and customers'. Not for me or any of the community of practitioners I know. Elsewhere there are 'clinical responsibility', 'treatment', and 'case material'.

This is not to be pedantic about language and style. There is an 'official' feel to this book; it could easily be a Department of Health or, more to the point, a British Medical Association document. I expect this is intended. I see it as part of the mould into which UKCP, BCP and BAC are pouring the concrete of a statutory psychotherapy profession. Spell out a series of procedural structures, label them as 'good current practice' and you define a form of accountability that intends to invalidate, and attempts to extinguish, other competing forms of practice. Perhaps the psychotherapists and counsellors devising these legalistic structures are well intentioned, but isn't it curious that their chosen approach is that of instilling fear of sanctions? Indeed, the whole edifice of complaints and grievances procedures as delineated in this book, and the discussion thereof, seem to me to

This article first appeared in *Counselling News*, November 1998 be rooted in fear. For example, the author's unquestioned assumptions about the necessity for practice insurance:

> ... adequate insurance cover ... the likely increase in litigation makes this all the more essential.(p. 36)

> clear and binding contracts ... may in the near future become helpful in *defence against legal action*. (p. 39, my italics)

> It is essential that all practitioners should have professional insurance. Without it they are acting recklessly. (p. 67)

The author appears to inhabit a vision of human nature that is filled with 'emotions that are powerful and often quite primitive', and which must be 'contained' if they are not to break out and wreak havoc in the world. The book seems to be saying ... 'be terrified of this possibility; construct a narrowed, conformist, restrictive, insured practice that will keep us all safe from the demons inside us (and our clients). And here is how to do it.'

It works. I felt terrified.

Background: This webpage fragment juxtaposes two events in the UK psychopractice Universe that at the time did not seem connected. With hindsight, the demand from the BCP that organisations from the psychoanalytic tradition cease their dual membership appears directly connected to the coup that Lord Alderdice was organising to capture control of psychotherapy regulation for the psychoanalytic community. This, I have always supposed, was a response to the emerging prospect of an Order in Council that could impose regulation on a profession.

CHAPTER NINE

Regulation ... By Order

Publication of the 1999 Health Bill opens the door to statutory regulation of 'professions' by Order in Council ...

> ... the social insanity of professionalising psychopractice in the UK moves on ...

> ... perhaps into a terminal phase ... depending on whether you think it is a great idea, or a big mistake ...

> ... or you were not consulted.

Take a look at the relevant pages of the Bill, Clause 47, and hidden away under Expenditure of Health Authorities and Primary Care Trusts ... Miscellaneous and Supplementary, Schedule 3 (weblinks page)

*****

<www.wannabee.theonlypsychotherapy.umbrella.org>
There is apparently no truth in the rumour that this is UKCP's new website address. However, anti-charlatan measures continue to be tested by the registration board ... the least attractive of these is the UKCP's hugely bureaucratic approach to complaints.

A close reading of Fiona Palmer Barnes' fear-drenched, semi-official handbook about Psychotherapy Complaints and Grievances ... (Chapter 8) reveals the not-altogether hidden-secret that: '... all investigations and inquiries into complaints against registrants are likely to be improvised by the people willing to put their heads in that particular can of worms ...'

So much for complaints 'procedures'.

*****

The BCP have imposed on training institutes who wished to have dual membership of both BCP and UKCP ... an 'us or them' choice, with a March 1999 deadline. And so I was intrigued to be invited to speak at their recent Summer Conference on *Statutory Regulation* at the Anna Freud Centre. In the same week that I gave the BCP talk, which focused on 'power relations in psychopractice', I did a presentation for the Bristol Psychotherapy Association that included the BCP material (Chapter 10).

This article first appeared in G.O.R.I.L.L.A. as Editorial # 4, June 22 1999

Background: This article combines a talk on professionalisation and the regulation of psychotherapy that I gave earlier in the year to the Bristol Psychotherapy Association with a similar presentation to a psychoanalytic audience at the Summer Conference on *Statutory Regulation* at the Anna Freud Centre. While I don't recall it being mentioned, the bid by Lord Alderdice to capture control of psychotherapy on behalf of the psychoanalytic community, which I touch on in this text, must have been well known to many of the analysts at the latter meeting.

CHAPTER TEN

Statutory Regulation:
Shrink-wrapping psychotherapy

The BCP billing for the talk that forms the basis of this article described me as an 'independent psychotherapist'. This phrase merits brief attention, since in a political debate of this kind the context from which an article is written matters a lot.

For the last fifteen years I have been in independent private practice in West London as a 'facilitator', 'psychotherapist', 'coach','counsellor': one of the hundreds, maybe thousands, of psychopractitioners in the UK with very diverse training and experience who developed outside the dominant psychotherapy training cultures. I work with people using a diverse mix of skills and orientations through which I attempt to find a close match for clients' needs. However, 'independence' doesn't mean isolation. During all this time I have been in one or another form of accountability structure, all of them based on self- and peer-assessment. For the last ten years I have been in open-ended personal therapy, and since 1995 I've been a founder-participant in the Independent Practitioners' Network [IPN] (Totton, 1995), to which I return below. From this perspective I see the professionalisation and statutory regulation of psychotherapy in the UK as the annexation, or colonisation—the theft—of a piece of the territory of psychopractice (Postle, 1998). For that reason this article is primarily about power.

The statutory regulation of psychotherapy means engaging the power of the state to endorse the values, practices and worldview of the organisations that seek it. As Ann Casement, the current Chair of the UKCP, recently put it in a radio broadcast:

> CASEMENT: At the moment, we're a voluntary register, but we are now in the process of moving to registration; by law, to statutory registration; we're actually in the process of doing that.
> INTERVIEWER: You would then be the professional body and without qualifications from you, people would not be able to practise?
> CASEMENT: Exactly so. We're seeking to protect the title of 'psychotherapist', so anybody after that, once we've registered by law, anyone who calls themselves a 'psychotherapist' will have us to deal with. (Casement, 1999)

The rather parental tone of the last sentence, more so in the original broadcast, is a further reminder that in choosing to accept, resist or ignore the statutory regulation of psychotherapy, it is vitally important, in our occupation of psychotherapy, to be vigilant about 'power', its varieties or qualities, and who is exercising it on behalf of which constituencies.

This article first appeared in the *British Journal of Psychotherapy*, September 1999, 16:3

In this article, as in the talk on which it is based, I offer a series of propositions about the way power has been deployed in the field of UK psychopractice. I extend some of the assertions and add support for them in ways that were impracticable in a short talk, and draw conclusions about the value of statutory regulation of psychotherapy.

Positional power

I begin by outlining my notion of 'positional power'. The power of the proprietor, the occupier, the owner, inherited privilege, or the licensed professional. Positional power is often arguably legitimate, as in the case of elected public officials; whether it constitutes a bulwark against disorder, a form of imprisonment, a refuge, or an enduring and valued form of social enhancement depends on how it is deployed. However, to suppose that accumulated positional power confers some intrinsic virtue would be naïve. The reverse seems to be the case with the rush to professionalisation, which often seems to be a form of licensing for incongruence (Postle, 1998). The above radio phone-in provides one cogent example of this in the first sentence, where the chair of the UKCP claims: 'At the UK Council we run the national register for psychotherapists …'

Elsewhere, UKCP ex-chair Digby Tantam provides another recently published example:

> There already exists a professional association for all generally accepted psychotherapy organisations in the UK—The United Kingdom Council for Psychotherapy. (Tantam, 1999)

As anyone who has followed the debate about psychotherapy professionalisation knows, these statements are simply untrue. The UKCP is *one of* the national registers for, or that includes, psychotherapists; the BCP has one and in its own style, and so does IPN; and there are also the BPS and the UKRC.

In the next breath Ann Casement goes on to assure her listeners that UKCP registered practitioners are: '… fully trained … qualified. They have to fulfil entry, training and ethical requirements.' Yet here are two supposedly 'fully trained', 'qualified' and 'ethical' practitioners making public statements that are factually untrue and very misleading for present or potential clients.

This is positional power in action and I believe it signals a deep, fundamental incongruence in the psychotherapy professionalisation project, and thus regulation, whether statutory or not.

Market forces

The proprietors of UK psychotherapy training schools have been accumulating positional power for a couple of decades by forming what I regard as trade associations: the UKCP, more recently the BCP, and also the BPS, a trade association for the more scientifically inclined.

In the last ten years the psychopractice training market has seen an explosive growth in counselling training. Is it coincidence that it is exactly this period during which the UK psychotherapy trade associations have worked hardest to consolidate their positional power—notably through attempting to inflate their trade association status to that of a 'profession'? It is as though this body of psychotherapists had no historical or political sense of the tendency of such bodies to gravitate towards self-serving clubs (Kendel, 1998). Plentiful evidence of this evolutionary tendency of professions is all around us, from medicine (Boseley, 1990), law (Dyer, 1998,1999), psychiatry (Kendel, 1998, Cassidy, 1999), and biomedical research (Boseley, 1990).

Trade associations, whether of psychotherapy trainers or cement manufacturers, have intrinsic legitimacy. However, for the former to inflate an understandable business agenda into the ring-fencing of a sector of the psychopractice prairie seems to me unforgivable—firstly on ethical grounds because, as I show here, it is contrary to the interest of clients. Secondly, it arbitrarily imposes oppressive and indefensible conditions on the occupation of psychotherapy that I and others practise, without either representation or consultation; and lastly because, for the registrants who have chosen to be herded into the 'professional' enclosure, it will constitute a form of imprisonment.

What often seems to disappear from sight in this debate is the range, extent and *value* of psychopractice as a whole. There seems to be little awareness of how much of it there is, e.g. counselling in its rich diversity (career, stress, trauma, bereavement), assertiveness training, coaching, stress management, the Alexander method, Tai Chi, massage, co-counselling, voicework, bodywork etc. Much of this mirrors or comprehensively overlaps with psychotherapy. Many of these modalities are locally just as effective and/or more economical than some varieties of psychotherapy and may often more accurately match some client's needs.

Insofar as we take account of the strength, diversity and richness of UK psychopractice as a whole, trade associations such as the UKCP, BCP and BPS and their professional ambitions amount to formidable concentrations of unelected, unaccountable positional power.

Dissent

How these organisations deploy this positional power and, especially, how they deal with *dissent* points to the ideology around power that they have adopted. And there has been considerable dissent during (at least) the last ten years, as UK psychotherapy professionalisation and the prospect of statutory regulation have emerged. Since many practitioners seem not to be aware of the extent and depth of this dissent, here are a few items from it, the tip of an iceberg.

First, and certainly the most influential, is *The Case Against Psychotherapy Registration: A Conservation Issue for the Human Potential Movement* by Richard Mowbray (Mowbray, 1995). This is a substantial, thoroughly researched book, well supported by evidence from a wide variety of sources, with an eighteen-page bibliography. I am going to quote at some length from a review of the text by Richard House (House, 1995), one of the more articulate dissenting voices.

[Mowbray] criticises UKCP for being dominated by training organisations with a vested interest in monopolising the market in training provision, with procedures which make it extremely difficult, if not impossible, for new entrants to establish themselves in the training market (pp. 55–6). He quotes the psychiatrist Peter Breggin, who has written that 'Overall, licensure laws enable groups of professionals to monopolise the psychotherapy market by locking out unlicensed competitors while guaranteeing a steady flow of clients and high fees for themselves.' (p. 142)

In a time of occupational uproar such as we have in psychotherapy at the moment:

' ... prospective trainees may avoid organisations which are not approved. Thus both training organisations and prospective trainees are under pressure to board the bandwagon, whatever its merits' (p. 55). With training effectively 'frozen' in the hands of established members and innovation effectively stifled, 'UKCP is essentially an exclusive club for the psychotherapy training business' (p. 57). Perhaps more damning still is the criticism that within the UKCP 'there is little involvement of the public interest, the consumer interest, the client interest, the trainee interest, or the non-trainer practitioner interest in the core institutions of UKCP'. (ibid.)

Market regulation protects vulnerable clients: so runs the populist litany of professionalisation:

Yet a close study of the experience of licensing in the USA reveals that 'disciplinary action is extremely ineffective as a means of protecting the public' (p. 81); and Mowbray quotes J. Pfeffer who concluded that 'It is difficult to find a single empirical study of regulatory effects that does not [conclude that the outcome is frequently not in the interests of consumers or general public'] (p. 85).

Not only can it be shown that licensing has harmful side-effects in terms of restricting the supply of practitioners, inflating the costs of services, stifling innovation and discriminating against minorities by raising market entry requirements (p. 86), but Mowbray goes on to show at length that none of the preconditions which should be fulfilled to justify the introduction of licensing (pp. 89–91) are in fact present in the counselling and therapy fields. Thus, psychotherapy does not have a clearly defined scope of practice capable of clear legal definition (pp. 92–3); it is not a unified field, there being no consensus as to values, goals and means (pp. 96–7); simpler and less restrictive methods that could accomplish the same purposes as licensing and regulation are available within existing laws (pp. 205, 215–16); there is no evidence of there being potential for significant harm from incompetent or unethical practitioners (pp. 10, 101, 103, 106, 148); it is not possible to demonstrate that practitioner incompetence is the source of harm to clients (pp. 106–8, 111); licensing laws do not necessarily prevent harm to clients (112–14, 116, 118, 124); and overall, it is very difficult not to conclude that the negative side effects of licensing more than outweigh the positive benefits (pp. 86, 214). (House, 1995)

Mowbray asks 'Is psychotherapy a suitable case for statutory treatment?' His book responds with a resounding 'No!'

One of the justifications for psychotherapy professionalisation and statutory regulation is that 'This is the best of all possible worlds and everything in it is a necessary evil', the 'inevitability' argument. But is the institutional infrastructure that supports and drives it forward 'inevitable', a necessary evil? Might it not signal a failure of awareness of group dynamics? A failure of creativity? A narrowness of institutional vision?

These topics, beginning with a critique of the current psycho-politics and moving towards worked-through alternatives to the 'necessary evils feature in another substantial text—*Implausible Professions: Arguments for Pluralism and Autonomy in Psychotherapy and Counselling*, edited by Nick Totton and Richard House (House and Totton, 1998). Twenty-four authors, many of them well known in the field, examine the dynamics of professionalisation from a variety of different points of view and in some detail. The challenge to the whole basis of professionalisation is comprehensive and sweeping. Can psychotherapy and counselling be reduced to a set of objective expert skills? Is a core theoretical model necessary or possible? What model of accountability is truly congruent with the values of therapeutic work? Are there viable practical alternatives to current models of professionalisation?

House and Totton assemble several chapters of critique that look at UKCP, BCP, BPS and BAC.

> In their different ways and with various degrees of cooperation and rivalry, these organisations all promulgate the idea that psychotherapy is a profession; that this profession needs regulation; and that they are the people to do it— preferably with the help of government. In our view, and that of many other practitioners and supporters, this would be a disaster.

Several authors then take up the theme of 'refoundation', which seeks to re-establish some values that have always been at the centre of the craft of psychotherapy. These chapters point to

> ... the 'normalisation' of psychotherapy and counselling which we aim to throw into question, returning to the clear perception of many of its founders that what they had created was 'wild', extraordinary and unsuitable for domestication.

The book concludes with several chapters which build on the notion of *refoundation* and arguing that it points to *new foundation*, alternative ways forward:

> What is new, we feel, is the argument that there is an inherent relationship between psychotherapy and counselling on the one hand, and pluralism and autonomy on the other.

This implies, they argue:

> ... ways of thinking and organising which we have referred to in our subtitle 'pluralism and autonomy'. Many other terms are relevant here—'self-regulation'; 'horizontal organisation'; 'networking'; even 'mutual aid'.

I continue this miniaturised survey of the articulated dissent to psychotherapy professionalisation with a mention of another text that will emerge around the time this article sees the light of day. In his forthcoming book, *Therapy Beyond Modernity*, Dr Richard House uses a deconstruction strategy to generate a long and scholarly critique of psychotherapy professionalisation. He identifies what he calls

> ... the culturally legitimated 'Professionalised Therapy Form' (hereafter, PTF), which, I will argue, can routinely not only of itself be intrinsically abusive, but which actively sets up a milieu in which abuse (be it emotional, sexual or professional/financial) may be a typical by-product, irrespective of the conscious intentions of the therapist.

But isn't the therapist, among other things, an agent for the resolution of abuse?

> Therapeutic abuse may occur because an artificial infantilising framework (the PTF) is created, in whose thrall clients or patients end up being unable to take responsibility for their own choices or behaviour. 'Abuse', then, may be uniquely attributable to, and enabled by, the PTF with its (sometimes deliberate) precipitation of power imbalances, transference dependencies and infantilisation experiences. In addition, 'abusive therapists' could be seen as being just as much subject to the 'regime of truth' that is artificially set up by the PTF ideology as are 'abused clients'—albeit, of course, in a different way.

He moves on to show how therapy, in its modern professionalised form:

> ... increasingly functions as a 'regime of truth', whose discourse actively creates identity and subjectivity (and, most centrally, the identities of 'therapist' and 'client'), and whose accompanying practices self-fulfillingly construct an ideological framework, which then reinforces and guarantees the conditions of its own existence. More specifically, the very way in which such therapy is structured (or 'framed') continually encourages and threatens to produce client infantilisation and dependency through the deep unconscious dynamics triggered within the PTF, and by the assumptive framework typically (and often uncritically) embraced by the therapist. (House, 2003)

Reading the chapters of this book interleaved between client sessions, as I happened to do, was initially a shocking and then a highly rewarding experience.

My own contributions to the professionalisation debate began with *Stealing the Flame* (Postle and Anderson 1989, Chapter 1), followed by *The Glacier Reaches Edge of Town* (Postle, 1994, Chapter 2) and *How does your Garden Grow?* (Postle, 1997, Chapter 4). The titles of these papers, and the present one, reflect my view of the value of metaphor in enquiries of this kind.

> The main task of research is to find images and metaphors which arrest the flow of automatic thoughts and actions and make taken for granted metaphors more obvious. (Riikonen and Smith, 1990)

More recently, *The Alchemists' Nightmare: Gold into Lead—the annexation of psychotherapy in the UK* (Chapter 6) employs a metaphor that conveys my settled perspective that psychotherapy professionalisation in the UK constitutes a form of theft, and the article contains a series of arguments that support and extend this perspective.

I was surprised and pleased that a major journal in the field was prepared to air these contentions, especially since the editors of *Implausible Professions* found that several obvious mainstream publishers were unable or unwilling to take that text:

> We offered the book to every major publisher we could find with a serious
> psychotherapy and counselling list. Many were encouraging; none was prepared
> to publish ...
> ... an editor for one of the leading firms in the field wrote: 'I am sure your book
> will be an interesting and thought-provoking collection. I'm afraid, though that
> ... would not be able to pursue the idea to publication. We ... have close links
> with the UKCP and BAC and other regulatory bodies, who are co-publishing or
> planning to co-publish with us, and it would not therefore be appropriate for us
> to take on this title. (House and Totton, 1997)

By way of sidestepping this institutional collusion, and to broaden the base of the
debate about psychotherapy professionalisation and statutory regulation, some
of the dissent has found a home on the internet. The G.O.R.I.L.L.A. internet site
that I edit—motto 'facilitate the power of love, confront the love of power' (Postle,
1996)—contains a large and growing archive of critical articles on
professionalisation that might otherwise sink from view. The thousands of visitors
to the site in the last year appear to demonstrate that these issues resonate with
psychopractitioners in countries other than the UK.

I will conclude this catalogue of dissent by introducing very briefly one of
the concrete outcomes of it: the Independent Practitioners' Network [IPN] which
currently has several hundred participants fairly evenly spread across the UK.
Founded in 1995, IPN is the indirect descendant of two Cambridge conferences
about professionalisation organised by the Norwich Collective, a grouping of
psychopractitioners in and around that city, in 1991 and 1992.

> Since the initial proposal was first published, the structure has been confirmed
> as a network of autonomous member groups, each linked to other groups; with
> no central administration and with no individual membership, but accessible in
> principle to any psychopractitioner who can meet the network criteria. The
> defining task of an IPN group is to get to know each other well enough personally
> and professionally *to be able to stand by each other's work*. This entails a lengthy
> process of support, inquiry and challenge.
>
> Refinement has led to, among other things, two mandatory requirements. One,
> that to be able to declare itself a Member, each group must have active links to
> at least two other IPN groups that are prepared to validate the process through
> which the group reached their agreement to stand by each other's work. And
> secondly, that member groups publish to the network the names of their members
> plus a statement of their ethical commitment.
>
> IPN has evolved with numerous centres of influence, but no centre of control. In
> its pursuit of 'power-from-within' for ourselves and our clients, it continues to
> sustain itself exclusively via 'power-with' social relations, with varying levels of
> elegance and certainty. (Postle, 1998)

I will return to these notions of 'power-with' and 'power-from-within' shortly.

This accumulated critique of psychotherapy professionalisation/statutory
regulation amounts to a formidable body of research/inquiry/practice. Almost all
of it expresses disapproval, yet this dissent has met with a very clear response

from the register-builders and promoters of statutory regulation:

Silence.

Or rather, as Nick Totton has pointed out, a special form of silence that Germans call *Totschweigen:* ignoring something to death. (Totton, 1999).

What is it that the promoters of professionalisation and statutory regulation don't want to hear? Principally that the move towards professionalisation/statutory regulation of psychotherapy is driven by considerations of economics, status and territory. Notice that I don't include clients' interests.

Economics

I am convinced that one of the fundamental economic drivers of professionalisation/statutory regulation has been the explosive growth in counselling training, up from 76 training organisations in 1990 to 545 in 1997 (*Independent*, 9 December 1997). This means that, increasingly, psychotherapy is part of a saturated psychopractice market. Seen from this perspective, several of the key features of professionalisation make good economic/business sense.

Raising the threshold of entry to psychotherapy training, i.e. to graduates only (UKCP, 1993), along with academically aligned, theoretical course extensions, contributes to the added value that psychotherapy might be supposed to embody compared with say, counselling, despite there being little or no evidence that either this academic threshold or the longer courses contribute to better client outcomes.

> A great number of outcome studies have shown that the results of therapies mostly correlate with the quality of the interpersonal relationship (measured by factors like 'warmth of the therapist', 'trust', 'hopefulness', 'a constructive nature of conversation', 'feeling understood', etc.), not with factors like the methods used, or the length of the training of the professionals involved. (Riikonen and Vataja 1999)

While promoting practitioner registration may enhance training-school product differentiation *vis à vis* other, supposedly less valuable modes of engagement with clients, it is also likely to stifle innovation (Postle, 1998), through imprisoning practitioners who sign up in professionalised therapy forms that, along with the accreditation structures, glaciate psychotherapy practice (Postle, 1998). Plus, as I have seen at first hand, psychotherapy registration forces training schools either to get into the register system, regardless of the profound values incongruence this can entail, or go out of business.

Lastly, professionalisation requires weed/charlatan creation, a chronic tendency of some of the professorial inhabitants of the UK psychotherapy universe that I have gone to some trouble to confront (Postle 1997, 1998).

> The public needs ... to be protected from charlatans by the existence of adequate

training standards codes of practice and complaints procedures ... we were also disadvantaged by the fact that anybody could set up as a therapist and in some cases practise erratically and irresponsibly, tarnishing our reputation. (van Deurzen-Smith, 1996)

It is easy to see why this makes good business sense. If non-registered psychotherapists can be made to seem unethical, unsound or dangerous then this underlines the supposed virtues of the expensively trained cultivars.

when a garden has been very fertile and has been left to itself for a long period of time it is overgrown. Sprawling plants obscure each other's light and deprive each other of nutrients. It is then necessary to cut the plants back, quite drastically and carefully select the ones that one wishes to encourage and make room for, at the same time as uprooting those plants considered to be weeds. (van Deurzen-Smith, 1996)

Such perspective, devoid of an ecological awareness of the importance of diversity (Slunecko, 1999), coupled with the presumption of a psychopractice 'gardener' whose values remain out of sight, together with the failure to notice that the notion of a psychotherapy 'weed' is a highly contestable social category, does not support confidence in its cultivar proponents. It may make business sense, but it doesn't make ethical or ecological sense.

Status

Psychotherapy professionalisation/statutory regulation is also, it seems to me, about *status*. In response to earlier articles, I have been reminded by several people that for some sectors of the UK psychotherapy training world, the status of psychotherapy within the NHS is a prime consideration and thus shapes and energises professionalisation/registration, statutory or otherwise. If you are training people who after spending, say, £15–20K on their training/therapy are denied access to work that, for example, less able psychiatrists control, then clearly the status of psychotherapy is a major business consideration. I was also told , in looking at what drives psychotherapy professionalisation, 'Don't underestimate the importance of envy and jealousy of psychoanalytic 'seniority'/patronage in the NHS' (Coulson, personal communication).

I suppose it is a matter of taste and/or orientation as to whether this understandable desire for parity with psychiatry and clinical psychology in the NHS will eventually constitute a debasement of the psychotherapy currency. In my experience, few UK practitioners know much about the managed 'care situation' in the US (O'Hara 1997). Were they to be better informed, they might realise that even in the more public-service UK environment, the result of these concerns with status will very likely be a compromised, 'tamed', 'domesticated' and probably 'manualised' form of practice that drives out 'wildness' and with it, innovation.

Chaos combines order and irregularity in a subtle way ... Too much order is bad for you! ... Living on the edge of chaos is the best place to be if you want to live a creative life. (Goodwin, 1997)

Territory

Satisfying the status concerns I have touched on above tends to require that there be a 'unified profession', so that psychotherapists are able to 'speak with one voice' to government and the other professions, as doctors, psychiatrists and lawyers do, on matters close to their hearts. As readers can hardly have failed to notice, the competition for who gets to be the psychotherapy umbrella organisation results in a tremendous struggle for control.

In the fight for this contested territory, one of the groups in danger of being marginalised, the BCP, issued an 'us' or 'them' ultimatum on dual membership which expired earlier this year. Elsewhere in the psychopractice landscape, UKCP enthusiasts are busy trying to create/lead/manage/control a 'European psychotherapy profession' with 'science' as a badge of merit.

Psychotherapy is an independent scientific discipline. Training takes place at an advanced, qualified and scientific level. (EAP, 1997)

As though the notion of 'science' in this context had not been thoroughly and comprehensively discredited:

Today even the most rigid scientific orthodoxy is ready to recognise the adverse effects of its own achievement, admitting as unintended consequences the evidence announced by movements in culture and society.(Melucci 1989,1996b)

Stephan Chorover, one of the two authors of this and the following statement, has long held tenure at the Massachusetts Institute of Technology [MIT], a fountainhead of technocratic expertise. Yet he is profoundly sceptical of the notion that science has universal efficacy.

... these adverse effects are an inevitable result of our uncritical acceptance of the paradigm guiding their creation. (Chorover and Melucci, 1997)

The EAP's use of 'science' as a form of up-market decoration seemed familiar, and I realised that it resembles very closely the way the transcendental meditation [TM] movement used 'scientific research' in the 1970's to legitimise their meditation routine (see also Chapter 29).

The more I have studied psychotherapy professionalisation and the desire for statutory regulation, the more it has seemed to be driven by these kinds of market-dominance business agenda. And of course I can appreciate that along with the proprietors of training schools, people in or seeking to work in this sector may even applaud this elbow work. But what about the benefits to clients that are supposed to be the prime focus of professionalisation?

Client benefits

Market-protection initiatives such as those I have touched on here need sound-bite-style rallying calls in order to gain and consolidate support. 'Protecting clients' continues to be the slogan of choice of the regulationists—this despite the weight of evidence that client abuse is endemic in professions (Pokorny, 1998); that licensing doesn't reduce abuse (Mowbray, 1995); and that professionalised therapy may be intrinsically abusive (House, 2003). I expand on this below. In addition, the populist quality of the 'client protection' argument contributes one component to the arguably authoritarian equation some inhabitants seem to ascribe to parts of the UK professionalisation social relations (Wilkinson, 1999). More on that below.

Clients' interests as a way of *justifying* professionalisation of psychotherapy have become separated from actual *benefits* to clients of either professionalisation or the proposed statutory regulation.

Are there going to be any benefits for clients?

Cost

As a result of psychotherapy professionalisation and statutory regulation, clients seem certain to be faced with increased costs; someone will have to pay for the increased levels of training, supervision and administration. Who else but clients?

Choice

There will be reduced choice for clients. The already strident insistence that only registered psychotherapists are any good, and above all 'safe', relies on the spurious definition of 'psychotherapy' in this market as being only what the training schools say it is.

To the extent that professional interests control or influence both the setting and enforcing of licensing standards, there is a risk that the standards will be set too high in order to restrict entry unduly and drive up the incomes of existing practitioners (thus shielding them from the competition of new entrants). The emphasis placed by most professional cultures on technical excellence over other issues of service quality and over issues of cost and access, is likely to increase this risk (Trebilcock,1982: pp. 98–9 in Mowbray, 1995).

This tendency to self-definition by training businesses also denies and avoids the untidy reality that many other modes of delivery of personal development overlap or mirror what the psychotherapy training schools teach. And more importantly:

> ... 'psychotherapy' in a very real sense is not in need of deconstruction—because there has never really existed any definable activity deserving that name. There are so many schools of therapy and so many varieties of activities calling themselves 'psychotherapy' that it is not easy to even start to look at their

> differences and similarities ... The situation is made even more complex when we observe that many of these activities can hardly be separated from what people do continuously in their everyday lives. (Riikonen and Vataja, 1999)

Perhaps because of the near certainty that no defensible definition of psychotherapy is possible, the UKCP appears to have decided, rather than confront this inconvenient obstacle, to ignore it: 'We're seeking to protect the *title* of psychotherapist'[my emphasis] (Casement 1999).

Safety

There will be no increase in safety. Ex-UKCP chair Michael Pokorny, flying in the face of the notion that his organisation is devoted to client protection, claims that:

> There is now a huge amount of research showing that about 10 per cent of all professionals abuse their clients sexually. This has been shown for all professions and in many countries ... The only constant index of the likelihood of a psychotherapist abusing a client sexually is to have been sexually abused during training by one of the training staff. (Pokorny, 1998)

Pokorny's view is supported by Jeffrey Masson:

> Something like 15 per cent of all male therapists in America self-admit that they have sex with a client whom they were seeing in therapy (the real figure must be higher since there must have been some who would not admit it to themselves or to a questionnaire no matter how assured of anonymity they were). (Masson, 1994)

So far as I can tell, the UKCP and other registration strategies intend to deal with this abuse mainly by detecting and dealing with this 10 per cent when someone complains—i.e. the quality control inspector, unpaid, is the client. Might not such a client ask why an institution that claims such privileged, indeed 'expert', knowledge about the human psyche has not revised its trainings to eliminate this abuse? And if they can't eliminate it, how 'ethically sound' are their 'qualifications'?

This evidence of sexual abuse also leaves out the other kinds of misconduct by other licensed professionals that are coming to the surface, for example:

> The editors of some of Britain's medical journals yesterday called for an independent body to be set up to counter fraud, plagiarism and other misconduct committed by doctors and scientists in their eagerness for academic status.
>
> Richard Smith, editor of the British Medical Journal ... said he was haunted by papers from 15 years ago which he had rejected rather than exposing. 'There was a GP who had a general idea that ECT (electro-convulsive therapy) was effective for almost anything—from arthritis to the menopause. He sent us a paper where he described how he had used this treatment on dozens and dozens of patients.' (*The Guardian* 9 September 1999, p. 8)

The editors appear to be asking for a regulatory body that is independent of a profession that has for several generations been regulated by statute.

I hope I have given some sense of the flavours and extent of the critique that has been mounted of psychotherapy professionalisation in general, and the statutory regulation of psychotherapy in particular. Yet, as I have pointed out, in the face of this critique there has been almost total silence from the psychotherapy trade associations. What does this refusal to engage with dissent tell us about their approach to power?

My notion of *positional power* accounts for much of it. If dissent is experienced as peas bouncing off the battlements, rather than as the valid and even vital expression of difference, then it can be ignored. Not a minor matter, because this is not the manufacture of cement but psychotherapy, in which sophistication about power in human relations might be supposed to be a feature. Many of those promoting psychotherapy professionalisation seem deaf or blind to, or ignorant of, the value of dissent.

What other notions of power are there that might help us with this silence or deafness? Here are Bachrach and Baratz, whose typology of power:

> ... embraces coercion, influence, authority, force and manipulation. *Coercion*, as we have seen, exists where *A* secures *B*'s compliance by the threat of deprivation where there is 'a conflict over values or course of action between *A* and *B*'. *Influence* exists where *A*, 'without resorting to either a tacit or an overt threat of severe deprivation, causes [*B*] to change his course of action'. In a situation involving *authority*, '*B* complies because he recognise that [*A*'s] command is reasonable in terms of his own values'—either because its content is legitimate and reasonable or because it has been arrived at through a legitimate and reasonable procedure. In the case of *force*, *A* achieves his objectives in the face of *B*'s noncompliance by stripping him of the choice between compliance and noncompliance. And *manipulation* is, thus, an 'aspect' or sub-concept of force and distinct from coercion, power, influence and authority, since here 'compliance is forthcoming in the absence of recognition on the complier's part either of the source or the exact nature of the demand upon him'.(Bachrach, P. and Baratz, in Lukes, 1976)

Pursuit of psychotherapy professionalisation has, by these definitions, involved 'coercion', 'influence' and 'manipulation'; statutory regulation extends the list through adding 'force'. It is perhaps noteworthy that because of this, for those of us outside the trainers' clubs, 'authority' as defined here has required the creation of a dissenting form of accountability—IPN.

And yet why the silence in the face of dissent, not only from the professionalisation institutions but also apparently from their registrants? Is it because, for many people, 'power', and thus dissent, are strongly associated with 'conflict' so that many of us, because of our distaste, or our lack of skill around conflict, don't want to touch it or be touched by it? And indeed, might the power relations of psychotherapy be one of the strategies that we deploy to avoid conflict?

At this point, it may be relevant to make the reminder that observable conflict is not a precondition for or, an indicator of, the exercise of power: 'The crucial point is that the most effective and insidious use of power is to prevent ... conflict from arising in the first place' (Lukes, 1976). And Lukes claims that this is particularly true if organisations give a lot of value to pluralism in their ways of constituting themselves: 'A polity ... that is pluralistic in its decision making can be unified in its non-decision making' (Lukes, 1976).

In these days of 'spin', if power is being exercised within the system to limit decision making to acceptable issues:

> Individuals and elites may act separately in making acceptable decisions but they may act in concert—or even fail to act at all—in such a way as to keep unacceptable issues out of politics ... (Lukes, 1976)

Following this we might even ask: is the 'umbrella' of psychotherapy regulation really grounded in the personal preferences of the individual registrants? Or is it an example of what Lukes calls 'the supreme and most insidious exercise of power'?

> ... to prevent people, to whatever degree, from having grievances by shaping their perceptions, cognitions and preferences in such a way that they accept their role in the existing order of things, either because they can see or imagine no alternative to it, or because they see it as natural and unchangeable, or because they value it as divinely ordained and beneficial ... To assume that the absence of grievance equals genuine consensus is simply to rule out the possibility of false or manipulated consensus by definitional fiat. (Lukes, 1976)

If this brief discussion of power comes as a surprise, or seems disagreeable or in poor taste, that may be because as a topic it is under represented-to-invisible in psychotherapy journals.

> With a few notable exceptions (Guggenbuhl-Craig, 1971; Embleton, Tudor and Tudor, 1994; Parker 1999) the issue of power seems hardly ever discussed in the therapy field. (House, 1999)

> ... there is a vast literature on the topic of power, but interestingly most of it is to be found within disciplines such as sociology, politics or philosophy and very little within psychology, psychotherapy and counselling; Clarkson (1997) describes the lack of literature on power in counselling psychology as a blind spot ...

> ... the discipline as a whole is deeply implicated in the maintenance and reproduction of power relations which it persistently refuses to make explicit— indeed actively obscures ...' (Kitzinger, 1991:111)

This being so, as psychotherapists we may be somewhat disabled when a major issue entailing the exercise of state power arises, such as the statutory regulation of psychotherapy. However, the inconvenience or distaste may be unavoidable.

> ... until psychotherapists address the issue of the abuse of power within their own ranks, they have not given any reassuring evidence that they care about the issue at all. Why, for example, did the evidence of Bruno Bettelheim's abuse of clients have to come from the clients themselves, though analysts in Chicago knew about it for years? (Masson, 1994)

We should endorse the sentiment expressed by family therapist Lynn Hoffman: 'Therapists of all kinds must now investigate how relations of domination and submission are built into the very assumptions on which their practices are based'

(Hoffman, 1999: P. 14 in Hart, 1999).

In seeking to follow this injunction I have found American psychotherapist and political activist Starhawk a rich source of nourishment. She offers a model of power that bridges both the personal and the political while honouring the spiritual. She proposes three varieties of power: *'power-from-within'*, *'power-with'* and *'power-over'* (Starhawk, 1990).

'Power-from-within'

When working with clients, most psychotherapists seek to evoke, enhance or awaken the *'power-from-within'* of the client. The *'power-from-within'*—to survive, to recover, to flourish, to heal, to belong, to love and be loved, to become self-directing, or responsible, etc.

'Power-with'

In relations with colleagues, family, friends and many clients, psychotherapists are likely to adopt *'power-with'*. *'Power-with'* refers to cooperation, negotiation, debate, parity, mutuality, consensus building, power sharing.

'Power-over'

However, in pursuing professionalisation and the statutory regulation of psychotherapy, it seems to me that UKCP, BCP and BPS, and to a lesser extent BAC, have adopted a *'power-over'* approach to each other, to their registrants, to dissenting psychopractitioners and, ultimately, to clients.

'Power-over' refers to bullying, coercion and domination—the use, or threat, of force/sanctions to ensure compliance, deference, obedience, discrimination or subjugation.

Here's how Starhawk describes it:

'Power-over' comes from the consciousness I have termed estrangement ... It is the consciousness modelled on the God who stands outside the world, outside nature, who must be appeased, placated, feared and, above all, obeyed.

The language of power-over is the language of law, of rules, of abstract, generalised formulations enforced on the concrete realities of particular circumstances ... (Starhawk, 1990).

Engaging the force of the State, through statutory regulation, to consolidate the power of a psychotherapy 'profession' is a 'power-over' approach to social organisation. It poses a special problem for psychotherapy because 'Power-over motivates through fear. Its systems instil fear and then offer a hope of relief in return for compliance and obedience' (Starhawk, 1990).

Is this notion that 'power-over' characterises the social relations of UKCP, BCP, and perhaps also BPS and BAC, some irrelevant fantasy on my part? I think not and I offer three strands of evidence.

A semi-official UKCP handbook (Barnes, 1998) attempts to bring order and reasonableness to complaints procedures. The text makes no attempt whatever to be client-friendly, and I infer from this that it is mainly directed towards the basket-weave of registrants, trainers, trainees and supervisors who remain under the influence of their original training bodies. Between the lines, perhaps unintentionally, the book oozes threat. Palmer Barnes delineates a huge, cumbersome edifice of complaints committees, adjudication panels, investigations and appeals boards.

> ... Standardised complaints procedures based on an adversarial, quasi-legal structure quite inappropriate to the sorts of situations which arise in psychotherapy and counselling. Grinding on for month after month, fitting the client to the structure rather than the structure to the client and producing at best a largely irrelevant verdict of 'guilty' or 'not guilty', complaints procedures are often disastrous for all involved. (Totton, 1999)

According to Palmer Barnes, the people who serve on such boards and panels 'need to be people of stature within the organisation'. Why? The answer is that what is being described amounts to a bureaucratically layered, top-down, seniority-driven 'big stick'. The message to registrants is highly parental: 'be good and everything will be OK; otherwise look what awaits you.' In other words, 'power-over'. For an account of one such enquiry, see Owen (1999).

Part of my chosen role in the last year or two has been to busy myself opening psychopractice doors and windows on matters that some people would prefer to be remain unaired; to let air and light in and, occasionally to let out what may have been kept in the dark. This talk/article is one such. 'The Alchemists' Nightmare: Gold into Lead' (Postle, 1998) (Chapter 6, this volume) was another. Thirty pages and 17,000 words long, it represented a carefully researched inquiry, with extensive peer review from colleagues, into psychotherapy professionalisation in the UK. It sought to confront some of the glaring contradictions and oppressive behaviour to which organisations such as BCP and UKCP seem oblivious. Despite its length and depth, it evoked only a derisory 481-word response (Pokorny, 1998) from one of the UKCP ex-chairs. Wearily, I responded with a polite but acerbic rebuttal of the inaccuracies and sheer inadequacy of his badly written half-page. Here was 'power-over' in action—dissent can be ignored or derided. However, I mention this here not out of point-scoring but because of the sequel.

Some issues later the editor, for reasons perhaps also of his own experience, I don't know, devoted almost all of a somewhat elliptical, academically framed eight-page editorial (Wilkinson, 1999) to the constitutional implications of certain aspects of psychotherapy professionalisation in the UK and the rest of Europe. All of it concerns what I have called the 'power over' posture of the promoting organisations, and his frame of reference throughout is 'national socialism'. 'Is "professionalisation" a mask for anti-constitutionalism?' Wilkinson asks, responding that:

The lack of constitutional ground on which to face our radical power issues and differences, in psychotherapy, leaves a vacuum for power-mongering, and marginalisation, paralleling the wider vacuum in our political world as a whole ... The fault line which opens the doors to National Socialism is the political equivalent of loss of memory, involving a direct alliance of central leadership (Führer principle) and populist base. This fascist defence against isolation is mirrored in the forms of schizoid concreteness experienced by the marginalised.

After this, as I suppose, indirect reference to my text, he goes on to discuss this assertion, posing a series of questions. Fascists? Surely an absurd and extreme claim? But one less absurd, he argues, when the implications of constitutional history are considered (which I take to be a coded reference to seminal agreements and negotiations within UKCP in particular). If psychotherapists do not engage with constitutional history, if we avoid these questions:

Are we democratic psychotherapy organizations destined ... to end up as mere bureaucracies, more or less united or disunited? Is the current catchword slogan of 'professionalisation' a mere mask for anti-constitutional, anti-democratic, centralism and autocracy?

Moreover, fundamental values are at risk for registrants:

As we engage in the processes of acquiring power as a Profession, we are inevitably caught up with all the issues of the practice of power, including the most questionable. In the institutional context, our naiveté and ignorance, our tendencies to deal with issues of power simply by control, our quietistic tendency to bury our heads, politically, ostrich-like, in the sand, our failure adequately to inform and consult, and our *consequent tendencies to take constitutional* short cuts, are all trends which alienate us from the roots of our values.

The ongoing dialogue in response to Denis Postle's paper, arguing the hegemonic style of the United Kingdom Council for Psychotherapy in particular, and by implication the national and international umbrella organisations in general, carries within it a *cry from the depths*, a cry of protest at elements of fascistic modes of marginalisation: for instance, *Totschweigen*, the German, as Denis Postle notes in this issue, for 'deathly silence'—an active, lethal form of silence, *ignoring something to death* (Totton, 1999), of which elements, the cry says, have even entered the pages of this Journal.

Wilkinson observes that all this might helpfully remind us of the significance of Adolf Hitler:

The most powerful forms of political counter-movement of this century have indeed been those *whose essence has been the direct annihilation of constitutionality*, but upon *a direct alliance of central leadership (Führer principle) and a populist base*, offering the apparent short cut to political identity which bypasses the laborious process of creating or maintaining constitutionality.

By this I understand Wilkinson to mean that UKCP registrants, trainees and students need to be in possession of the constitutional means with which to supersede its present hierarchy, and that this is currently not secured. It would be unfair and inaccurate to suggest that Wilkinson is equating UKCP and BCP with national socialism in a one-to-one way; but that the discourse should be chosen at all strongly supports my contention that, notwithstanding their federal internal structure, a 'power-over' style of social relations is the norm in these organisations.

Lastly in support of this view, I want to ask: is it not curious that in its attempt to dominate psychopractice in this way, professionalised psychotherapy so willingly embraces the 'power-over' domination that is threaded through the society around us? A recent study of bullying in the UK found that:

> Children expect bullying to be a regular feature of school life, with eight out of ten having suffered at least one sustained attack.

> Just over 85 per cent of those who had been bullied said it happened at least twice a week, with more than 51 per cent saying that they had suffered both physical and verbal abuse. (Chaudhary, 1998)

> Power in Britain is firmly regal in character, as befits a country where the monarch remains head of state; it is centralised, undevolved and top-down. (Hutton, 1998)

Look, for instance, at the 'power-over' language of the 1999 Health Bill, which was intended to open the legislative door for professions such as psychotherapy to become regulated by the state: *'Her majesty'* may by order in council make provision ... regulating any other profession which appears to *her* to be concerned wholly or partly with the physical or mental health of individuals and to *require* regulation in pursuance of this section. (Health Bill, 1999)

This is the 'power-over' embrace that the statutory regulation of psychotherapy seeks.

At the time of writing, September 1999, a private members bill (see Chapter 12) is being prepared to regulate psychotherapy; it is presently out for 'consultation' to BCP and UKCP, and probably to BPS and BAC. As a significant feature of the psychotherapy accountability landscape, IPN voices sought to be included in this consultation process. Access was denied.

Who is the progenitor of this bill? And what is its provenance? Its promoter declares his 'interests' as British Medical Association, he's a doctor; the Royal College of Psychiatrists, he's a psychiatrist; and a psychoanalytic psychotherapist, though unregistered so far as I can discover. Lord Alderdice is also a member of the House of Lords. If origins matter—a value I would suppose many psychotherapists share—here again is the unaware assumption that the existing 'power-over' constitutional status quo, even the House of Lords, is a tolerable, or even the only, way to structure the working life of thousands of psychopractitioners, whether or not they have chosen to assent to the process. And many of us, probably the majority, have not.

Again, 'power-over'

How could what I outline somehow pass without notice as involving dominance and subordination? My presumption is that perhaps—because as practitioners, psychotherapists are one-on-one orientated—there is a tendency for power/political social relations to be out of awareness, so that when choosing a constitutional form there was never any consideration of alternatives to the 'power-over' status quo.

While it could be argued that these are unimportant local shenanigans, they have value because of the way the 'micro' is often an indicator of the 'macro'. Nevertheless, I don't want to get lost in them, because there is a deeper form of bad news in all this—especially for clients. Why does this ubiquity of 'power-over' matter? It matters because *domination* and the long list of 'power-over' correlates, threat, coercion, subjection, subjugation, victimisation, discrimination, exploitation, manipulation, bullying, deference, exclusion, dependency, normalisation, obedience and collusion—*are the fundamental factors in most client abuse.*

As Jeffrey Masson asks:

> What lies at the heart of child sexual abuse? Sexual pleasure in dominating a weaker person. Sexual pleasure in being on top. Sexual pleasure in the unequal distribution of power. (Masson, 1994)

Many, if not most, clients seek to survive or recover from some form of 'power-over' social relations: grown-up children whose parents manipulate/control them through giving/withholding family wealth; women who seek to survive the dual violence of being beaten by partners and being threatened with worse if they leave; employees whose employer removes out-of-office lunch breaks and hints that to object would be interpreted as 'lack of commitment'; employees promised bonuses in return for unpaid overtime who find the offer withdrawn later for trivial reasons; women terrorised by casual acquaintances who repeatedly make heavy-breathing phone calls.

All are struggling with how power, both personal and institutional, is deployed in their lives. If the psychotherapist they hire, whether willingly or not—and my guess is it is often very unwillingly—structures his/her 'professional' life around, or tolerates a 'power-over' form of constitutionality (as is exemplified by BCP, UKCP, BPS) how can the practitioner fail to remain uncontaminated by this incongruence? Worse, if they are asleep to this issue, how can they fail, as House points out (House, 2003), to perpetuate some form of 'power-over abuse' *in the therapy* through its 'regimes of truth'?

Conclusion

That proponents of psychotherapy professionalisation deny, avoid, side-step, absorb, ignore but do not generally engage with the body of argument against their project that I have outlined here, eloquently delineates the approach to power that they have chosen. And this 'ignoring to death' has increasingly reinforced my settled sense that there are two overarching arguments against the statutory regulation of psychotherapy, either of which should be enough to ensure that it is dropped.

One, there is a massive incongruity between 'power-from-within'/'power-with' practitioner/client relations and 'power -over' occupational politics. This generates a lot of fear in practitioners that will inevitably contaminate work with clients, if it hasn't already done so. As Wilkinson asks: 'If the *power structures* of psychotherapy are totalitarian, how can our practice fail to be contaminated in significant measure by them?' (Wilkinson, 1999)

Two, statutory regulation is intrinsically a 'power over' constitutional form. Installing it at the heart of psychotherapy will cement in place the very factor common to both the presenting experience of many clients and the abuse by practitioners that it claims to minimise or eliminate—the societal norm that dominance is OK.

References

Bachrach, P and Baratz (1970) Power and Poverty. Theory and Practic. In S Lukes, *Power: A Radical View*, pp.17–18. New York: Oxford University Press

Barnes, FP (1998) *Complaints and Grievances in Psychotherapy: A Handbook of Ethical Practice*. Oxford: Routledge

Boseley, S (1990) Fraudsters needed to curb dud research. *The Guardian* 9 September

Boseley, S (1990) Regular check-ups on doctors agreed. *The Guardian* 11 February

Casement, A (1999) Straw Poll, *Talkback*, 4 September BBC Radio 4

Cassidy, J (1999) A professor's caring touch *Observer* 13 June

Chaudhary, V (1999) Children expect bullying at school *The Guardian* 22 January

Chorover, S and Melucci, A (1997) Knowledge and Wonder: Beyond the Crisis of Modern Science? Conference Proceedings, The Center for Frontier Sciences (May)

Dyer, C (1998) Solicitors on fiddle stay in business. *The Guardian* 2 December

Dyer, C (1999) Solicitors get final warning to clean up their complaints act. *The Guardian* 22 March

Goodwin, B (1997) Challenges to Darwinian orthodoxy, paper presented to the Scientific and Medical Network conference on 'Heresy and the Challenge of Revolutionary Ideas', London (May)

Guardian, The (1998) Editorial, 'A patient's right to know' 11 June

HMSO (1999) Health Bill, Schedule 3 Regulation of Health Care and Associated Professions

House, R (1995) Review of R Mowbray's The Case against Psychotherapy Registration. *Clinical Psychology Forum*, December pp. 43–4

House, R (1999) 'Limits to professional therapy: deconstructing a professional ideology', *British Journal of Guidance and Counselling*, 27: 377-92

House, R (1999) The place of psychotherapy in a healthy European social order: a commentary on Tantam and Van Deurzen. *European Journal of Psychotherapy, Counselling and Health*

House, R (2003) *Therapy Beyond Modernity Deconstructing and Transcending Profession-Centred Therapy*. London: Karnac

House, R and Totton, N (1997) *Implausible Professions: Arguments for Pluralism and Self-Regulation in Psychotherapy and Counselling*. Ross-on-Wye: PCCS Books

Hutton, W (1998) *The Observer* 3 May. *The Independent* (1997) 9 December

Kendel, RE (1998) What are Royal Colleges for? *Psychiatric Bulletin* 22, 712–723

Kitzinger, C (1991) Feminism, Psychology and the Paradox of Power. *Feminism and Psychology* 1:1, 11–129

Lukes, S (1976) *Power: A Radical View*. London: Macmillan Press

Masson, JM (1994) A Question of Power in *Psychotherapy Existential Analysis*, 5

Mowbray, R (1995) *The Case Against Psychotherapy Registration: A Conservation Issue for the Human Potential Movement*. London: Trans Marginal Press

O'Hara, M (1997) Emancipatory therapeutic practice in a turbulent transmodern era: a work of retrieval. *Journal of Humanistic Psychology* 37:3, 7–33

Owen, N (1999) More Gold into Lead: Further observations from the alchemists lab - UK psychotherapy developments in the 1990s G.O.R.I.L.L.A. archive <http://g.o.r.i.l.l.a.postle.net/confrontUKPP/owengn2l.htm> WLR London

Pokorny, MR (1998) Alchemy, daydreams and fictions: Psychotherapy in Britain today. *International Journal of Psychotherapy,* 3:3

Postle, D (1994) The Glacier Reaches Edge of Town. *Self and Society,* 23:6

Postle, D (1996) (ed) G.O.R.I.L.L.A. world wide web psychotherapy professionalisation archive <http://g.o.r.i.l.l.a.postle.net/confrontUKPP/carppp.htm> WLR London

Postle, D (1996) A Client's Guide to Psychotherapy. G.O.R.I.L.L.A. archive <http://g.o.r.i.l.l.a.postle.net/clientcorner/cliegide.htm> WLR London

Postle, D (1998) The Alchemist's Nightmare: Gold into Lead—the annexation of psychotherapy. *UK International Journal of Psychotherapy* 3, 53–83

Postle, D and Anderson, J (1989) Stealing the Flame. *Self and Society, 18*:1

Postle, D (1997) How Does Your Garden Grow? *Counselling News,* June, 29–30

Richardson, A (1997) Psychotherapy Registration A view from the Department of Health: paper given at the British Confederation of Psychotherapists Conference: Regulation of Psychotherapy in Europe, 7 June

Riikonen and Vataja (1999) Can (and should) We know how, where and when psychotherapy takes place? In I Parker (ed) *De-constructing Psychotherapy.* London: Sage

Slunecko, T (1999) *International Journal of Psychotherapy,* 4:2

Starhawk (1990) *Truth or Dare: Encounters with Power, Authority, and Mystery.* San Francisco: Harper

Tantam, D (1996) *International Journal of Psychotherapy,* 1:1, 97–100

Tantam, D (1999) Registration benefits and is necessary to the public and the profession in C Feltham (ed) *Controversies in Psychotherapy and Counselling,* p. 223. London: Sage

The Strasbourg Declaration (1996) *European Association for Psychotherapy International Journal of Psychotherapy,* 1:1

Totton, N (1995) Independent Practitioners' Network

Totton, N and Edmondson, E (1994) Proposal. Independent Therapists' Network

Totton, N (1999) *The Water and the Glass.* London: Rebus

UKCP (1993) Training Requirements

van Deurzen-Smith, E (1996) Registration—what it will mean to you the counsellor? Presented at the Fifth St George's Counselling in Primary Care Conference 12 June

Wilkinson, H (1999) Editorial: Psychotherapy, fascism and constitutional history. *International Journal of Psychotherapy,* 4:2, 117–126

Background: I came away from *Summer Conference on 'Statutory Regulation'* at the Anna Freud Centre and the Bristol Psychotherapy Association meetings (see Chapter 10) convinced that what would benefit clients most was not squabbling about 'standards' and 'regulation' but education—consumer advice about how to handle buying psychopractice services—what to expect, and how to get value for money. In 2003 I published a comprehensive self-help guide to personal development, *Letting the Heart Sing*, a CD-ROM edition of an earlier volume, *The Mind Gymnasium*, that gave client education the attention that I believe it deserves (see weblinks page for details). *Letting the Heart Sing* includes an updated version of this user guide.

CHAPTER ELEVEN

Protecting the Client *Experience*:
A user guide to psychopractice*

Hiring a psychotherapist can be a daunting task and the need to find someone often occurs at times of distress when we are least able to choose wisely. Deferring to the power of an expert is tempting, but it is wiser to be adequately informed about what to expect from the relationship with your psychotherapist and what sort of commitment it requires from you.

Starting psychotherapy means above all beginning a relationship. Unfortunately, qualifications provide little guarantee that a psychotherapist will be right for you. This is because the breadth and depth of their lived experience matters as much as their technical and academic knowledge; and what matters most is their ability to get into a rapport with you and your concerns. If you are someone who presently meets with a counsellor or psychotherapist, or who is contemplating it, these guidelines are intended to help you both with your initial choice of practitioner and with getting the best from the psychotherapy relationship.

Clarify your intentions

Use your practitioner to reality test what you want out of your time together. In this sense, 'paths', and having maps and nourishment for the 'journey' may be more relevant than destinations.

Be aware ...
... that counselling/psychotherapy meets a wide range of needs in many different ways. For example, there is fire fighting/rescue work; helping you get through tomorrow/next week; recovery work; letting go of redundant learning; and flourishing work, re-inventing yourself, or creating a new piece of life.

Be aware also that your practitioner is not there to meet your needs, but to help you to identify your needs and find ways of meeting them yourself.

---

* Psychopractice here includes psychotherapy, counselling, coaching, mentoring and personal and professional development, but not psychoanalysis or psychoanalytic psychotherapy.

First published on the G.O.R.I.L.L.A. website in 1997. A revised updated version can be found in Letting the Heart Sing—The Mind Gymnasium, CD-ROM 2003.

Feel free

To check out your practitioner's life experiences that may be relevant to your issues. Does s/he have children? Is s/he in a relationship? Has s/he been divorced? Been in business? Worked on an assembly line? Had a job in a large corporation?

Feel free to ask your practitioner where, how, and with whom s/he trained. Remember, in listening to his or her response, that one of the functions of a psychotherapist or counsellor is to model being fully human. Zest, vigour, love, delight, wit and even vulnerability may matter more to you in the long run than their PhDs, psychology degrees or other formal qualifications, including psychotherapy and counsellor trainings.

Questions to ask yourself

- Is there a clearly defined contract between you for the work you are doing?
- Is the work you do with your practitioner being driven by your needs?
- Is the work confined to your sessions, with no homework between them? The effectiveness of the work is dramatically improved by your carrying it into your life—and in the long run it costs less.
- Does your practitioner encourage you to take yourself seriously? To regard yourself as a project?
- Does your practitioner hold a good balance between supporting you and challenging you?
- Does your practitioner negotiate directly and openly?
- Does the room you meet in unnecessarily limit the kind of work you could do together? Is it full of valuables, or so cramped, small or public that you wouldn't feel able to make loud sounds or vigorous body movements?

Good practice

Good practice comes in a wide range of varieties. There are many different styles of psychotherapy and counselling, probably hundreds. Some involve physical contact; many don't. Some are primarily verbal; other styles favour imagination and play-acting. These differences are often more a matter of starting points rather than fundamental differences.

It is good to remember that, while life experiences are widely divergent, our body-minds are strikingly similar. Because of this, therapies or counselling that are effective in helping us for example, deal with grief and anger, or fear, seem likely to share many common elements.

Pointers to good practice

- Your practitioner has good rapport, by which I mean s/he has good attention, listens well, responds warmly and with feeling where appropriate.
- Your practitioner acknowledges/values a variety of ways of working with clients. S/he presents from time to time an array of models, maps, schemes or other nourishment for the work you do together.
- Your practitioner is careful to distinguish between propositions, suggestions, advice, recommendations, and their opinions, whether personal or as a practitioner.
- Your practitioner holds a balance between psychological, political and historical origins of the issues you bring to the sessions.
- Your practitioner is actively engaged in helping you take charge of your work in, and between, the sessions (essential for primal and other deep/ advanced levels of work).
- Your practitioner holds that healing and change come less from the therapist than from you as a client; and more than either, from the rapport between the two.
- Your practitioner will be open to objections from you and will be able to admit to any mistakes s/he happens to make.

Some basics of good practice

Expect your practitioner to be scrupulous about the confidentiality of what goes on between you. This confidentiality extends to any supervisor with whom s/he discusses your concerns. (Perhaps the only exception would be a situation where your practitioner believes that a third party may be in danger.)

Expect clear agreements about:
- How much you have to pay.
- How long the sessions are.
- Arrangements about cancellations.
- Whether and when you can phone.
- How many sessions you may need.

Be sceptical of:
- A practitioner who creates entanglements between you around agreements/ disagreements, session etiquette, arrangements/bookings/payment, etc., which then have to be unravelled in the sessions.
- A practitioner who doesn't openly and directly negotiate changes in the contract between you, including implicit contracts based on custom and practice—especially if this involves physical contact.
- A practitioner who constantly talks in medically related language, i.e. about health, sickness, pathology, cure, normality, etc.
- Too much analysis of causes and origins.

- No analysis of causes and origins, no maps of the territory you are exploring.
- A practitioner who psychologises everything, including the relationship between you and him/her, particularly when you express dissatisfaction with lack of progress/development/change.
- A practitioner who politicises everything, so that all your difficulties are ascribed to capitalism, 'men', 'women', 'the state', etc.
- A practitioner who too often pours out the riches of their knowledge and skill, so that you feel swamped.
- A lack of significant disclosure by your practitioner.
- A practitioner who is rigid about cancellations, postponements, or changes to session times when there is adequate notice of the alteration.
- A practitioner who often seeks to tell you what to do outside the meetings through advice, recommendations or judgements.
- A practitioner who never offers advice, suggestions, recommendations or opinions.
- A practitioner who constantly directs all your work towards catharsis and who is unwilling to help you with planning, problem solving, etc.
- A practitioner who seems unwilling, or unable, to handle your deepest/ strongest emotions.
- A practitioner who seems unwilling, or unable, to openly discuss/deal with sexuality.
- A practitioner who seems to rely a lot on authority in a way that invites you to defer to their expertise.
- A practitioner who seems to lack a spiritual and/or political perspective.
- A practitioner who seems unable to demonstrate the qualities that s/he recommends.
- A practitioner who seeks any kind of contact outside the meetings: more specifically, one who offers or accepts sexual contact.

If you feel mistreated:
- If you can, raise your concern right away.
- Even if your concern is unclear, or has been growing gradually over a period, try not to let this stop you from raising it.
- Leave the relationship, and find another practitioner. If you can, say why you are leaving.
- Keep in mind that an actual present-time grievance may also carry an emotional overlay from some similar episode from your past.
- If raising your grievance is not given a hearing, or there is not enough recognition of your concern from the practitioner, ask to make contact with their supervisor or practitioner support group.

Part II

Couch Wars: Defending the Walled Gardens of Professional Eden

Background: If the psychotherapists gathered under the UKCP umbrella looked to be ethically incongruous in their imperious and domineering exclusivity, events in 1999 demonstrated that the previous psychoanalytic partners in UKSC, who had quit in 1992 to form the BCP, were several times worse. Anne Casement, UKCP chair at that time, devoted almost four pages of Issue 16 of *The Psychotherapist*, the UKCP's house journal, to detailing the astonishingly abusive institutional elbow-work that lay behind support for the Alderdice Psychotherapy Bill.

> Almost all the individuals around the table are psychoanalytic ... other modalities were being deliberately excluded ... It became crystal clear that many of the individuals on the Steering Group had no intention of allowing anything to take place that was not advantageous to the BCP's psychoanalytic position ... The same issues arose around power and control that were around at the time of the BCP leaving UKSCP in 1992 ... The idea of a Security Council has been put forward again ... people calling for equal representation for their own modalities are labeled 'extremists' who are incapable of trusting anyone to represent them ... an attempt was made to muzzle free speech and transparency ... The meeting of 1 December was so acrimonious that several representatives threatened to withdraw their organisations. (Casement, 2001)

CHAPTER TWELVE

Psychoanalysts Attempt a Regulatory Coup

In G.O.R.I.L.L.A Editorial #4 (see Chapter 9) I mentioned that last summer's Health Bill opens the door to statutory regulation of 'professions' by Order in Council ... Surprise surprise ... while that Bill was being enacted, John (Lord) Alderdice, psychiatrist, doctor, erstwhile Speaker of the Northern Ireland Assembly, and LibDem health shadow, was crafting a private members bill to regulate psychotherapy (and head off ministerial initiatives to unilaterally regulate psychopractice that might ruffle seniority and vested interests?). The Psychotherapy Bill emerged into the daylight in September 1999 and has been 'out for consultation' with interested parties such as the BCP, the UKCP, and probably the BAC and PBS too. Attempts to widen the consultation to include IPN, a feature of the UK psychopractice landscape, were rebuffed.

The Bill is available via G.O.R.I.L.L.A. (weblink page) if you really want to see it, but I recommend my comprehensive, detailed descriptive review (weblink page).

The word in G.O.R.I.L.L.A.'s ear is that the consultation ended on the last weekend (of 23 October 1999) with a decisive rejection of the Bill in its present form; and I guess that anyone who has paid attention to the material in this archive would come to the same conclusion. In looking for a cogent image to describe the Psychotherapy Bill's qualities, I kept coming back to the Berlin Wall. If the Alderdice Bill, or anything resembling it were to become law, it would build a similar fence around the title of 'psychotherapist'.

Is this 'over the top'? Not in the least; read it for yourself (weblink page). All the persons mentioned are, without exception, men. The authority to delineate and investigate offences, specify tests, hold examinations and define what counts as competence is vested in the Privy Council, no less. And yet all the key contentious issues, like defining psychotherapy, are simply left to the Council (appointed by the Privy Council) to settle at some future date. In sounding off like this, I don't want to neglect a clear sense that the author is well intentioned and that this Bill represents a great deal of hard slog and care ... but psychotherapy?

Not much sign of it, either in the writing, or in what would remain of psychotherapy if the Bill became law. If you are anxious or sceptical about the statutory regulation of psychotherapy, take a look at the Bill. Your scepticism will evaporate, to be replaced by the unpleasant aroma of the grim reality of what SR would mean on the ground, on the day, in practice.

This article first appeared in G.O.R.I.L.L.A. as Editorial #5, 25 October 1999

A shift of balance

The Independent Practitioners' Network [IPN] was five years old in November 1999. Coincident with this birthday, G.O.R.I.L.L.A., which will continue as an archive of psychopractice texts, has cloned itself ... the result being an internet journal <www.ipnosis.org>, which provides a window into and out of IPN.

IPN is a remarkable piece of social innovation. Notwithstanding Lord Alderdice's arrogant ignorance of its value, an increasing number of people inside UKCP and the BAC see IPN as a relevant and legitimate feature of the UK accountability culture. I hope that *Ipnosis* will consolidate and extend that view.

References

Casement, A (2001) Chair UKCP, Letter to all Registrants, *The Therapist, 16*

Background: The G.O.R.I.L.L.A. website began in 1995, parallel with the founding of IPN. I saw it as a way of finding out what this new medium, the internet, could do, and it also offered the possibility of a more flexible alternative to the hegemony of printed journals and books. Four years on, a parallel site that might provide a voice for IPN and help consolidate it in the psychopractice landscape seemed essential.

CHAPTER THIRTEEN

Conversations About Power

This first edition of *Ipnosis* arises at an interesting time for IPN. Five years on, we are growing steadily. Many of us have just about recovered from the fear that kept us locked into the agendas of professionalisation; now we face the perhaps quite different task of consolidating the fascinating social innovation that is the IPN. Will we freeze as an organisation? Can we find the courage to engage with the rest of the world that the task of deepening our knowledge and practice may require? *Ipnosis* hopes to initiate and sustain conversations about all of this.

Power, its varieties and its deployment continues to be a preoccupation at this time in the evolution of psychopractice. It is nonetheless a topic that is noticeable by its absence from psychotherapy journals. Why should this be? Is it due to embarrassment? Is it due to a lack of insight, or of theory? In the coming months I hope *Ipnosis* will contribute to remedying this deficit. Power is also an issue close to home. Does *Ipnosis* on the internet and the increasing use of e-mail by participants unduly privilege some people in IPN?

In this inaugural edition of *Ipnosis* I have tried to hold the balance between the agendas of confronting professionalisation and 'creating', making the accountability culture we want. Yvonne Bates *Still Whingeing* (weblink page) picks up the weariness that some of the convinced supporters of professionalisation have with objectors, and her title points to the way that language can be used to marginalise while failing to attend to the argument. Her article, rejected by *Counselling*, usefully lists some of the reasons why statutory regulation of psychotherapy is bad news.

IPN is a lived critique of professionalised psychotherapy in the UK. However, as John Heron points out towards the end of *The Original Theory of Co-counselling and the Paradigm Shift* (weblink page)—one of the two pieces by him that I include here—there is a danger in political engagement of becoming overdefined by the entity that is being opposed or resisted. Do we have the balance in IPN right between resisting oppressive developments in psychopractice and creating what we want?

At one of the early IPN gatherings, a straw poll indicated that about half of those present had experience of co-counselling, and there is much about IPN that I suspect may have been shaped by it. Historically, co-counselling has been an important contradiction of the myth that there is an inherent divide between clients and the 'professional' expertise of counselling/psychotherapy. Anyone who has had experience of teaching a group of completely naive participants to use

This article first appeared in *Ipnosis*, October 1999

co-counselling and see it take root, is likely to be aware of the inflated value that psychotherapy expertise, especially in its professionalised forms, seems prone to.

John Heron's revision of the theory of co-counselling has several notions that may be of interest to *Ipnosis* readers; the primary relationship of cathartic exploration to subsequent transmutative work and the consequences of the first being left out; the interrelations of oppression and spirituality; and the reiteration of the value of a learning perspective as a core theoretical framework for psychopractice of any variety.

From an altogether different direction, in *More Gold Into Lead: Further observations from the Alchemist's Lab. UK psychotherapy developments in the 1990s. a response to Denis Postle, May 1999* (weblink page), Nick Owen, a psychotherapy trainer and formerly an active promoter of UKCP and its antecedents, writes at length about his experiences of being the object of a (sustained) complaint from members of a UKCP-accredited training course. His experience of the UKCP's complaints procedures suggests that they are very likely to be dominated by 'adhocery', i.e. who is willing to take on the task and how much time they are prepared to give. Clearly, the UKCP way of dealing with complaints can be a damaging and unhelpful experience for everyone involved.

By way of underlining the importance of the 'creating' agenda, making the institutions we want to have, I include two pieces which refer to cooperative inquiry, one of the more thoroughly developed and theoretically well-supported ways of doing what IPN broadly does. *Bringing Research to Life: From Survival and Recovery to Flourishing* (Chapter 26) is about a residential cooperative inquiry which included several members of an IPN group; and the second is about *Primary Theatre and Lean Ritual* (weblink page), from a more recent inquiry at John Heron's centre in Italy.

Elsewhere, and not to be missed, are *Tidbits*, which has an apposite quotation from Iris Murdoch (weblink page); and *History* (weblink page), which has a revealing account of medical life in Paris in the 1880s.

Lastly, I hope that as it evolves from this starting point *Ipnosis* will set a culture for the open exchange of knowledge, practice and comment about psychopractice. Look on it as a window both into, and out of, IPN.

Background: I had originally intended to cut most of the references to the Alderdice Psychotherapy Bill from this book because it seemed now to be merely history. Revisiting the documents convinced me that the shenanigans around its development and the structure of regulation it favoured (it has a family resemblance to current proposals for a Psychological Professions Council), coupled with its imperious, ambitious superciliousness, was indeed how many psychopractitioners experienced and continue to experience themselves socially. Apparently unaware of the deep-seated incongruity of institutional bullying and client relations, they felt able to try to unilaterally impose the Psychotherapy Bill's arrangements on the rest of us. Six years later it is reasonable to suppose that most of the Bill's proponents are still working, organising and teaching; in other words, those oppressive social relations are still with us.

CHAPTER FOURTEEN

Registering the Psychotherapy Bill

I have been deeply touched in the last month or so by two things. The Alderdice Psychotherapy Bill turned my heart to stone for the best part of a day (weblink page for a detailed and comprehensive review). Secondly, I heard Daniel Hogan, author of a justly famed 4-volume study of psychotherapy accountability, speak about what he calls 'licensure', at a conference to launch Susan Greenberg's excellent book *Therapy on the Couch: a shrinking future* (Greenberg, 1999).

The Psychotherapy Bill tempted me into irony ...

> Happily there is nothing here that need worry ethically sound practitioners. Lord Alderdice, author of the bill, is after all speaker of the Northern Ireland assembly and LibDem Health Shadow, a psychiatrist, a doctor and an analytical psychotherapist—a professional background that means he can be trusted to be even-handed and fair in his approach to protecting the public. His decision to omit any mention of women, either as practitioners or members of any of the Bill's regulatory body, underlines his deep personal commitment to the ethical standards that the Bill will make Law.

> Similarly, there is nothing that need worry or concern us about the Bill's assignment of ultimate continuing authority for psychotherapy to the Privy Council, not least in defining the starting membership of the regulatory council and thus its statutory committees. The Privy Council has centuries of experience of the exercise of power and we can trust the people who have gravitated to it to ensure a smooth uncomplicated downward flow of control. Top-down authority of the kind the Bill embodies, cascading through layers of deference, is exactly the kind of relating that ethically sound psychotherapists model for their clients. And the safe, competent, proficient standards of practice of any psychotherapist who has followed a four-year recognised training will easily ensure that this professional structure will never affect how they relate to clients.

> Indeed, the minimising of personal autonomy in how psychotherapists ensure safe and competent practice will be a major factor in convincing public opinion that psychotherapy has rid itself of any last vestiges of the social pathology that has seen so much division and schoolism in the last few years. Equally one of the underlying motivations for preparing the bill, 'that UKCP had better get on with statutory regulation before the voluntary schemes unravelled' (Casement, 1999) is just the kind of motivation foundation that the professionalisation of psychotherapy needs in its development of better client accountability.

> Certainly any practitioner reading this Bill who finds their heart turned to stone, or who sees it as about as aesthetically appealing as the Berlin Wall, is evidently either inadequately trained or has a deep vein of unworked material around power and authority.

This article first appeared in *Ipnosis* Editorial, November 1999

A bird's-eye view of psychopractice suggests that there are twin needs that it needs to meet: the requirements of clients, and also the requirements of psychopractice employers with statutory obligations, such as the NHS, the Probation Service, the Prison Service or Social Services. The latter appear to need a shorthand of diplomas, registers and qualifications so that, without being competent in these matters themselves, they can hire people to whom they can legally delegate, or refer on, their statutory responsibilities for clients to other statutorily approved practitioners.

Registers, statutory or not, are a form of currency, of legal tender, which facilitates this referral or delegation of statutory responsibility, under, say, the Rehabilitation of Offenders Act, to an unknown but statutorily bar-coded practitioner.

The Psychotherapy Bill is so heavily weighted towards meeting these employers' requirements that it appears to have missed how many of them are directly contrary, even harmful to, the interests of many clients, not least those who pay directly for psychotherapy services.

Certainly it would be hard to find a way of organising accountability that is more *in*congruent with the way practitioners actually relate to clients; as I point out elsewhere (see Chapter 16), the 'power-over', coercive style of the Bill and of its co-creators UKCP and BCP installs at the heart of psychotherapy the very approach to power at the root of almost all abuse: that domination is normal, tolerable and 'natural'.

Contrary to the two mendacities prevalent in this debate—that statutory regulation is inevitable and that it is nothing to do with politics, i.e. power—there are other, better ways of meeting clients' needs. IPN represents one of them and in a recent talk Hogan (1999), author of a justly famed four-volume study of psychotherapy accountability, outlines proposals for licensure—as he calls it— some of which are replacing the immensely restrictive arrangements in several US states.

Hogan argues that:

> Instead of an almost exclusive emphasis on control and discipline, which restricts practitioners from entering the field, we need to focus on how regulation can help the profession develop. This means moving away from restrictive licensing laws to a system of simple registration embracing the entire range of therapists.

He reminds us that:

> Little evidence exists that current entrance requirements have any bearing on necessary skills or any relationship to performance. Even if it were, it seems clear that the requirements are way above what is minimally necessary to be competent.

Also, and relevant to people such as Lord Alderdice who are confident they can test/examine psychotherapist competence and proficiency:

> Since psychotherapy is such an ill-defined field, since reliable and valid standards do not exist to determine whether practitioners are competent, since not enough is known about how to train practitioners effectively, and since methods of

measuring competence and selecting practitioners have not been agreed upon, restrictive licensing laws are inadvisable.

Lastly, Hogan argues that restrictive regulations are likely to cripple the field they control.

> Licensing laws are not meant to ensure a high level of professional competence, only that a practitioner is not likely to harm the public ... *In this regard, licensing laws should emphasise the regulation of output, not input. Hence, they should be concerned with a person's actual skills, not how those skills were obtained.* [*Ipnosis* emphasis]

References

Hogan, D (1999) Protection Not Control. In, *Mindfield: Therapy on the Couch*. London: Camden Press

Background: If they got past the first page, the sheer obnoxiousness of the Alderdice Psychotherapy Bill's provisions seemed likely to blind readers to its damaging underlying presumptions. To contradict this I added to a detailed review of the Bill for *Self and Society,* (weblink page), a short article that addressed what I continue to feel is a core objection to state regulation of psychopractice—it legally endorses registered practitioners' take on human nature, on what is 'human' and 'natural'.

CHAPTER FIFTEEN

Registering Human Nature

Weary of the task of confronting the professionalisation of psychopractice, I often remind myself that vigilance about how, and by whom, human nature is being defined is always honourable and necessary. Thus is it is no exaggeration to say that the Psychotherapy Bill is a very important document. It attempts to put certain of the definitions of what constitutes human nature, what is 'human' and 'natural', beyond argument.

There is a literal assumption in the Bill that its registrar and all practitioners are male. This Achilles heel is a pointer to the Bill's male-dominant, hierarchical, autocratic view of what is human and natural in the form of its regulatory infrastructure.

That such views of what is human and natural are seeking to be privileged over any other is surely highly incongruent with the ways in which psychotherapists actually work (Wilkinson, 1999). Yet it is clear (Casement, 1999) that this Bill, or something very like it, is high on at least the UKCP's wish list.

Might the Bill square the circle that the UKCP's 70+ training schools face, owing to the impossibility of advocating both pluralism and restrictive regulation? This looked promising. But wait a minute: insofar as these schools sign up to statutory regulation, won't their definitions of human nature suddenly have the status of law? What was previously local will become global and legal. And also by giving, literally, the 'force of law' to a handful of definitions of human nature, does not the Bill demean, denigrate and demote the rest of the field of psychopractice? Might this indeed be one of the Bill's intentions? So much for pluralism.

Regulation, as we are often told, is for the protection of clients; and now surely, with this Bill, for them everything in the garden is now rosy. Or is it? Just as doctors know what is 'normal' and 'healthy', and psychiatrists know about 'disorders' and 'mental health', so now psychotherapists (state-registered, for there will be no other) claim to 'know what is good for us', 'how we should live' (Tantam and van Deurzen, 1999): in other words, what is human and natural.

That many clients may welcome this is unsurprising—but isn't it a poisoned promise? Part of the price of the Bill's legal enforcement of who is and who isn't a 'psychotherapist' involves the modelling of domination as a preferred form of social relating. As a result, one of the definitions of human nature that psychotherapists regulated under this Bill inevitably bring to their clients is that domination is tolerable, even natural, because that is the organisational style they have signed up to.

This article first appeared in *Self and Society*, January 2000

134 REGULATING THE PSYCHOLOGICAL THERAPIES

As I point out elsewhere in more detail (Chapter 10) domination (and subjection, subordination, victimisation, etc.) is a defining feature of almost all client abuse. Yet here is a Bill that has domination running through it like 'Blackpool' through a stick of rock: a *Psychotherapy* Bill, no less.

References

Casement, A (1999) Chair remarks, *The Psychotherapist*, Autumn

Tantam, D and van Deurzen-Smith, E (2000) In A Howard, 'The place of psychotherapy and counselling in a healthy European social order: Further commentary on Tantam and Van Deurzen' *European Journal of Psychotherapy, Counselling and Health*, Summer. See also <http://ipnosis.postle.net/pages/alexhowardipnosis.html>

Wilkinson, H (1999) Editorial: Psychotherapy, fascism and constitutional history. *International Journal of Psychotherapy*, 4:2, 117–126

Young, R (1997) The Grand Leading the Bland <http://www.psychoanalysis-and-therapy.com/human_nature/papers/pap101.html>

Background: At the time this *Ipnosis* fragment was written, I wasn't aware of how acrimonious the contact between the British Association of Counselling and Lord Alderdice had been following BAC's realisation that counselling was somehow beneath his radar (and beneath contempt?). My BAC source told me that they were 'poorly received' at a first meeting with Lord Alderdice. Following an email row during which, one might speculate, the size of the BAC membership was mentioned, a later meeting was more cordial. BAC heard that 'regulation was inevitable', that Lord Alderdice 'thought that he could just about get psychotherapy in the bottle, but to get counselling in too would break it'. There was a choice: either a Bill like this, or have the government do it to them through an Order in Council.

CHAPTER SIXTEEN

Domineering, Sexist, Archaic: A *psychotherapy* bill?

The Psychotherapy Bill was given its first reading in the House of Lords on May 18th.

One of the fictions that the regulationists would have us believe is that the Psychotherapy Bill will magic into place a unified psychotherapy profession ... some chance! In a statement in the last issue of *Counselling*, the Chief Executive of the BAC revealed that, like IPN, BAC had had haughty treatment from Lord Alderdice and they too had been refused a voice in the discussions on the Psychotherapy Bill draft.

Speaking of which, the published Bill is virtually identical to last autumn's draft, even down to the continued use of male pronouns to describe all practitioners mentioned in it: an archaic parliamentary convention? Perhaps. But what are all those women registrants doing signing up for a grossly sexist document? And I remember a senior UKCP person being reported as saying that she had as yet failed to get equal opportunities on the UKCP agenda.

A surprising number of people in and around the Psychotherapy Bill think it has no chance whatever of becoming law, and at least one MP we know is likely to block any attempt to bring it into the Commons; so why go to so much trouble? Unless your intention is a dry run of the topic in the Lords—run up the SR flag and see who salutes and who blows raspberries; perhaps, as some Machiavellian fantasists suggest, for the Bill to become law is not high on Lord Alderdice's agenda. Perhaps it is primarily a stratagem to heal the split between BCP and UKCP.

And if there is little interest in the Bill's way forward from now on—a General Psychotherapy Council modelled on the General Medical Council—might that have some connection with the continuing evidence of the gross inadequacies of the medical model of regulation that the Psychotherapy Bill mimics? Bristol ... Ledward ... Slade.

This article first appeared in *Ipnosis* editorial, 12 June 2000

Background: My recurring theme of power–over dominance in the institutional approaches to regulating psychopractice was reinforced by the way in which *Lord* Alderdice's Psychotherapy Bill was dropped by the government. *Lord* Wedderburn, in the presence of a cluster of *Noble Lords*, hears from *Lord* Hunt that they are minded to create and use the Health Professions Council for the purposes of regulating psychotherapy.

CHAPTER SEVENTEEN

Psychotherapy Bill 'Bombshell'

In this extract from Hansard, 19 January 2001, Lord Wedderburn of Charlton concludes his supporting remarks on the Psychotherapy Bill with news of the government's position on the regulation of psychotherapy and related trades.

LORD WEDDERBURN OF CHARLTON:
... I have omitted many points that I wished to address. However, none of them affects my warm support for the Bill. What was the bombshell for me last night? It was this. On an open fax I received a communication from my noble friend Lord Hunt, the Parliamentary Under-Secretary of State at the department. It is an issue on which we have had several general discussions. The Minister said:

> The Government is currently considering proposals for consultation on an Order under Section 60 of the Health Act 1999 ... This would create a new federal and multidisciplinary Health Professions Council, with the power to extend its remit to other groups not currently registered.

He continued:

> ... statutory registration using the powers of the Health Act is the most appropriate way to deal with the regulation of psychotherapists, counsellors and other related groups. We will also assess other important factors, such as their readiness for registration and the availability of Parliamentary time with a view to positive and early moves to secure their regulation'.

I believe—my belief is shared by others—that an Order in Council under the Health Act 1999, which the Government has lawful authority to produce, would wreck the progress with the Bill that the noble Lord, Lord Alderdice, has made. It is not right for Whitehall simply to grab a convenient area to apply to psychotherapists, counsellors and goodness knows who else. It needs patient work, not an Order in Council, with those who treat patients and want to know—I named earlier such a foundation—where to send their patients and what advice they can obtain. There are two informal registers. Is there a register where they can look up the training of different modalities with regard to particular people?

I do not believe that that objective can be best achieved by an Order in Council. I am sorry to throw in this dissenting note but we would fail the objectives of the Bill and fail the person who drew up the Bill with such hard and patient work if we accepted that the right way forward is by regulation by Order in Council. I am sorry to end on a note of asperity. However, I can avoid that by repeating my congratulations to the noble Lord, Lord Alderdice, on the Bill to which we shall now give a Second Reading.

This article first appeared in *Ipnosis*, 25 February 2001

Background: Part of the role that I have inhabited through *Ipnosis* has been to give voice to aspects of the professionalising of psychopractice that insiders would rather kept unheard. This fragment from *Ipnosis* chronicles some of the institutional leakages that dissenting outsiders depend on, especially when, owing to overvalued civility, some of the very strong feelings are carefully screened from public view.

CHAPTER EIGHTEEN

Fear as a Psychotherapeutic Organising Principle?

An intriguing new dimension to the Psychotherapy Bill has emerged in recent months. *Ipnosis* had assumed, wrongly as it turns out, that the so-called 'stakeholders' for the Psychotherapy Bill included BAC. Not so. Indeed BAC, it appears, were offensively cold-shouldered by Lord Alderdice and only after considerable pressure, including some mention that there were several thousand members of BAC who considered themselves psychotherapists, did contact warm up. This late development might be supposed to wonderfully complicate the task of coming to agreement about the composition and membership of any Statutory body regulating pychotherapy, since it would require considerable ongoing intimacy between BCP and BAC adherents.

A year or so ago an anonymous well-wisher sent *Ipnosis* a copy of the draft Psychotherapy Bill. For some considerable time it was the only place outside the registration ostrich farm where this bizarre legislation could be tasted.

Recently, a very different but perhaps more remarkable document arrived at *Ipnosis*.

In her 40-page *Open letter to Janet Boakes [UKCP chair]*, Petruska Clarkson details very comprehensively the anger, rage, hurt and damage that have arisen from her pursuit of complaints against UKCP and one of its member organisations. You wonder what the glue is that holds UKCP together, that holds you in it if you are registrant? It's fear. Fear that what has happened to Petruska could happen to you. This is why UKCP/Alderdice try to 'ignore dissent to death'. The dissent constantly points to the bizarre incongruity of a *psychotherapy* accountability deploying fear as an organising principle. Petruska's chilling and deeply felt personal account will no doubt already have been dismissed as pathology. Not here. In tone, vigour and directness Petruska's 'voice' epitomises the wildness that the UKCP seeks to tame and domesticate. As others before her have found, the price of challenging highly collusive herd behaviour can be very high. Petruska details the ruinous damage she has suffered with sadness, fury, exasperation and not a shred of hatred. The message rings out loud and clear: that there are people in UKCP who are willing to wreck the working life of anyone who threatens its progress to statutory salvation.

This internet text is unmediated by the tidying of editors. It feels like book-length; it's uneven; it digresses; and yet it shimmers and sparkles with exactly the life—the 'physis', as she calls it—that the hard hats of the UKCP training schools are busy crushing in their rush for market share. (Following Petruska's death in

---

This article first appeared in *Ipnosis*, 16 February 2001

2006, this text is no longer available on the internet; however, in honour of her institutional confrontations I have included a short section from her Open Letter document at the end of Chapter 2).

Psychotherapy Bill continued

Strong insider reports two weeks ago that the government intended to regulate psychotherapy via an 'Order in Council' seemed for a while in curious conflict with the fact of the second reading and committee stages of the Alderdice Psychotherapy Bill, 19 and 22 February respectively. However, a close reading of those proceedings leaves little doubt—if there was any previously—that happily, the Bill is dead. It's likely replacement? A 'General Psychotherapy Council' modelled on the General Medical Council that has been so successful in 'regulating' the practice of medicine ...

Background: I have never been able to find out what caused the exodus that I outline below. Does it matter? Probably not, but what seems certain is that following the failure of the Alderdice coup, for it was such, there seemed to be a change in presentation, if not in overall strategy, in the mainstream accrediting bodies. In September 2000 BAC changed its name to BACP, giving the psychotherapists on its books public (and political) recognition, and perhaps for the first time in a decade, the UKCP seemed more open to dissent around statutory regulation.

CHAPTER NINETEEN

Old Drawings in New Colours:
The statutory regulation of psychotherapy (continued)

One or two apparently unrelated happenings in the last year or so suggest that morale may be sagging among some of the officials hitherto strongly committed to the statutory registration of psychopractice.* The Chair of the UKCP and several officials quit, without explanation to the membership, in autumn 2001. The Chief executive of BAC(P) left unexpectedly, also apparently without explanation to his members. Of course these could be career moves, positioning themselves for the plum administrative roles of actually implementing a DofH clone of the osteopathy regulatory body.

But back to the 'decline in morale' theory—perhaps more accurately, slippage—in the hitherto psychotherapy organisations' spin that statutory regulation would be a 'Good Thing'. One piece of evidence for this might be the recent inclusion in UKCP's house journal, *The Psychotherapist*, of an article by Richard House entitled: 'The statutory regulation of psychotherapy: still time to think again' (weblink page). A follow-up to this in the March 2002 issue prints some letters in response, plus, at House's suggestion, a 'debate' featuring six paragraphs—two from people who are pro-statutory regulation, two who feel neutral about it, and two from people opposed to it.

This openness, though overdue, is very welcome. *Ipnosis* was delighted to contribute to the debate; my 'paragraph' consisted of the headings in this expanded *Ipnosis* version.

The statutory regulation of psychopractice—

—creates a religion of priests verified by the state as the only legitimate guardians of the secret knowledge about transference:
The admission to 'qualified' psychopractice too often resembles a process of anointment, especially in the psychoanalytic territories (Young, 1999), and of 'schooling' in a 'regime of truth' (House, 2003) that overvalues what can be taught i.e. sold as a course. It denies the value of more scattered, more accumulative

---

* Psychopractice. I coined the label 'psychopractice' to contradict the spin that statutory regulation of psychotherapy does *not* imply regulation of the whole field. Regulating one part of the field necessarily determines, or shifts, the terms of trade for the whole field. Happily there have been signs that the Department of Health shares this view.

This article first appeared in *Ipnosis* 3 July 2002

mixes of life experience and self-directed learning which seems more likely to benefit clients.

'Schooling' seems to install a one-legged-stool approach to practice that favours 'psychologising' and/or the 'spiritual/transpersonal' to the exclusion of the 'socio/political' so that the processes through which institutional power is deployed are rendered invisible or unimportant. This tends to undermine the courage needed to voice and act from the misgivings that many, maybe most, practitioners have about statutory regulation.

—creates multiple walled Gardens of Professional Eden.

The extent to which the whole statutory regulation project recapitulates archaic models of power and authority are well expressed in a cartoon that appeared in the *New Yorker* a while back. Adam and Eve are disporting themselves in the Garden of Eden, while in the Heavens a placard appears saying 'RULE NUMBER ONE: DON'T PISS ME OFF'. As I have pointed out elsewhere, current and recent proposals for statutory regulation will impose a culture of domination on the whole field of psychopractice.

Alongside this, as some of us have found, the walled gardens of registerable psychopractice inhibit or disallow dissent, and inhibit or marginalise 'out-of-the-box' thinking, contributing to a failure of creativity so that colouring in old drawings (the GMC) in new colours (the HPC) is the best that can be envisaged.

—institutes discredited quality control: find and bin rejects.

Perhaps because of the decline of manufacturing, few practitioners seem to have enough experience of industry to know that quality control in any remotely efficient manufacturing these days means pro-active quality control of the continuing process. Such modern quality assurance has a feedback loop (or loops), so that any drift away from the specified practice leads rapidly to corrective action *before rejects are produced*. The notion that CPD and/or supervision is adequate to this task seems very naïve.

The essential feedback loop for an adequate practitioner's quality assurance process, i.e. one that would fully honour clients' interests, seems to me to require a high level of ongoing self-disclosure with peers. At the moment the only organisation I know of that provides this is IPN.

—belongs to the same family of 'security herdangst' as electronically gated and fenced housing developments.

What people who live in such developments near me (how nice for them that they have the 'wild' river close by) seem to fail to notice is that from the outside they resemble prisons (I don't exaggerate; inside the walls house after house has lift-gates over the windows). Statutory regulation has long seemed to me to be some kind of imprisonment. I suppose that, like gated housing developments, it provides a literal guarantee that you have only to relate to BMW-, SAAB- or Mercedes style-peers.

It's curious that, in our society, many people of the two extremes of privilege and under-privilege get to inhabit prisons— except that imprisonment is one of the structural ingredients of cultures of domination.

—as currently proposed, extends and deepens the hegemony of the medical model: psychopathology—diagnosis—treatment, yet sidelines, or excludes, non-medical approaches that emphasise learning, education and self-directed personal development.

Anyone who had any doubt that this is what is afoot should read the transcript of the talk that Anne Richardson, senior advisor to the Department of Health, gave to IPN last autumn (weblink page).

—enables practitioners to avoid the detailed self-disclosure *to clients* that would enable them to make informed choices.

After watching and trying to resist the glaciation of the field of psychopractice in the UK over the last 12 years, I have come to the conclusion that effective accountability *for* clients (that they would experience as effective) requires a different approach from those that have been pursued. Development of this is still embryonic but the two components that seem essential are:

1. The ongoing peer-disclosure that I refer to above, presently implemented by IPN.

2. A comprehensive, public form of 'full disclosure' by practitioners of their training, life experience, supervision arrangements, working style, client population (with whom they don't work), complaints routing and references, i.e. formal statements from people who are prepared to assert that they 'stand by their work'. Entry to this 'full disclosure' model would be open to any practitioner and would be available to clients via an internet database with local client/practitioner/support group initiatives providing paper listings (see Chapter 22).

—appeals to the feudal monarch in us.

Just as the 'feudal monarch' lives on in society in the shape of royal families, holy fathers, Houses of Lords and Privy Councils, so it lives on in us, too. We may be inclined to think that the temporal power of such monarchies is so narrowed as to be unimportant, and yet they still shape key social agendas; look at the bishops in the House of Lords, and the 'establishment' of the Church of England. The trouble is that so long as these archaic models of power continue, and thus continue to inhabit us psychically, we may be inclined to think that their power, the domineering tendencies of our inner House of Lords, or Royal or Holy families too, are similarly so slight as to be unimportant. Therefore, we fail to see that statutory regulation institutionalises these feudal remnants and the damage that dominance inflicts.

Such a sleep of complacent compliance commits those who are prepared to inhabit the feudal monarch roles to a poisonous mix of reverence/worship (as an apparently essential continuing bulwark against social disorder), but also to fear (as a source of punishment or retribution for transgression). Either way, as in the historical past, it generates victimhood.

—enables practitioners to continue to avoid confronting and engaging with issues of political power.

Yes, politics is time-consuming, often tedious, frequently unrewarding, and often means spending time with people with whom you profoundly disagree; and yet, isn't some engagement with the exercise of power in its social forms essential, i.e. appreciating directly the influence that the exercise of power has on identity and behaviour? Isn't that what lots of clients bring to meetings? To work with their power issues? If we take the ostrich option around the organisation of our own trade, how can we expect that decision not to unhelpfully skew our client work?

—invites us to sign up to a culture of domination that mimics that which afflicts many, if not most of our clients.
Cultures of domination continue to shape UK government and many, if not all, of our social arrangements. The statutory regulation of psychopractice asks us to sign up to these damaging cultures, despite the evident threading through of daily life of approaches to power that are facing the other way, i.e. child care that is less domineering in style; anti-discrimination initiatives; much greater public awareness of the value of feeling and emotion; and so on. The proposals currently out for discussion seem in Canute-like denial of these benign developments; some of them even perhaps the fruits of our labour.

Further reading (see also weblinks page)

Heron, J (1990) The Politics of Transference: an essay of the AHPP. *Self and Society*, 18:1
Hogan, D (1990) Protection not Control. In, *Mindfield: Therapy on the Couch*. London:Camden Press
House, R (2001) The Statutory Regulation of Psychotherapy: Still time to think again.*The Psychotherapist*,17, 12–17
House, R and Bates,Y (2002) (eds) *Ethically Challenged Professions: Enabling Therapy beyond Modernity*. Ross-on-Wye: PCCS Books
House, R (2003) *Therapy Beyond Modernity Deconstructing and Transcending Profession-centred Therapy*. London:Karnac
Howard, A The place of psychotherapy and counselling in a healthy European social order: Further commentary on Tantam and VanDeurzen. *European Journal of Psychotherapy, Counselling and Health*.
Postle, D (2000) Shrink-wrapping Psychotherapy. *The British Journal of Psychotherapy*, 16:3
Postle, D (1998) The Alchemists Nightmare: Gold into Lead, the annexation of psychotherapy. *TheUK International Journal of Psychotherapy*, 3:1
Richardson, A (2001) *Statutory Regulation of Psychotherapy, Psychology and Counselling: The way forward*. Transcript of talk given to IPN London gathering, 13 October
Richardson, A *Getting Fit for Regulation by Deputy Head*. Mental Health Services Branch, Department of Health
Totton, N (1999) The baby and the bathwater: Symposium: Critiques of Psychotherapy and Counselling. *British Journal of Guidance and Counselling*, 27:3
Whan, M (1999) Registering psychotherapy as an institutional neurosis: or, compounding the estrangement between soul and world. *European Journal of Psychotherapy, Counselling and Health*, 2:3, 309–323
Young, RM Psychoanalysis and Psychotherapy: The Grand Leading the Bland <http://www.psychoanalysis-and-therapy.com/human_nature/papers/pap101.html>

Background: Post–Alderdice, keeping track of disparate and apparently unrelated events in the ongoing regulating of the soul of counselling and psychotherapy became problematic. The overarching fear of government control meant that organisations that had previously been psychically at each other's throats, or behaving as if the others didn't exist, were now, following shifts in personnel, often in fearful but private dialogue. The BACP, which appeared to understand taxonomy very well, had the idea of mapping who was actually out there and approached the DoH for funding. They received only a small proportion of what they requested from the DoH, which I guess made it a condition of the funding that the UKCP be partner in the work. In an ethically dubious reversal, the mapping research was presented as having been initiated by the DoH. The BCP told me they had been excluded from the research; their attempt to negotiate directly with the HPC (see below) was refused.

These fragments from *Ipnosis* give an impression of the growing turbulence in the psychopractice field and the difficulty stakeholders such as IPN, who were out of sympathy with the regulation project, had in finding out what was being done in their name.

CHAPTER TWENTY

First Quarter 2005 Developments in
UK Psychopractice

News 1

10 March 2005: The British Confederation of Psychotherapists [BCP] intends to negotiate directly with the Health Professions Council [HPC] to create a statutory register for their member population. The source for this information, the College of Psychoanalysts website, includes much fascinating and relevant detail of the continuing elbow work between the contenders for statutory psychopractice status (weblink page).

News 2

10 March 2005: British Association of Behavioural and Cognitive Psychotherapies [BABCP] leaves the UKCP (weblink page).

News 3

In autumn 2004 IPN heard that 19 psychopractice organisations were meeting to promote the Statutory Regulation of Psychotherapy and Counselling in the UK. Not having been invited, many of us in IPN wondered what was being arranged by these organisations.

Finding out what they were up to proved surprisingly difficult. Letters to Rosalind Mead, the relevant DoH person, went unanswered; copies of books mailed to her setting out the context and research on regulation went unacknowledged. When I tried to phone Ms Meade the DoH switchboard refused to give me her phone number, or an email address, even when I insisted I was calling on behalf of IPN, a stakeholder in UK psychopractitioner accountability.

News 4

A BACP press release was more informative. After listing the 19 member organisations, it went on:

This article first appeared in *Ipnosis*, 28 March 2005

... various organisations representative of the whole profession have come together and united in a course of action ... A meeting was held of the NATIONAL ACCREDITING BODIES FOR COUNSELLING AND PSYCHOTHERAPY, representing the Chairs and CEOs/Directors of all groups in the mainstream therapy spectrum. Present were key players Rosalind Mead, Project Manager for New Professions Regulation, Department of Health (D.H), and Marc Seale, the CEO/Registrar of the Health Professions Council. With their support, it now looks as though this Register will form the nucleus of Statutory Registration and Regulation, which is currently anticipated in 2008.

'All groups in the mainstream therapy spectrum ...' Why not 'all groups in the therapy spectrum'?

News 5

A letter to my MP drawing her attention to the lack of openness of the DoH produced the following reply from Lord Warner, Parliamentary Under-Secretary of State, Department of Health:

The Department has this year funded two of the main umbrella organisations within psychotherapy and counselling, the United Kingdom Council for Psychotherapy (UKCP) and the British Association for Counselling and Psychotherapy (BACP). These organisations have been asked to map existing training and qualifications to identify agreed roles and competencies within the professions. This is a necessary first step towards defining standards of competence, training and practice that will form the basis of statutory regulation in the future.

Lord Warner went on to say that IPN should approach either of these organisations in order to register its interest and contribute to the work that is being undertaken:

My officials have passed the Independent Practitioners' Network's name to BACP and UKCP and asked them to be inclusive in taking this work forward. We expect that once this work is complete and nationally agreed training and qualifications are available, statutory regulation of psychotherapists by the Health Professions Council should be possible by 2008.

News 6

Parallel to this, an IPN participant discovered on a discussion list that someone had emailed the Health Professions Council about a BACP press release that claimed statutory regulation under the HPC was on the way, and received this reply:

Dear Mr ...
I am not aware of the BACP or UKCP or any other counselling body applying to the HPC for statutory regulation. We certainly have not recommended to the Department of Health that they be regulated by the HPC. Please see our website for further details about aspirant professions and our role. If the title 'counsellor' was to be protected by law, it would make no difference whatsoever which professional body or organisation they belonged to; if the HPC were to ever regulate counsellors, it would be a legal requirement for them to be registered

with us to use the title.
Regards
Victoria Nash
Health Professions Council

Activity and Title
A colleague reminds me: what is missing from the discussion is the improbability
of actually policing the *activities* of psychotherapy or counselling, even if the *title*
(calling yourself a psychotherapist or counsellor) were to become a legal entity.
However, regulating the title will have an impact on the field of practice, though
this may be self-correcting through the introduction of alternative names for the
'activity'.

*****

News 7

Dr Graham Cocking, registrar of the International Society of Professional
Counsellors [ISPC] claimed in a discussion at www.counselling.ltd.uk that the
list of relevant organisations in UK psychotherapy and counselling was more like
46, not the shortlist of 19 orchestrated by the BACP and UKCP. A forum member
backed this up by offering a much longer list of excluded organisations.

News 8

In mid-February 2005 an IPN participant phoned a contact at the HPC and was
told that:

> Even if a body wished to make an application, that in itself would take at least
> 18 months. The Privy Council is booked until at least 2008, so any application
> from Counsellors and Psychotherapists may well take until 2010 or longer to be
> looked at. No psychotherapy organisation has applied to join HPC; there was a
> discussion with BACP in 2004, but no more has been heard of it.

In a later conversation with the DoH, the same IPN participant formed the
impression that:

> The DoH are well aware that in regulating psychotherapy and counselling they
> have a huge and complex situation to deal with. In an ideal world they wouldn't
> want anything to do with it; hence their strategy of asking BACP/UKCP to try to
> draw things together. Essentially, someone started a very-much-not-wanted ball
> rolling and everyone is trying to keep out of its way!

The decades-long pattern of trance-induction—'*Be sure your are signed up otherwise
you won't be able to practise*'— misinformation, disinformation and self-righteous
exclusivity on the part of the UKCP, BACP and allied regulationists continues.

Background: If you wonder about the polemical tone of this fragment from *Ipnosis*, keep in mind that it reflects something of a collective sense of exclusion. This was how it felt to be at the mercy of a group of training and accrediting interests (still in place in 2006), meeting privately to plan and implement control of the UK psychopractice market. It was easier if you knew nothing about it, as was the case I guess for most practitioners; certainly being a participant in the IPN accountability process helped keep the 'compulsive hegemonic disorder' of the mainstream accrediting institutions in perspective. There were some wonderful, even hilarious ironies to come (see Chapter 32), but they weren't in sight in late spring 2005.

CHAPTER TWENTY-ONE

An Established Church of
False Promises

Having been a UK psychopractice regulation watcher for over 16 years, *Ipnosis* finds the current attempts by a self-selected group of trade associations to fence off and claim exclusive legal rights over a sector of the territory of counselling and psychotherapy the most shameless and corrosive to the credibility of the field in all this time. Yes, Lord Alderdice: even including your attempted coup.

Why shameless? Because the culture of domination that the active exclusiveness entails is bizarrely incongruent with core notions of psychopractice such as mutuality, nurturance and cooperation—and I might add tolerance of, and respect for, dissent. Especially and particularly they are shameless because what they are up to is claiming the exclusive and legal right to manage the transference of the population of this nation. I don't exaggerate. This is what it means:

> ... it is fear that has, in my experience, characterised the response of psychotherapists to the whole political process of professionalisation. They fear loss of livelihood, loss of status and recognition, loss of legitimacy. And in this fear I detect a strong element of transference itself: the acting out of infantile survival patterns in the face of all-powerful authority figures. So the political argument for professionalisation, based on legally accredited competence in handling transference, is itself a rationalisation of a more deep-seated transference phenomenon. This is the paradox. One can scarcely have much confidence in psychotherapists whose need to have their management of transference government-approved is itself a sign of unresolved transference material.
>
> Competence in handling transference, by its very nature, is the one thing that cannot, without serious distortion, be professionalised and legalised in an emotionally repressive society. The professionalisation of it takes it away from the public domain into mystification and expert knowledge accessible only to the few—and this exacerbates and reinforces the very processes which it is supposed to be dealing with. There is no better way to sustain compulsive infantilism in society (and thus an endless supply of clients) than by setting up a highly specialised, government-protected profession that alone is qualified to deal with it. This is the ancient corruption of priestcraft: to organise your hierarchy in such a way that you generate the sins you are appointed to redeem. It is significant that the pressure for statutory registration in this field always comes in the first instance from those who are already caught up in some kind of transference abuse and want to preserve and protect the improper exercise of professional power (Heron, 1990) (weblink page).

This article first appeared in *Ipnosis* Editorial, 12 June 2005

Statutory regulation of psychotherapy and counselling would mean that only registrants would be legally able to sit with people and explore their inner worlds and their projections onto family members, partners, workmates and you, the practitioner.

Do you realise that if you are a member of the 19 colluding organisations, this is what you are signing up to? Can you not see that this is hubristic beyond imagining? As though licensing a single grouping of people to exclusively manage the fallout of the multiple trance inductions (projections, transference) of political life, advertising, marketing and daily imaginal and emotional life were a benign, let alone practical proposition?

Have you no knowledge of the impoverishment that such regulatory straightjackets have caused in the US (weblink page), and Germany and other parts of Europe (weblink page)? How would this Established Church of False Promises be more capable in 'managing' the nation's transferences than the Established Church of England is in 'managing' the nation's spirituality?

Coupled with this is the equally astonishing lack of awareness of how buying into state power is likely to corrode the credibility of activities such as psychotherapy and counselling, which often mediate and explicate matters of power for many, if not most clients. How you do power in the institutions you sign up to shapes how you do power in your practice. Sign up to the safety of an archaic hierarchy headed by the Privy Council, which is what is likely to be on the table—become an exponent of 'risk-averse' practice—how does this protect clients' *experience*?

And then there is the unquestioned assumption that the proposed 'Health Profession' framing is even remotely appropriate for an activity such as psychotherapy or counselling—as though the medical model was an unchallenged and fixed North Star that everyone else had to steer by.

The shamelessness of cherry-picking a list of organisations, who then collude to keep the group exclusive, is compounded by the extent to which, across at least the last decade and a half, these groups have steadfastly ignored the cumulative evidence that the competencies claimed are overvalued, that none of them will significantly protect clients, and that statutory regulation of activities such as psychotherapy and counselling is not primarily about professional and economic aggrandisement for administrators and trainers with courses to fill. See also Douglas McFadzean's excellent 'Warning' (weblink page), a short account of why the government's present approach to Statutory Regulation is bad news.

If you feel that these moves towards statutory regulation are mistaken, discriminatory, and bad news for clients' interests—what to do? If you are unhappy about your organisation's participation, write to the Chair and ask them to justify their actions.

Background: One of the challenges posed by oppressive social institutions such as the mainstream UK psychopractice accrediting bodies is that they tend to annul fresh thinking about alternative ways of holding civic accountability. IPN provides a handy platform for out-of-the-box thinking about the practitioner/client interface, and this quite widely circulated proposal for a practitioner list offers a more open approach than is presently available. The Vermont State *nonlicensed* and *noncertified* psychotherapist legislation (weblink page) provides a US pointer to how such a form of accountability could be implemented.

CHAPTER TWENTY-TWO

Psychopractice Accountability:
A practitioner *'full-disclosure list'*

What does a prospective psychotherapy/counselling client need and deserve from a process of practitioner accountability? Revising my last book, *Letting The Heart Sing—The Mind Gymnasium* (Postle 1988, 2003) for republication has repeatedly put me in the position of adopting a client perspective—what do people seeking help with the human condition need to know when hiring a psychopractitioner? They need to know a lot more than they are likely to now.

Many practitioners and employers and consequently, we might expect, most clients/service users still see accountability through the narrow, professionalised lens of hoop-jumping—'qualification' and 'training'. Two other lenses are likely to be more relevant: *effectiveness*, and how we maintain our *capability* as practitioners.

First, then, effectiveness. Psychotherapy and counselling do not generally subscribe to the practice, commonplace in management and technical training, consultancy and language interpretation, of eliciting client feedback after events. Asking for feedback on our presumed effectiveness, and paying attention to what we hear, makes it more likely that clients will benefit from their time with us. This is not to argue that psychopractice is free of feedback on effectiveness, only to note that it is usually informal. For example I, and I imagine other practitioners, invite clients to take time at the end of the year or end of the quarter to review progress or development.

Recent enquiries based on more formal approaches—that in effect asked 'Did it work?', 'Did I get the help I needed?' (Duncan and Sparks 2002; Lambert et al. 2001)—point to a handful of effectiveness factors that challenge the sacred cows of professionalised psychotherapy. For example, the value of academic and technical competence—credentialling—in terms of 'qualifications', training and Continuing Professional Development (CPD) is seen as contributing as little as 15 per cent to client outcomes. Placebo effects—hope and expectations—are held to be at least as important. The quality of the rapport between the partners in the therapeutic or, as I prefer, educational alliance counts for as much as these two together; and furthermore, what the client brings in the way of support, resourcefulness, education, and lived experience of survival and problem solving accounts for approaching half the outcome.

So if the *resourcefulness of the client* makes a very high contribution to therapy outcomes, how can this be facilitated or enhanced? Apart from underlining the

This paper first appeared in: Y. Bates and R. House (eds), *Ethically Challenged Professions: Enabling Innovation and Diversity in Psychotherapy and Counselling*, pp. 172–8, PCCS Books, Ross-on-Wye

importance of a facilitative/client-centred approach, *client education* seems one obvious answer—an option that is almost entirely neglected by the bodies that dominate accountability in the UK, such as the UK Council for Psychotherapy (UKCP), the British Association for Counselling and Psychotherapy (BACP), the British Psychological Society (BPS) and the British Confederation of Psychotherapists (BCP).

When they seek a practitioner, the vast spread of self-help books, magazine articles, radio programmes and websites that refer to psychological matters are likely to mean that clients may be well informed, if haphazardly, about the *territories* of counselling and psychotherapy. They are not likely to be knowledgeable about what to expect, how to choose someone fitted to their needs or what is involved in hiring a practitioner. Personal recommendation aside, clients finding a practitioner through medical referral, the Yellow Pages, or checking out one of the psychotherapy organisation directories in the public library, are likely to know little or nothing about the person with whom they are starting to work—a recipe for a poor match between what the client needs and what the practitioner offers. After all, the psychotherapy/counselling relationship may affect how the whole of the rest of their life plays out. As I see it, the issue from a client's perspective is not getting it absolutely right or eliminating risk, but *increasing the chances* of a fruitful match.

Alongside effectiveness there is the question of how to sustain practitioner competence. How can practitioners be helped to navigate life's swamps and precipices and still be present for the clients who bring their lives to us? I borrow from industrial quality assurance the notion of *capability*: if we become, through a mix of education and experience, capable of delivering effective psychopractice, how do we stay capable? Supervision, the ongoing discussion of current concerns and declaration of potential risks; plus some form of CPD certainly helps us stay capable. However, I want to argue that both CPD and supervision are limited in their support of capability, because disclosure of where a practitioner is *as a person* tends to be optional or absent.

To summarise, present forms of psychotherapy/counselling accountability rely too much on input 'qualifications', on training, and on CPD events, plus supervision to support and sustain practitioner capability, while neglecting client education and information. How could they be replaced by, or become transformed into, a new kind of accountability structure, one more congruent with what is now known about outcomes and client/practitioner power relations, and consequently more attuned to clients' interests?

I am convinced that the missing element in present approaches to accountability is *disclosure*. Full disclosure to peers of information about where the practitioner is in their life, as well as how their practice is going; and disclosure of relevant information to clients about available practitioners.

The UK Independent Practitioners' Network (IPN) has pioneered Continuing Self- and Peer-Assessment and Scrutiny (*CSPA and S*; House and Totton, 1997) as an ongoing process of quality assurance that in my experience wonderfully supports and maintains practitioner capability. *CSPA and S* requires continuing (eye) contact with practitioners, not only as people who deploy models, skills and experience; but also with the practitioner as a person with a life; so that contingencies that might skew, distort or undermine the quality of alliances with clients can be surfaced, supported or confronted. *CSPA and S* itself depends on practitioners getting to know each other very well in a safe enough and confidential enough forum for *non-disclosure* or *resistance to disclosure* to become a focus for attention. For example, a practitioner who, not for the first time, casually says they are so tired they could scream might be disclosing something about their current life that is likely to affect the quality of their work with clients and that merits confrontation by peers.

In addition, and as the main but related focus of this chapter: how can disclosure of information about practitioners be extended and deepened so as better to support consumer choice? I propose that this requires development and installation of an innovative accountability process through which practitioners publish, in some detail, who they are, how they became practitioners, what their life experience and working orientation are. This needs doing on a scale sufficient for a *client* to be able to make some kind of informed guess that this is someone with whom *they* could work.

On the following pages I outline a proposal for such a psychotherapy/counselling accountability process. It requires, I believe, a switch of gestalt from the present secretiveness/reticence of professionalised psychopractice to what has been called a 'full disclosure' model. Mowbray lists Will Schutz, Dan Hogan, Roberta Russell and S. J. Gross as advocating full disclosure as a basis for accountability (Mowbray, 1995: pp. 205–9). Since such shifts of paradigm are often hard to grasp in the abstract, I will describe my proposal for a full-disclosure accountability structure as if it existed.

A practitioner 'full disclosure' list [PFD*list*]

What would be the key elements of disclosure?
Participation in the PFD*list* requires a statement in each of the following categories. (*NB: Practitioners may choose to make minimal or detailed statements.*)

LIFE EXPERIENCE: work, jobs, roles, responsibilities; relationships—single, married, divorced, separated, partnered; children, grandchildren, adopted children, stepchildren; sexual orientation. A recent photograph.

PRACTITIONER DEVELOPMENT: education, training, relevant life experience/skills transfer, competency process (qualification, accreditation, self- and peer-assessment, etc.).

PRACTITIONER STYLE: approaches/orientation(s) statement; ethical statement; terms and conditions including charges; weekly client load, specialities and preferences, who they wouldn't work with; confidentiality, note-keeping, supervision.

PRACTITIONER COMPETENCE: supervision, continuing practitioner development, client feedback.

PRACTITIONER 'REFEREES' STATEMENTS: documents from three peers who:
> 1. attest to the accuracy and integrity of the claims to competence of the practitioner in the statements made in the disclosure.
> 2. provide a brief account of the process through which they keep this information up to date.

PRACTITIONER CONFIDENTIALITY: note-keeping, supervision.

PRACTITIONER/CLIENT DISPUTES: details of practitioner's conflict resolution/ mediation process and details of whom to contact.

PRACTITIONER TRADE ACTIVITIES: publications, journal contributions, research, books, interviews, trade association roles.

What form should this information take? What would be mandatory?

The *categories* of disclosure should be mandatory, but practitioners need to be free to say as much as they like (but not nothing) in response to each of the categories. Similarly, the style of presentation is also a matter entirely for the practitioner. Styles seem likely to range from the purely factual to more discursive, or narrative. The openness to, and ease of change of, entries by practitioners (see below) is intended to encourage a 'disclosure culture' that is both self-sustaining and self-correcting through its appeal to clients and service purchasers.

How would the PFDlist be implemented as an institution?

The PFD*list* information would be held in a *government-funded computer database* accessible through any standard web browser. Access to this database would be free to users and, because the task of preparing and updating an entry is considerable, to practitioners also. Since the PFD*list* entries would be in the public domain, local initiatives to publish *paper directories* for the IT-challenged would be likely and desirable. A sector of the PFD*list* would make available a moderated *user forum* where users and practitioners could exchange information and experiences. The PFD*list* would be managed by a small secretariat charged with the maintenance of the List and its functions. They would *not* be responsible for conflict resolution but would maintain a mediation/advocacy resource (see below), which might from time to time be drawn on for disputes that could not be locally resolved.

How could we ensure that clients experience it as user-friendly?

The user-friendliness of the whole system would be a commonplace IT design task. The 'friendliness' or otherwise of the entries would be entirely a matter of practitioner capacity and choice. Easily accessible, though password-protected, access to the PFD*list* would mean that practitioners could edit, add to and develop their entry as the need or occasion demanded. Non-IT practitioners would be able to mail additions or amendments to the PFD*list* manager.

How would it be administered/financed?

The PFD*list* is a service enhancement for psychopractice users that needs to be free at the point of access. To enable this, government funding would be essential. However, this should be taken to imply government participation/support/

facilitation rather than control. The database function is a commonplace IT function for which tenders could be invited. The layer of necessary management could be subcontracted to an existing contractor responsible or adjacent to the Department of Health. The *list* manager and staff would be charged with maintaining the database, promoting it and taking action on abuses or deficiencies in List entries (see below).

Does PFDlist *amount to statutory regulation by another name?*

The PFD*list* applies to the task of accountability what we know about the uses and abuses of power, both interpersonal and institutional, while at the same time respecting the lack of agreement on what constitutes competent or effective psychopractice. Out of that it seeks to make available the widest range of psychopractice offerings, while at the same time giving users adequate information about who/what, may or may not, meet their needs, and how to complain and seek redress if they experience an abuse of power and trust. Government-supported, but not government-controlled.

Which practitioners would be included/excluded from the PFDlist?

Any person offering services in the psychopractice area would be entitled to an entry on the PFD*list*. Non-registration should be tolerated, but not encouraged.

How would practitioner statements be verified?

Practitioner statements have to be verified by the referees who are named and posted with the entry. If the accuracy of the statements is significantly challenged, the PFD*list* manager in the first instance would invite the referees to check out the challenge/objection. Their response might lead to the PFD*list* manager requiring that the entry be edited or withdrawn. However, the intention of the PFD*list* would be to display carefully framed statements by practitioners that have been peer-assessed sufficiently well for accuracy before posting as to generally eliminate significant challenges. Indeed, such a challenge would indicate a failure of the refereeing process.

What sanctions might there be for inaccurate or misleading statements?

The aim of the PFD*list* is not to eliminate risk, but to honour users' needs for personal safety and value for money, without eliminating the 'wildness' and unpredictability implicit in effective psychopractice. If disputes arise, the PFD*list* will seek to enable all parties to reach some resolution through mediation and advocacy, rather than adjudication of guilt and blame, i.e. 'sadder and wiser' being more important than 'right/wrong'.

The PFD*list* management *would not be responsible for resolving disputes*, but they would develop and maintain access to legal and advocacy/mediation resources to enable clients and practitioners to progress disputes. The costs of such facilities could be contained through an insurance charge on PFD*list* participants.

Disputes about misleading or inaccurate statements, or allegations of fraud or abusive practice, should be explored and resolved by the practitioner's designated dispute process and his/her referees. If they are unresolved, then they should be referred to the PFD*list* manager's layer of advocacy and mediation services. Persisting with misleading, fraudulent or inaccurate statements should lead to removal from the PFD*list*.

The List management would maintain pages on the PFD*list* web domain for posting apologies, explanations, notices of agreement, settlement, or failure to agree.

What sanctions might there be for abusive behaviour?

Complaints or allegations of abusive or other behaviour by a practitioner in contravention of her/his stated practice description should in the first instance be pursued via the practitioner's stated dispute process. If redress or satisfaction is not reached through these means, then the management can be asked to invoke mediation/advocacy services. If the dispute/complaint is resolved as an instance of abuse, i.e. behaviour that the practitioner's referees cannot support, this would result in removal of the practitioner from the PFD*list*.

Reinstatement onto the list would require the re-establishment of the initial criteria, including the support of the same referees.

*What would be the PFD*list's *relations to other 'lists', such as those maintained by the IPN, BPS, UKCP, BPS and the BACP's UK Register of Counsellors?*

Multiple lists of practitioner offerings appear to be in clients' interests since they maximise choice. A single, government-sponsored listing that is inclusive of the wide range and variety of psychopractice offerings would go a long way towards securing a free market in these services.

The PFD*list* is intentionally inclusive: for instance, practitioners would be free to specify dispute procedures that lead to existing accountability bodies such as the IPN, BPS, UKCP, BPS and BACP. The PFD*list* is intended to promote benign co-existence between these and the dozens, possibly hundreds, of other institutions whose members might be participants.

*How would the PFD*list *resolve the range and divergence between the styles of psychopractice that are currently available?*

Client education would be an essential feature of the PFD*list*. The list would publish and maintain user-orientated information about how to hire a practitioner, what to expect, and guidance on how to negotiate with them. Several divergent, even contradictory guides might be expected to co-exist side by side in reflection of the comprehensive disagreement in the field about routes to competency and the kinds of contracting that psychopractice entails. In addition, organisations and individuals would be free to take web space to present the claimed virtues of their particular way of working with clients. The intention of this would be informative/educational, and a role of PFD*list* management would be limited to discouraging, and if need be removing, organisational statements that amounted to advertising or promotion, while encouraging the display of articles, research, personal experiences, etc.

Drafts of the proposal that I have outlined in this chapter have produced mixed reactions. Some people missed the point of the integration of practitioner accountability and client choice and saw the PFD*list* as a form of advertising; others warned that psychodynamically inclined practitioners wouldn't want to disclose anything at all because it 'would distort the transference', as though a client's ignorance of what they were getting into didn't also distort (or generate) transference. Two people were concerned that this amount of disclosure 'would provide clients with ammunition'; there were understandable anxieties that any government involvement would amount to a takeover and that the internet format would exclude too many clients. An objection that I feel has validity, but which is also a reminder of the purist reaches of psychotherapy, is that in helping clients find someone who was a good match for their needs, the PFD*list* would promote collusion through eliminating or reducing the chances that clients benignly meet a practitioner whom they *wouldn't* consciously choose. The trouble with the present randomness is that it too often seems to lead to unhelpful mismatching, ineffectiveness, and clients struggling to adapt to the practitioner's style.

My aims in devising the PFD*list* have sought to satisfy two criteria. First, further to confront the creative inadequacy of the Department of Health and the UK trade associations, the UKCP, BCP, BPS and BACP. Their notions of hierarchically structured accountability, based on archaic and discredited input forms of quality assurance, without ongoing face-to-face contact, mimic existing, deeply flawed, medical-style accountability (Totton, 1997). Like the GMC and the medical Royal Colleges, the psychotherapy trade associations are intrinsically exclusive and imperious in their relation to both registered practitioners and clients. Contrary to their assertions about client safety, through their claims of privileged, superior knowledge, they harm clients' interests by undermining the credibility of the very broad reach of personal and professional development work of which they are only a small part. As outcomes research seems to show and as others have argued (Mowbray, 1995), this supposed virtue and its false promise of client safety is an 'emperor's new clothes' assertion.

Secondly, after more than a decade of resistance to, and confrontation of, the professionalisation of psychopractice, I have sought to answer a personal question: Might there be government-sponsored form of accountability for counselling and psychotherapy and their relatives in the field of personal development that I could sign up to? And if so, what form would it take? I feel that the PFD*list* would be good enough.

References

Duncan, B and Sparks, J (2002) *Heroic Clients Heroic Agencies: Partners for change.* Nova Southeastern University

Gross, SJ (1977) Professional disclosure: alternative to licensing. *Personal Guidance Journal,* 55: 586–588

Hogan, DB (1979) *The Regulation of Psychotherapists,* 4 vols. Cambridge, MA: Ballinger House, R and Totton, N (eds) (1997) *Implausible Professions: Arguments for Pluralism and Autonomy in Psychotherapy and Counselling.* Ross-on-Wye: PCCS Books

Independent Practitioners' Network (1999) Principles and Procedures, *ipnosis: a journal for the Independent Practitioners Network*, <http://www.ipnosis.org>

Lambert MJ (2003) The effectiveness of psychotherapy: What has a century of research taught us about the effect of treatment. In *American Psychological Association: Updates from the Devision of Psychotherapy*. APA: Riverdale

Lambert, MJ, Whipple, JL, Smart, DW, Vermeersch, DS, Nielsen, SL and Hawkins, EJ (2001) *Handbook of Psychotherapy and Behavior Change*, 5th edn. New York: Wiley

Mowbray, R (1995) *The Case Against Psychotherapy Registration: A Conservation Issue for the Human Potential Movement*. London: Trans Marginal Press

Postle, D (1988) *The Mind Gymnasium*. London: Macmillan

Postle, D (2003) *The Mind Gymnasium: CD-ROM edition*. London: WLR

Russell, R (1981) *Report on Effective Psychotherapy: Legislative Testimony*. New York: Hilgarth Press

Shutz, W (1979) *Profound Simplicity*. USA: Joy Press

PART III

State Regulation of Counselling and Psychotherapy: The End Game?

From taxonomy to taxidermy: mapped… measured… captured… and stuffed?

Background: This *Ipnosis* page hints at a decisive, mid-course correction by the convoy of mainstream psychotherapy and counselling organisations as the destination just visible on the horizon starts to take shape as the Health Professions Council.

CHAPTER TWENTY-THREE

Rowing Away from the
Statutory Regulation of Psychotherapy

The end of the holiday season has seen a shower of activity in the UK psychopolitics territory. Apart from the July COSCA text (see below), three other items have appeared pointing to changes in regulationism priorities.

The College of Psychoanalysts, shocked perhaps by the British Confederation of Psychotherapists' attempt to negotiate directly with the HPC, appears to have woken up to the way the UK psychopolitics landscape was beginning to be eroded and is promoting a conference next year: Psychoanalysis and State Regulation.

Just as intriguing are the arguments put forward in a College of Psychoanalysts text handily passed on to *Ipnosis*—State Regulation and Psychoanalysis: The Position of the College of Psychoanalysts. This is essential reading for anyone interested in the debate about how, or whether, psychopractice would survive the state regulation that now seems to have become the government's preference (weblink page).

> The government wants state regulation under the Health Professions Council (HPC) instead of the original preference of the professions for statutory regulation via a Psychotherapy Bill. Almost by default, that now appears to be the direction in which both professions are heading.

Added to this, the College of Psychoanalysts catalogues some of the details of psychoanalytic practice. These, while at the extreme of the psychopractice spectrum, echo much of what many practitioners will be doing, if they are lucky enough to have clients with the courage and resource to dive deeply towards the often unforeseeable, unimaginable depths of human hurt and distress. As the College of Psychoanalysts correctly guesses, such open-ended psychic enquiry would be beneath the HPC's regulatory radar and thus potentially illegal. The text is a useful outline of why clients' interests are unlikely to be well served by any form of state regulation.

Alongside this, though they make curious bedfellows, a press release from the BACP reveals that the *Director of Workforce*, a sector of the DoH previously unknown to Ipnosis, is promoting a *Review of non-medical professional regulation: Call for ideas*.

BACP's response to this call (IPN has yet to be asked) supports the sense that, as though they had taken part in some long-overdue vision quest, the BACP

This article first appeared in *Ipnosis* Editorial, 27 September 2005 now seek to move away from, rather than embrace, statutory regulation of psychotherapy and counselling. Here is Point One from the BACP text:

1. The Professions
Regulation has served a number of purposes for the professions in the past. It represented recognition that a particular occupational group had gained jurisdiction over an activity to the exclusion of other groups. It gave legitimacy, status, respectability and greater bargaining power in the workplace and with user groups. It was the mark that showed that an occupation had become a profession.

Today, so many diverse occupations are regulated (from physiotherapists to radiographers to night-club bouncers), that regulation no longer confers the kind of status it once did. However, through the protection of title, regulation does close an occupation to the unqualified and thus provides some advantage to registrants, along with some public protection.

Further, statutory regulation results in a profession yielding significant control over its educational and continuing professional development (CPD) standards, and therefore, over its future development.

Bearing all this in mind, it is difficult to see why any currently unregulated profession would seek statutory regulation under the existing models with their tendency to stifle innovation. [*Ipnosis* emphasis]

After reassuring the DoH that despite this: '... BACP supports the concept of statutory regulation ... BACP's Alan Jamieson goes on to ask whether:

... there is an underlying assumption in this Review that statutory regulation ensures public protection. Given that there appears to be little evidence to support such an assumption, we would be interested to explore that premise further.

He adds that: 'The protection of a title, which is the main means by which statutory regulation operates, is proven to be ineffective ...'.

On the Health Professions Council [HPC], apparently the government's preferred vehicle for counselling and psychotherapy regulation, the BACP is less than enthusiastic:

Taking the HPC as an example, it seems to us that the developmental functions relating to the professions it regulates, i.e. review of curricula, approval of placement agencies and definitions of CPD, can only have a detrimental effect on the development of best practice and innovation in those professions. Whilst the purpose may have been to address professional self-interest, we believe the resulting exclusion of professional expertise can only result in stagnation in the longer term.

Their submission to the Foster review of non-medical professions bears witness to an attempt by the BACP to try to row away fast from the emergent state regulation of counselling and psychotherapy via the HPC—as though the damage to client and practitioner interests this would entail had not been thoroughly explored (and ignored to death by BACP et al.) over the last 16+ years.

An IPN participant recently posted the following message from Brian Magee, Chief Executive of COSCA:

Regulation of Counselling and Psychotherapy

Recently I attended a meeting in London of the UK Government's Department of Health Project concerned with the statutory regulation of counselling and psychotherapy. From my previous correspondence on this Project, you will recall that a Liaison Group comprising of the British Association for Counselling and Psychotherapy (BACP) and the UK Council for Psychotherapy (UKCP) was established and funded to work with a Reference Group comprised of all accrediting professional bodies in the field of counselling and psychotherapy in the UK. COSCA is a fully active member of this Reference Group.

*****

In the course of carrying out the above work, there have been increasing doubts cast by the Liaison Group on whether counselling/psychotherapy should be regulated by the Health Professions Council (HPC). One of the main reasons for this is that the above work showed that most professional bodies already have higher standards for counsellors/psychotherapists compared with those that the HPC would apply.

If the mood of the last London meeting was anything to go by, there now seems to be a shift in thinking not only away from HPC as the regulator, but also away from statutory regulation itself and a return to focusing on working together as professional bodies on self-regulating the activities of counsellors and psychotherapists. Depending on the UK Government's response to the above report, this shift may or may not be developed further. I will try to keep you informed about any developments on this matter.

Brian Magee
Chief Executive (COSCA)
July 2005

References

State Regulation and Psychoanalysis: The position of the College of Psychoanalysists. <http://www.psychoanalysts.org.uk/regulation.html>

Background: In 2004/5 my MP, Ann Keen, was immensely helpful in getting sensible responses from the Department of Health about otherwise inaccessible stirrings in the UK psychopractice universe. Was it necessary, we wondered, to have to engage an MP and the Minister himself to ensure that as stakeholders, IPN participants were included in the inquiries outlined below? I did not realise at the time (see Chapter 31) that this was the first 'mapping' stage of a taxonomy process that was to begin in earnest at the end of 2006, through which the DoH would attempt to 'map, measure and capture' psychopractice.

CHAPTER TWENTY-FOUR

UKCP/BACP Mapping Research into Psychotherapy and Counselling: Initial mapping project for the Department of Health

Brief review and selected quotes

Published in mid-November 2005—but note the date on the file, '30-06-05', five months after it was delivered to the Department of Health—the interim mapping project weighs in at an onerous 82 pages.

Though it could be taken as a Department of Health [DoH] initiative, the report appears to be the outcome of concerted effort by the UKCP and BACP to progress statutory regulation of psychotherapy and counselling in the UK and, if *Ipnosis* guesses correctly, to defend these organisations against the prospect of regulation via the Health Professions Council [HPC]. Since it was delivered to the DoH, it appears that HPC regulation of counselling and psychotherapy is off the UKCP/BACP agenda and that 'state regulation' by an independent body is being promoted as an alternative.

Here are some *Ipnosis* selections from the report, but keep in mind that they are no substitute for reading at least the first 14 pages of it (weblink page).

> The intention to create this project was announced at a meeting of accrediting and registering organizations in September 2004.
>
> BACP and UKCP agreed to create a Liaison Group to oversee the project.
>
> Consideration was given to the possibility of extending this group. A number of organisations expressed interest in this. However, it was not clear that there was a justification for any one particular addition.
>
> Although a small number of groups were not, in practice, cooperative these were a small minority and most participated willingly and with great good will. The impact of whatever short-fall in cooperation has occurred has not been great.
>
> A BACP/UKCP Liaison Group met to construct the project and arrange a funding bid.
>
> In a letter of 4 February 2005 the DoH offered £60,000 to carry out a project with the aim of delivering four objectives:
> —A map of existing training and qualifications in the fields of psychotherapy and counselling

This article first appeared in *Ipnosis*, 25 November 2005

—A map of the standards on which these programmes of training and qualifications are based
—A sample code of conduct and ethics based on existing codes and with regard to the HPC code of conduct, performance and ethics, for use by psychotherapy and counselling organisations currently without one ·
—A toolkit covering competences and processes

A proposal was put to the reference group aimed at seeking to carry out research at the level of fundamental processes in counselling and psychotherapy. This was rejected as too ambitious for the timescale and funding of this project.

SUMMARY OF FINDINGS

1. Training
1.1. Training is the major entry route into psychotherapy and counselling. Ninety-five per cent of counsellors and psychotherapists are trained and the majority practise within the scope of their training.
1.2. This would support the use of training standards and training requirements as the basis for regulating the professions.
1.3. There is no one route of entry to either psychotherapy or counselling in the UK through training. We have identified 570 different practitioner training courses. However, 63 per cent do not have professional-body recognition, although many of these are validated through the Further or Higher Education system.
1.4. There are a large number of titles for both training courses and individual counsellors and psychotherapists. This can only cause confusion to the public.

2. Standards of education and training and standards of proficiency
2.1. The HPC's focus on the Health Service and university education does not closely match current patterns of practice or of training provision.
2.2. There are a variety of approving bodies for training: academic, vocational and professional. There are a significant number of training providers linked to no external quality-assurance systems.
2.3. There is a spread of training between the sectors and recognised educational levels, both academic and vocational.
2.4. The development of psychotherapy and counselling training in Higher Education is significant, but there remains a substantial group of trainings not validated within Higher Education.
2.5. Thirty per cent of counselling training is in the Further Education sector.
2.6. Consideration would need to be given to the place of a core curriculum and to the nature of that curriculum.

3. Conduct and ethics
3.1. All organisations responding to the research have complaints and conduct processes; however, levels of lay representation and public accountability are low.
3.2. Codes of conduct and ethics fulfil or exceed HPC requirements.
3.5. There is need for a separate regulatory body for psychotherapy and counselling.

4. The size of the occupational field
4.1. For this research twenty per cent of a potential 37,500 members were sent a questionnaire and forty-four per cent of those replied.
4.2. The level of training activity suggests that the number of counsellors and psychotherapists in the UK is growing rapidly.

4.3. There are a large number of small psychotherapy and counselling organisations.

4.4. Ninety per cent of counsellors and psychotherapists are in paid work.

4.5. Over twenty-five per cent of all psychotherapists and counsellors work with children and may not necessarily have received appropriate training.

The professions of psychotherapy and counselling have been developing as separate but closely associated professions over many years.

In recent years some have argued that their similarities outweigh their differences, to the extent that they should be regulated together. Others are opposed to this proposal. It has not been part of the brief for this report to arrange a consultation exercise on this issue. It is hoped that this report will inform the debate. The commonalities are sufficient for there to be concern that if one profession were to be regulated and the other not, a significant number of counsellors or psychotherapists might transfer to the non-regulated profession. It is recognised that there will be those who work in a similar way to psychotherapists and counsellors who will not register and will use alternative titles. The judgement to be made concerns the public interest in regulating particular titles. The basis of this project is the proposal that there is a public interest in regulating the titles 'counsellor' and 'psychotherapist' either used alone or in combination with other terms.

Indicative registration rests on the protection of titles and the benefit to the public of this system rests on public understanding of the meaning and value of the protected titles. Simplicity is important to the clear communication that this requires. This report is therefore set within the frame of the two titles psychotherapy and counselling. The diversity of the field is recognised. The question of whether a more complex range of titles would serve the public interest is a matter for further debate.

1.4 The individual questionnaire

An individual questionnaire was developed by a small group of experienced members of UKCP and BACP, with input from representatives of the wider group of accrediting and registering bodies. The individual survey questionnaire was sent to twenty per cent of the membership of 34 professional associations: that is twenty per cent of circa 38,000 counsellors and psychotherapists, and had a forty-four per cent response rate. This high response rate means that the findings are robust and have a high level of validity in relation to psychotherapists and counsellors organised within professional associations.

The research identified 154 organisations in addition to the 94 referred to in the questionnaire itself. At 4,126, the number of respondents to the questionnaire is, in itself, larger than all but the largest of counselling and psychotherapy organisations

1.5 Observations on the participation of organisations

The consistent aim of the project has been to be inclusive. The project was managed on a very tight timetable set by the funding constraints faced by DoH. A consultation meeting on the questionnaire was held in March and the approach to the questionnaire was substantially changed as a result. Not all the organisations invited were represented at that meeting. Due to the timetable further consultations were not possible.

Background: Continuing help from my MP, Ann Keen, during 2005 helped secure access to this BACP/UKCP 'mapping exercise'. As IPN voices began to be heard by Department of Health officials, IPN became a little more visible on the psychopractice landscape and eventually our efforts were rewarded by seats at the table of the meeting described below.

CHAPTER TWENTY-FIVE

Roles, Competencies and Complacency: Mapping the territory of psychotherapy and counselling with the Department of Health

At a presentation on Friday, 18 November 2005, James Pollard of UKCP and Sally Aldridge of BACP introduced the findings of the BACP/UKCP-run, Department of Health [DoH]-funded research project to map UK counselling and psychotherapy. Further up the agenda was a presentation by Rosalind Mead of the DoH's take on all this.

The meeting had a notably low-key, polite, amiable and, it seemed to *Ipnosis*, complacent tone. This complacency was a sharp reminder of the extent to which we can inhabit tremendously divergent cultural universes, and the pair of us from IPN left the meeting in a state of culture shock. So let us say a few things that the meeting format appeared designed to suppress, or to be attended to in less public gatherings.

First, that in its 'classroom' format—a panel behind a table (albeit all of them women) and people in rows facing forward with minimal contact with each other—it reproduced the top-down, 'power-over', old hierarchical model of human community. It wasn't even the more face-to-face 'horseshoe' of so many management trainings. Despite the opportunities for comment, there were none for interaction with the rest of the group. Why not?

Ipnosis felt that the top-down dynamic of the meeting mirrored that of the mapping exercise, which was research *on* people, not research *with* people: old paradigm research of a kind that is deprecated by, for instance, institutions such as the Centre for Action Research in Professional Practice, University of Bath (weblink page), which look at such matters, as ethically questionable.

This research, which was being conducted by a team of people seeking to identify and install the ethical standards that clients need from psychotherapy and counselling practitioners, had a logo that read 'Towards the statutory regulation of counselling'; this was coupled with explicit claims to one IPN participant, that in the conduct of the research:

> ' ... *The question of any bias* in favour of BACP's regulatory processes, or the processes of any other professional body in the field of counselling and psychotherapy *does not arise* ...' [*Ipnosis* emphasis]

Why was the mapping research, and the meeting to present it so top-down, so unidirectional, so from-us-to-you? Might not a psychotherapy and counselling

---

This article first appeared in *Ipnosis*, 29 May 2006

community be supposed to have some awareness of how power is expressed in client work and client lives, and thus in professional institutions and research agendas?

Is it because, as I have pointed out elsewhere here, research *with* people is unpredictable, and often comes up with off-message findings? For example, one that contradicts the claim that counselling or psychotherapy clients and practitioners want or need state regulation. On the other hand, training/accrediting institutions certainly do need it, and so research methods that at least would not contradict that foregone conclusion were deployed. And here we were, listening to the findings.

Some of the details of the bean-counting aspects of the mapping research were intriguing— around 5000 people a year are joining the psychopractice field; there are at least 570 training/accrediting organisations in the UK; and about a third of the courses are part of, or under the wing, of higher education/universities. This is a reminder, were one needed, for those of us watching the psychopolitics field for 15 or more years, that the desire for regulation continues to be training-driven. In a notable bit of leakage of this agenda, the report claims: 'There are a large number of titles for both training courses and individual counsellors and psychotherapists. *This can only cause confusion to the public'* [*Ipnosis* emphasis]. But only to a public that is held to be naive or inadequate by 'professions' claiming unique knowledge of the human condition.

Unsurprisingly, this proliferation of counsellings and psychotherapies was one of the things the government did not want to see, and James Pollard floated the idea that perhaps they could be reduced to five: HIPS, CBT, Psychoanalytic psychotherapy, Systemic Family Therapy, and Hypnopsychotherapy; plus, perhaps because the research showed that a quarter of practitioners worked with children (and not all were trained for it), Child Psychotherapy. Around this point, a voice from the floor said, 'Yes we are all going to have to compromise.'

It sounded to me as though this was the kind of compromise, i.e. a decision to close down or relocate, that small businesses find themselves making when a national hypermarket opens in their area and actively seeks to eliminate local competition.

I did at times have the feeling that I could indeed be present at a national managers' meeting of a large supermarket chain, where the upfront task was improving service to the consumer, while the unspoken agenda was rigging the market. Yes, I know that people attending this meeting really believe in what they are doing, but this doesn't mean that, to someone from a groupwork tradition, they didn't seem to be in some kind of consensus trance—not least, I guess, due to being in the presence of a potentially powerful government official, i.e. entranced by the expectation that 'at last they were getting somewhere'. As one of the presenters put it, 'The task is to get into a place where the government would like to see us; we are not there yet.'

The politeness of the surface dynamics of this meeting reminded me of an anecdote attributed to Henry Ford, who announced to a board meeting: 'Gentlemen I'm leaving, there is too much agreement here.' It was as though, in the five months since the report was delivered to the DoH, the behind-the-scenes wrangling between the two lead institutions, the reshuffling of attitudes as evidenced by the *BACP evidence to the Foster Review*, the organisations who had refused to cooperate in the research, the are-they-in-or-are-they-out matter of the hypnotists—not to mention the psychoanalytic tendency, and the dissent expressed about the whole project had all evaporated. It was very reminiscent of swans gliding effortlessly on the river where I live, with the furious paddling of their feet hidden beneath the surface.

Hidden, perhaps, because of the presence of Rosalind Mead, New Projects Regulation Manager, Department of *Health*: as though psychotherapy or counselling had been, could, or should be a matter of 'health' rather than whatever it finds happening in the clients who show up.

Ms Mead outlined her civil-service, DoH approach to the government's 'wishes', as she described them, around psychotherapy and counselling. What was being looked for were 'standards', 'public protection', and 'discipline'. She also mentioned that the government was committed to 'improving access to talking therapies', adding that there had never been an intention to regulate psychotherapy and counselling together.

Ms Mead eloquently reiterated her department's position that, because they had to be written into law in a way that did not contravene human-rights legislation, state regulation required clearly identified 'Roles', 'Competencies' and 'Training'. This notion, and its double underlining by Ms Mead, seemed to be received by the meeting as 'The Problem'. For *Ipnosis* it seemed more like a solution, i.e., while the Roles and Competencies, let alone Training of counselling and psychotherapy were being defined, we could go away and tend our window boxes and forget about psychopolitics for the next couple of decades!

Ms Mead then outlined how the DoH proposed to progress matters. Perhaps, *Ipnosis* guessed, because of their impatience with the unruly, tedious dynamics of the psychopractice institutions they had hitherto been dealing with, the DoH planned to 'involve UK-wide external facilitators with expertise in competence mapping and development'. Under this proposal, national training organisations, such as Skills for Health and the Qualifications Authorities, would coordinate the production of a competence map for counselling and psychotherapy, using existing competence frameworks. These would be used to compare existing roles, to see how they fitted against the map and then to use this study as a basis for agreeing standards.

In *Next Steps*, Ms Mead spoke of taking this agenda forward by convening a planning meeting. This would engage the national training organisations, the Qualifications Authorities, representation of the four countries' health departments (since devolution, the government does not have reserved powers in these matters; Scotland, Northern Ireland or Wales could decline to support state regulation of psychotherapy and counselling) and some representatives of professional organisations.

Ms Mead followed this by listing issues to consider:

- Statutory Regulation must reflect roles at the point of first qualification not later career specialization.

- Standards must reflect what is needed now, not what may be in process of development; they can be reviewed over time.
- Roles must reflect what service users and providers need, not just what professions provide, or aspire to.

At around this point she tentatively listed what the latter might amount to: 'general mental health counsellor', plus 'bereavement', 'relationship', 'school/student', 'drug and alcohol abuse' and 'trauma counselling'. This is what service users want to see, she claimed. Reactions from the audience indicated that some organisations might see this as several bridges too far. There also seemed to be a medical-model presumption here: that first you qualified, and then specialised. In my experience the reverse is true for many psychopractitioners.

Do you see what I mean about divergent cultural preferences? On the one hand there are those of us who inhabit IPN's self-generating, power-with cultures of accountability, who see core psychopractice education as including the capacity, with peer support, to assess our own competence, and who see face-to-face contact and external validation of how we run our processes as essential. On the other hand here was what felt like a supermarket management team discussing its place in the high street; what was to be the brand name that would match Dixons, HSBC, Mothercare and M&S? There was talk of 'watertight public protection' while the reality, as the quotation from the report above suggested, felt like the infantilisation of service users. There was also talk of 'a register of professional membership being a selling point', and of how statutory regulation would help with 'damage limitation to professions'.

As I have outlined in *Gold into Lead—The Alchemists' Nightmare* (Chapter 6) and *Registering Human Nature* (Chapter 14), there seems to be an ideology, a model of human nature, running through statutory regulation proponents that still sees persons as 'fallen'—even persons such as psychopractitioners, who might be supposed to be free of, or at least aware of, such entrancement. The model of human nature driving statutory regulation assumes the necessity and dominance of a 'power-over' rather than 'power-with' approach to community. And yet was this not a meeting mostly of psychopractitioners, many, even most, of whose clients, as I have indicated in *Shrink-wrapping Psychotherapy* (Chapter 10), come with some form of victimisation—the harm or damage that results from a 'power-over' upbringing and life experience? Not to see the disconnect between that client victimisation and the hierarchical, top-down, power-over bureaucratic state regulation that is being sought, continues to seem massively incongruent.

Later in the meeting, points of dissent from the IPN participants seemed defensively met. Question: is it likely that state regulation of psychotherapy and counselling will be more successful in eliminating abuse than medical regulation? Response from Ms Mead: you cannot compare medical regulation with psychotherapy and counselling regulation (as though, with their proposals to regulate psychotherapy via the HPC, this was not what they planned).

After Ms Mead had very reasonably admitted that mistakes had been and could still be made, my IPN colleague asked her: 'Might you not be making a huge mistake with statutory regulation?' This was rebutted quickly, defensively, it seemed to *Ipnosis*, by James Pollard, UKCP chair: 'Might you, IPN, not be making a huge mistake?' Principled dissent, and a corresponding positive programme, the creation of IPN, a lived alternative: a 'mistake'? Really? And if a client doesn't agree with what is being suggested, is this 'resistance', not dissent?

Background: Throughout the debate around state regulation of the psychological therapies, the notion of evidence-based practice constantly surfaces. But what are the origins of this evidence? Too often it appears to be the result of old paradigm, positivist research ... research *on* people as opposed to research *with* people. The 'evidence', from the BACP/UKCP mapping exercise (Chapter 24), arises from such a form of 'power-over' research where the researchers unilaterally decide the research agenda, administer the inquiry protocols and then collate, analyse and publish the 'results'.

Is there an approach to research that better matches the form, dynamics and subjectivity of psychopractice? Is research something that only expert elites can do? It need not be; Cooperative Inquiry—or one of its many varieties, such as Experiential Inquiry, or Participatory Research—can provide a rigorous, ethically sound way of bringing research to life that anyone can learn.

For readers who may not have experienced the delights of research *with* people, I include here an account of a residential cooperative inquiry that Annie Spencer, a fellow IPN participant and I led in France in 1998. It looked at how we might get from 'survival' and 'recovery' in our lives, and maybe our therapy, to 'flourishing'; and what was 'flourishing' anyway?

CHAPTER TWENTY-SIX

What Counts as Evidence?
From survival and recovery to flourishing—
a residential cooperative inquiry, May 1998

High in the sky a short-toed eagle floats effortlessly, as though the silence thickened the air and made flight easier. Under the stone archway bathed in early morning sunshine, two women weave a garland for a birthday celebration.

In the hills nearby are etched the corrugations of terracing that once carried the almond and olive orchards of a self-sufficient and still hidden valley. Mulberry trees, the green debris of a once thriving silk industry, nestle against stone walls.

Beneath us and around us is the land, ancient, prolific with the ruthless mysteries of life. By night a land under the gaze of the Milky Way, wearing a silence the colour of bullfrogs, distant dog fights, wild boars digging for roots, and nightingales. By the bright light of day, a land sown, tended and harvested by countless generations.

In a few minutes, honey from the surrounding hillsides, coffee and fresh baguettes and butter spill out onto the table, courtesy of the breakfast crew.

Gradually the scene accumulates eight, then nine, then ten people, as the long-distance runner returns from her exertions and the naturalist puts away his binoculars.

We eat.

We are gathered to carry out research. Action research. Participatory research. Cooperative Inquiry. Research *with* people, not research *on* people.

That this land has been lived with for at least 300 centuries frames our task in ways that keep us close to our research topic. This is a Cooperative Inquiry into Human Flourishing. What does it mean to flourish? Is it an impossible dream? And, especially, what does flourishing mean for those of us with some experience of psychopractice? As our brochure for the event put it, 'What if, for all their value, mainstream therapy and counselling proved irrelevant and even an obstacle to moving on from survival and recovery into flourishing—creating the life you want?'.

If there is such a therapeutic mindset, is it not likely to be fed by conventional research methods and their illness-based medical antecedents? To find out seems to require that we break ' ... the ancient mould, still upheld by the majority of researchers today, that only an expert elite know how to acquire real knowledge, and how to apply it? (Heron, 1996).

This article was first published in *Counselling News*, November 1998

Cooperative Inquiry provides a way of contradicting, even supplanting, the top-down way in which knowledge is commonly generated and shared. It can even provide a forum where, as in this event, both clients and practitioners can participate. This matters because participation is an essential political process.

> (Participation) honours the basic right of people to have a say in forms of decision making ... institutions need to enhance human association by an appropriate balance of the principles of hierarchy, collaboration and autonomy, deciding for others, with others and for oneself ... The challenge is to design institutions which manifest valid forms of these principles and to find ways in which they can be maintained in self-correcting and creative tension. (Heron, 1989, 1993a; from Heron and Reason, 1995)

Cooperative Inquiry is such an institution; it provides a way of doing research into the human condition that incorporates what we know about feeling and emotion and the exercise of power, and that challenges the belief that domination—and particularly male domination, commonly expressed through overvalued intellect—is 'natural' and inevitable. But I am getting ahead of myself.

I have been describing a nine-day, residential event with ten people housed in Mas Marguerite, a large sixteenth-century farmhouse in the Ardèche *département* of France, about 60 miles north of Avignon. Despite its remoteness, it is a surprisingly accessible venue; high-speed trains through France mean that you can leave London (or Brussels or Barcelona) at breakfast time and be in these foothills of the Massif Central by late afternoon.

In the library the sun streams in, drawing a bright patch on the carpet. At the other end of the room D. sits, his hands dancing over the keys of the piano. As he plays, the soft rhythmic pulse of the blues reaches out to a handful of listeners.

In the kitchen, a huge, square, stone-floored room stands C., giving instructions to one of the lunch team. Or rather, struggling out of a giggling failure to find the words for instructions and commands, from a mind more familiar with deference and pussy-footing.

Leaning over a table overflowing with the purple thread and fragments of cloth of an appliqué picture, B. is practising ruthlessness; ruthlessly not anticipating other people's sensitivities, ruthlessly contradicting her belief that the world expects her to take care of them, to be available. Ruthlessly doing what she likes.

Upstairs, S. clicks away at her Powerbook computer: *From time to time along the road, animal or bird bodies were strung up on overhanging boughs; these were the work of hunters who hunted as their forefathers had always done, with bow and arrow, trap and snare and these overhanging boughs were their refrigerator, show window and advertising leaflet.* These are the stone-age African scenes of her first short story, brought to life under the ancient black oak beams of the room under the roof.

'Co-operative Inquiry rests on a participative view of the world, a world not of separate things but of relationships which we co-author' (Heron and Reason, 1995). Annie Spencer, my co-initiator, and I have a long and varied experience of cooperative inquiry. As initiators, both of us have long sought a way of approaching what it means to be human that would allow us to articulate and bring into being the spiritual, the transpersonal and the political (including the ecological). We want to be able to do this in ways that are congruent with, and that incorporate, the emotional, transmutational and body work necessary for well-grounded action.

'Flourishing' is a metaphor that provides a promising start for this task. It seems to carry enough of the qualities of well-rootedness and environmental rapport to keep the project earthed, particularly if both individual and community are kept in the flourishing focus.

In a secondary but relevant way, it challenges the restrictiveness and ineffectiveness of 'mainstream' therapies that support recovery and survival but provide poorly, or not at all, for flourishing or thriving. Many therapeutic modes, spellbound by the medical 'illness' model, take clients to the threshold of flourishing and then make great play of 'ending', leaving clients sadder possibly, wiser hopefully, poorer certainly.

In this inquiry, we delineated and explored this new territory of flourishing, honouring the problem solving of survival and recovery but, seeking to move on from them to 'creating': creating the life we want.

This particular inquiry was unique in its combination of an awareness of the importance of power in human flourishing, and support (and challenge) for the flourishing theme itself from its setting—kilometres of wilderness, populated by wild boar and richly carpeted with dozens of varieties of wild flowers.

How can I flourish as an individual? How can a community flourish? Is flourishing a mode of being with its own identifiable character, plus theory and practice?

The variety of Cooperative Inquiry that Annie Spencer and I introduced to pursue these questions has two easily learned components: an *inquiry cycle* and, running parallel, a set of *validity checks*.

The inquiry cycle begins with *propositions* that enable flourishing, our chosen theme, to be looked at. These range from the generic: 'whoever takes on the task of cooking gets to decide what is cooked', to the particular: 'wine is OK with the evening meal, but not before then'.

These lead to *actions* which test, shed light on, raise awareness of, these propositions. For example, some participants prepare and present meals.

A third, *review* phase evaluates these actions and the propositions that precede them. We reviewed the timing and presentation of the meals and how well they met our needs, and out of this review modified the original proposition a little before putting it into action again.

Parallel to this inquiry cycle, which can be both macro and micro in form and short or long in timescale, is the second component, a series of *validity checks* through which the participants can keep the inquiry on track. Is there enough variety in what we are doing? Are we making enough sense? Are we meeting our needs as inquirers? Has everyone internalised the inquiry method? Has there been enough chaos? What might we be avoiding? Is distress due to the topic or process interfering with the inquiry?

Intrinsic to CI is an awareness of power in human relations. Deference to real or imagined authority and letting others set priorities runs very deep in us. How we perceive, experience and deploy our own power can be a window into what enhances or inhibits our flourishing.

In this CI as in others, as the cooperative basis for it sank in—that it *was* cooperative—several people felt very unsettled, frustrated, impatient and uncertain. As initiators, should we have done more to ease the transition from leading to cooperation? Perhaps; but as the group learned the inquiry method and began to apply it, everyone seemed to find their feet. A turning point came with the decision, after characteristically awkward negotiations, on how we would cooperatively make decisions. Following the dissolution of our role as leaders/initiators, we began to sink into the rich and often chaotic mix of self-direction and negotiation and community participation that characterises CI.

How did the Inquiry compare with my expectations?

I felt I flourished through it. I had the idea for it and promoted it for twelve months; it came in on budget, and participants found that it strongly supported their individual flourishing. One of the things that quickly became clear to me was that I couldn't directly know much about what other people in the inquiry were up to. I found that I had a deep connection with three or four other people around their individual flourishing issues but little sense of what other people where actually doing. This bothered me for a little while. As the days passed, I began to see several strands of activity. Yes, there was intense and sometimes very highly charged individual inquiring going on and this was complemented by the community inquiry, grounded initially in how to manage the household and moving on to looking at how a community can flourish.

Was this enough? I had an appetite then, and have still as I write, for wider, deeper, more grand realisations about flourishing; and our CI could be criticised I feel, for perhaps not being convergent enough, for not making enough sense of its deliberations. But is this true? I went back to my notes and gathered the headlines of what seemed to be, or to point to, the fruits of our inquiry, or what at the time seemed worth recording. These tell a different story.

Here are a selection of them. A few are my own; most are gathered from our reviews and discussions and dinner conversations. Flourishing:

- requires participation in community
- is fun
- involves creating something that doesn't exist: order—relationship—connection
- requires that we (occasionally) dance chaos thoroughly
- means recovering lost intentions
- is undermined by fear
- is about identifying, owning and naming our inner inklings
- implies ruthless focus
- requires courage. It is being yourself in the moment and going for what you want with your whole being all the time, using your will to be alive. To regain your joy over and over again, however dire the circumstances
- is about taking care over whether, and how, we name our experiences
- is about grounding your dream
- depends on an ability to dance between distinctness and whole-hearted participation

- prerequisites for flourishing include preparation, rooting, support, opportunity, climate, good psychic weather, nourishment
- is a value, a direction in life, an orientation, a myth to live by
- may be expected to be intermittent
- when we see others flourishing we don't see the rest of the iceberg of life and preparation, or the courage or the origins that precede it
- arises in a life that is awarely created
- the grain of our flourishing may run parallel to or be congruent with early learning, or may be in a different direction altogether, even in a different psychic universe
- may not apply to all, or even much of life, but it reminds me of the possibility that I can extend flourishing to more and more of my life
- is dancing on the edge of precipices
- is hopping about
- is daring to be different
- is knowing what I want and seeing who congregates around it
- requires planning, the minimum needed to take us forward to the next choice point
- is a cyclic process. The iris bulb, invisible in the bog, becomes the flower we see, and the scattered seed, following which it shrinks back into its bulb. If we are connected to this flourishing cycle then we won't despair at being in the dark quiescent part of the cycle
- life lived as an inquiry would really loosen up life.

So much for my feeling that we were not making enough sense of what we were doing.

One of the items on this list says that flourishing requires that we take care with whether, and how, we name our experiences. I want to conclude with an example of this from the Ardèche.

I have never much fancied long-distance walking, so choosing to join a three-hour walk across the hilly wilderness of shrub oak and box trees to meet the rest of the group for an evening meal felt quite risky for me. It produced an example of how naming and/or framing experience affects flourishing.

After more than two hours climbing the trail to the top of a ridge overlooking the next valley, we descended very steeply, to discover that between us and the restaurant was a roaring torrent of storm water. Rainfall, 13.5 cm of it, had accompanied 14 hours of thunder and lightning two days earlier.

We found a concrete ledge over the torrent just wide enough to scramble across, only to discover that the road from the bridge to the restaurant was flooded; it had become a shallow river of clear, very cold mountain water. At that point in time, the promise of food and drink did not balance the excruciating pain of walking barefoot the three hundred metres on the cold, sharp gravel of the flooded road required to reach it.

How we name such an event is likely to give to, or detract from, its value. I had begun the walk feeling that it was a test of endurance; the task was to keep going. This perception shifted sharply to one of potential nightmare when the bridge appeared broken, i.e. dusk was falling and we faced a long walk back through the forest. The walk through the water was very painful indeed, but at least the meal afterwards was amply and deliciously French.

That was the experience. As a person cooperatively inquiring into how I flourish, how might I handle this event? What did I bring to it? This is always a point of choice but one that I guess, well greased by habit, I often slip through. As I reflected on it, the feelings of 'near nightmare', 'never again', 'not my kind of thing', were in the foreground. Then as I heard informally how others felt about it, the aversive naming that was becoming installed around the event shifted to a more flourishing description, as I realised that I could call it 'an adventure'.

Cooperative inquiry is an adventure too. It starts from the known, the familiar; it is likely to include both pain and delight; it calls for self-confrontation with our predispositions and deficiencies; it may enable us to create new strategies for flourishing in ways we have painted over, or in ways previously unimaginable.

In France this spring, we cooperatively created the conditions for flourishing, checked out whether we had brought any with us and whether we could create it on the spot.

Background: As I have previously mentioned, ensuring a hearing for IPN voices in the Department of Health was a struggle. Contributing to the Foster *review of non-medical regulation—'a call for ideas'* was no exception. When we approached the DoH for details of the review, Andrew Foster, conducting it, said 'No, too late'; the Minister, following a prompt from my MP said 'Yes', but his letter was sent after the revised closing date that Foster didn't tell us about. However, we decided to send submissions anyway, so as to be on the record. The following *Ipnosis* briefing document that I submitted to the Foster Review was one of two from IPN participants.

CHAPTER TWENTY-SEVEN

Accountability for Client–Practitioner Relationships in UK Psychopractice

Client protection examined

Psychopractice trade associations have been promoting Statutory Regulation [SR] for around 20 years. During this time their training needs, especially those of sustaining and consolidating trainee streams, i.e. of keeping courses in business, have been the overwhelming but unavowed, tacit need driving their desire for SR. SR would add incomparable added value to training products.

A second, related dynamic has been the desire on the part of some practitioners, particularly those connected to the NHS, for the enhanced status and career/pay structures that a state-regulated profession is believed to convey.

Client protection has been a convenient smokescreen behind which these economic and status factors could be hidden. (When, recently, I asked the BACP/UKCP registered participants of an IPN group what the benefits of registration were, their unanimous response was 'You get more work.')

Evidence-based legislation?

Discussions about psychopractice regulation often invoke the need for 'evidence-based practice'; yet the need for client protection still appears to be based on hearsay and anecdotal evidence. If we presume 37,000 UK psychopractitioners, each with say, 10 or 12 clients, this amounts to approaching half a million working alliances; then multiply this by the number of client hours, say 40 per client per year, and we have a figure of getting on for 15 million contact hours, year after year, which is also probably a very conservative figure. *(If we take the recent claim by a BPS press release (BPS, 2006) that '100,000 non-regulated practitioners say "No" to government regulation plans,' then based on that population the total annual contact hours rise to around 40,000,000.)* Considering the scale of these estimates, the number of disputes—let alone the instances of actual abuse in psychopractice—appears to be quite insignificant or even negligible.

But are they insignificant? Ros Mead appeared to maintain, at the recent meeting to hear the results of the BACP/UKCP mapping research, that they are significant: but where is the evidence for this? If the DoH has evidence, why has it not been disclosed? If the DoH doesn't have research evidence from across the

Ipnosis submission to Department of Health Foster Review of non-medical regulation, 2005

client population to demonstrate that client abuse is significant, why is it planning to spend public money and tie up already scarce resources on measures to regulate psychopractice based on a need for client protection?

Here, it appears, is a gaping hole in the proposals for psychopractice regulation—one that requires research to establish, through independent inquiry across the client population, that psychopractitioner abuse is significant. Such research could establish how many clients/service users feel they have been abused, (and in what way), how many have had disputes, and how many have been generally/well pleased with the practitioners they have worked with. Without such research, regulation of any kind seems likely to lack credibility other than as support for trade-association control of a market for services. (There is of course a sense in which any abuse is significant for the abused, but we are not yet such a risk-averse society that every conceivable instance of abuse is necessarily assumed to require legislative intervention.)

Compliance

Developing regulation without an evidence-base of the actual scale of client abuse is one thing. Using what is likely to be seen as a 'combine harvester' approach of the external application of the categorising techniques of NVQ, QAA and Skills for Health to reap and thresh psychopractice competencies, standards and training seems highly likely to be seen as anathema by many practitioners (and training institutions). Taken together, these two proposals seem certain to result in low compliance with any resulting legislation/regulation, and a flight by practitioners to other, unregulated titles—of which there are many—leaving the official mainstream occupied by practitioners asleep to the downside of professionalisation. It is difficult to imagine how this could conceivably be of net overall benefit to the client/service-user population.

Criteria for adequate client/service-user accountability

Rather than regulation, civic accountability is a better and more widely acceptable way of framing ethically sound client/practitioner working alliances.

Over a decade of IPN theory and practice has identified several key elements of effective accountability:

- Ongoing, long term, face-to-face contact with a settled group of peers that demonstrates a practitioner's capacity to form working alliances based on respect, negotiation, mutuality and rapport.

- Declaration by each participant to the peer group of their training, competencies, special area of expertise if any, the client population for whom they are competent, their client workload, their continuing personal/ professional development commitment, and their supervision arrangements.

- Mutual disclosure in the peer group of challenges, deficits, difficulties, achievements, and significant developments in their practitioner work, coupled with disclosure of any developments in their personal life that might affect their fitness to practise.

- Agreement between the practitioner group members about how disputes with clients should be handled.

Self- and peer-accreditation in such a group institutionalises practitioner/client, i.e. civic accountability in a way that greatly increases the likelihood of client satisfaction, and reduces to close to zero the chances of abusive or exploitative practitioner behaviour.

Some people have objected that the close personal contact of this process invites collusion. In the IPN model, when such a group has formed they contract with other similar groups to establish external validation of their accreditation/ dispute resolution processes and possible collusive agendas. There is also a vested interest carried by every group member that their group colleagues' practice is sound and ethical (not least because if it is not, then that will reflect unfavourably upon their own judgement and practice). Moreover, this approach to accountability also draws fully upon what is commonly a very well-developed intuitive and perceptive sense in therapists and counsellors, such that our 'peers-in-relationship' are best placed by far to 'pick up' concerns about any given practitioner's fitness to do this demanding work.

As IPN demonstrates, such a framing of psychopractice civic accountability can be orchestrated in innumerable different ways.

If a regulation process lacks this mix of autonomy and external validation how can it avoid being perceived by practitioners as coercive and stressful, and an unwarranted imposition? Will it not prove to be lacking in credibility, resulting in low compliance and low effectiveness in protecting clients, should the latter indeed prove to be a significant, evidence-based requirement?

Incorporating the key elements of a self- and peer-accreditation approach into DoH policy recommendations (to be implemented in a variety of ways by all the diverse organisations presently in the psychopractice field) could ensure that quality assurance of practitioner/client relationships would be intrinsic—i.e. eliminating abuse through continuous monitoring—and not as the Department of Health *Next Steps* proposals seem to indicate, extrinsic, via the detection, investigation and adjudication of complaints. Insofar as quality assurance is intrinsic, state regulation of psychopractice would be redundant.

Such an outcome would be strongly supported by what is a missing ingredient in the whole discussion of psychopractice regulation, namely education.

Education—the missing ingredient

In the recently outlined plans for taking forward SR, the DoH seems to be adopting a dominance and subordination approach to institutional power that mirrors the difficulties many clients bring to practitioners. I accept that it may not feel like bullying to the DoH, but that is how the underlying posture of the *Next Steps* looks to those of us with a professional training in and around power relations in groups.

External control as the paradigm for professional regulation is an archaic take on quality assurance whose lack of efficacy has, in recent years, been demonstrated only too well in the medical world. Industrial quality management long ago moved away from external quality control, where production is monitored for rejects that are then scrapped (the present psychomedical institutional model) to designing accountability processes that minimise the possibility of producing rejects in the first place. IPN is an example of this well-established industrial paradigm.

A less expensive and much more effective approach to addressing the concerns that may be politically important around supposed client abuse is to commit major resources to educating the UK population on the benefits and limitations of psychopractice; making available through publications, helplines, websites and publications the why, when and for whom psychotherapy, counselling or other modalities are relevant, and what are reasonable expectations as regards outcomes and practitioner behaviour.

In addition, I believe there would need to be a comprehensive, publicly available listing of all psychopractitioners, whatever their accreditation, who are prepared to declare in some detail their training, experience, orientation, capability, terms, complaints procedures and accreditation status. I have published a detailed proposal for how this can be implemented in my proposal for a Practitioner Full Disclosure List (see Chapter 22).

There are two other reasons why regulation of psychopractice should not take legislative form, and why it will continue to meet with both determined resistance and low compliance. They deserve greater space than I have time for here, but are likely to exert a vital influence on the shape of any psychopractice-wide accountability settlement.

Defining human nature

Though many psychopractitioners appear unaware of it, all psychopractice involves the constant renegotiation of what is 'human' and 'natural', an ongoing task that many people see as being a core element of all acceptable political settlements. For a grouping such as psychopractitioners, very diverse but perhaps only 50,000 in number, to be licensed by the state as the people who know about human nature and who are implicitly experts in the definition of human nature, and yet for other, unlicensed practitioners who conduct such negotiations with clients to be criminalised, is politically unacceptable. This perception, though not often clearly articulated, is I believe at the root of the deep disquiet and continuing resistance of many psychopractitioners to SR.

Compromised creativity

There is considerable informal evidence that across the last decade, the 'getting ready for regulation' components in the accreditation of psychopractice training courses, have resulted in the inhibition of psychotherapeutic creativity and a corresponding shift towards a 'pasteurised', risk-averse practice. Two examples will illustrate this. Discussing touch in US therapy, Babette Rothschild (Rothschild, 2000) says 'Many malpractice insurance policies will not cover treatment methods that use touch *and the licensing boards of most US states forbid it* [my emphasis]. Describing the end of his long training, a psychotherapist I work with said recently that, 'It wasn't an inquiry; it was a regulation framework I was being pushed into.' That this process will be dramatically accelerated by a state licensure that requires the definition of 'roles', 'standards' and 'discipline' seems overwhelmingly likely. If this is the price to be paid for 'client protection', is it not far too high, both for the field of psychopractice and for clients?

References

BPS (2006) Press release, Friday 10 November <http://www.bps.org.uk/media-centre/press-releases/releases$/statutory-regulation/100000-reject-government-plans.cfm>

Rothschild, B (2000) *The Body Remembers The Psychophysiology of Trauma and Trauma Treatment*. New York: Norton

Background: That many UK practitioners have felt alienated from the institutional manoeuvering around psychopractice regulation—'Shall we, shan't we get into bed with the government?'—is not surprising. Even with resources and some support, *Ipnosis* found it difficult to keep track of the often out-of-sight elbow work and mindset re-engineering that has been going on. This *Ipnosis* page is an example of the mix of competing perspectives.

CHAPTER TWENTY-EIGHT

Roles Analysis, Expropriation, Exclusion and Evidence

Ipnosis has lately been preoccupied with a series of indicators on the current state of play of proposals for the state regulation of psychopractice in the UK.

At the Reference Group meeting on 18 November (see the *Ipnosis* report, Chapter 25), Ros Mead of the DoH introduced her Department's *Next Steps* proposals for psychotherapy regulation. Diligent regulation watchers will know that because in the last five years the profession hasn't been able to meet the DoH wishes around State Regulation of Counselling and Psychotherapy, *Next Steps* introduces the prospect of Competencies and Roles analysis to be carried out by external facilitators.

A friend, not from the psychopractice world, recognised the notion of Roles Analysis and sent me documentation of the role analysis, written by a US commercial consultancy, that has been running through dozens of UK educational establishments in the last few years. Since I wrote this *Ipnosis* page the Skills for Health *Roles Analysis* documentation has become available and I discuss it in later pages. What may not be clear to many practitioners is that this is taxonomy. Think of the trays of butterflies/moths/insects, pinned in rows according to their likeness/difference, and arrayed in trays in natural history museum collections. Moreover, it is an approach to the taxonomy and hierarchical categorisation of the nuances of life that is very suited to contemporary computer analysis. The following quote gives a taste of the mindset that shapes Roles Analysis inquiries.

> *Roles* are what any concept (or class) would play within the context of its related concepts (or classes). For instance a 'company' would be the 'supplier' of some specific 'product'. 'Supplier' is a *role*. All *role* problems can be easily solved by selecting one of the following five *role patterns*: Role Inheritance, Association Roles, Role Classes, Generalised Role Classes and Association Class Roles. Each *role pattern* contains its own blend of power, flexibility and complexity. Together, they offer a complete solution to all role problems. (Francis G. Mossé)

If you are a practitioner registered with the UKCP or allied organisations, look forward to filling in documents based on this kind of thinking to enable the people at the Health Professions Council [HPC] to tell you whether your psychopractice role is one they are prepared to endorse.

This article first appeared in *Ipnosis*, 29 May 2006

Colonisation of psychopractice territory—continued

The National Institute for Clinical Excellence [NICE] Guidelines for the treatment of Generalised and Panic Anxiety Disorder, published late last year, specify that: If a 'psychological treatment' is to be used, *'it should be CBT'* (p. 71); and 'CBT should be delivered only by suitably trained and supervised people who can demonstrate that they adhere closely to empirically grounded treatment protocols.'

On p. 72 there is a list of modes of psychological 'treatment':

> Hypnosis, interpersonal therapy, neurolinguistic programming, problem solving, progressive muscular relaxation, psychoanalysis, solution-focused therapy, stress control, stress management, psychodynamic therapy, bilateral stimulation.

The NICE recommendations assure us that there is no evidence that any of these ways of working with people who suffer panic attacks have any value.

On p.117 there is the statement that for Generalised Anxiety Disorder: 'If a psychological treatment is offered it should be CBT.' On p.126 we are told that: 'There is a lack of evidence about the effectiveness of counselling for individuals with generalised anxiety disorder or panic disorder.'

Alongside the overall dominance of NHS psychological services by psychiatry, CBT—the latest in a series of imperial colonisers of the UK psychopractice landscape—has emerged as its secondary and apparently only partner. The NICE 'evidence' for CBT seems to be entirely based on literature review, as though empirical, client–practitioner, in-the-consulting-room experience didn't exist.

Psychopractice client harm—the evidence?

Harm due to psychopractice is used to justify the public protection stance of the DoH on psychopractice regulation.

> The Government's overriding reason for the introduction of statutory regulation for these or any professions is to provide a mechanism for protection of the public against practitioners who are unfit to practise and who may therefore cause harm to those who use their services.
> Service users themselves have called for such protection to be made available. It is in response to such calls that Parliament and the Government have supported the introduction of regulation for some five years. Email from Ros Mead, DoH, December 2005

Is it reasonable to presume that this decision, as with the NICE recommendations on panic and general anxiety disorder, was based on evidence, i.e. on research, which has established beyond reasonable doubt that psychopractice is significantly harmful? If so, essential ingredients in the continuing debate about the value of state regulation of psychopractice would be: who did the research, what is the name of the institution to which the researchers belong, and when and where was the report published of their findings on the extent of harm? Are these unreasonable expectations if, as is claimed, the regulation of a whole set of occupations is predicated on the harm they cause?

In preparation for a presentation at the College of Psychoanalysts Conference on Psychoanalysis and Statutory Regulation, *Ipnosis* asked Ros Mead, an accessible and very reasonable DoH official, for sight of their evidence of harm to clients. Despite two prompts, neither evidence, nor pointers to it, were forthcoming. I'll ask again.

That there is harm is not at issue, and of course any level of harm matters— but is it significant? As I have estimated here previously, based on 50,000 practitioners in the UK there are probably around 20 million contact hours. In relation to this number of contact hours, is there really a significant level of harm? Moreover, if a whole raft of regulatory frameworks is being constructed on the premise of significant harm to clients, where is the research evidence for it?

S—p—l—i—t—t—i—n—g

Looked at from the non-denominational, bird's-eye perspective that IPN provides, the landscape of psychopractice looks to be gradually starting to divide. On the one hand there is a highly bureaucratic NHS form of psychopractice; and on the other are people in independent private practice who don't expect, or wish, to work for the NHS.

If the DoH has its way, to carry out psychological work in or for the NHS is going to mean embracing the audit/surveillance culture that has been visited upon it and the UK schooling system, with the probable result that working alliances with clients will be similarly compromised.

What of the more or less private sector? Curiously it seems interested, even enthusiastic, in signing up to the HPC/NHS style audit culture. As a participant at a recent UKCP AGM reported, 'there was unbounded enthusiasm' for the idea that 'all sections would be expected to prepare a list of competencies to describe exactly what they do'. 'At last it would be possible to speak a language the HPC would understand', and 'doubts raised about this framework' got 'a chilly reception'.

At the same meeting, along with the UKCP's move to Islington, another structural makeover was announced: the foundation of a series of UKCP colleges, one for each modality and one a company, which will function as a vehicle for outsourcing the otherwise intractable structural difficulty of dealing with complaints that would otherwise prevent the 'colleges' from being plugged into the HPC.

If you are a private, independent-sector practitioner who continues to support this corporate wriggling to match the DoH/HPC specifications for accountability, expect to have the essential qualities of your psychopractice compromised in much the same way as those of the teaching and medical professions have been.

The Foster Review?

What happened to that? As I have previously noted (Background: Chapter 27) IPN was deviously excluded from making a submission to the Foster Review of non-medical professional regulation, a topic about which IPN has legitimate concerns. Richard House and Denis Postle ignored the deadline and made submissions anyway (see Chapter 27). The BACP sneaked in under the August holiday-period deadline with their document (weblink page); The College of Psychoanalysts submitted this text (weblink page) several weeks after IPN was denied access to the Review and, especially and offensively, we were kept in the dark about its terms of reference.

In December 2005 Andrew Foster wrote to IPN telling us that:

> The review has completed its process of taking evidence and I am now considering the advice I will give to Ministers. We expect that Ministers will publish a document setting out their decisions in the New Year.

But how does the Foster review relate to the DoH *Next Steps* and its externally facilitated research into Competencies and Standards? Does the left hand know what the right hand is doing? And why do both Andrew Foster and The Minister, Lord Warner, talk about 'Statutory Regulation' in their correspondence with IPN when the HPC route, currently much favoured, would amount to '*State Regulation*'? There is a useful discussion of the difference between Statutory Regulation and State Regulation on the College of Psychoanalysts' website (weblink page).

References

Mossé, FG *The Six Role Patterns*, Object Discovery Corporation <http://www.objectdiscovery.com/papers/roles/index.html>

Background: As I mentioned earlier (see Chapter 25), on several occasions in the last couple of years I heard chairs or officials of UK accrediting bodies warming to the prospect of regulation by the state. There seemed to be an eagerness to present themselves in ways that the government would be pleased to see, for example as 'scientific'. Organisations 'on the pull' so to speak, like people, are inclined to over emphasize virtues and keep quiet about deficiencies. The normal currency of a hearty life, perhaps, but not, I would argue, tolerable in organisations that claim to occupy some moral/ethical high ground as the UKCP does.

We might suppose that NICE and the medics of the DoH could be expected to put a high value on 'science', but how many counsellors and psychotherapists share this view? Very few, in my experience, including those I know in the UKCP. And especially if, as seems to be the case in this document, 'science' often comes in the shape of taxonomy, i.e. when is a counsellor not a psychotherapist? However, this further example of a lack of mandate did not impede the UKCP from making the submission reviewed below to the DoH.

CHAPTER TWENTY-NINE

UKCP's Love Affair with the State:
The second decade—science as decoration

Late last year, parallel with the joint mapping exercise it conducted with the BACP, the UKCP undertook some work that the DoH had also paid for, on restructuring itself. In a perhaps characteristic omission in the report Ipnosis reviews below, no mention is made of the size of the financial support, or how it was spent, or indeed why a trade association with 80 member institutions needed to have taxpayers finance its internal metamorphosis into a regulation-ready institution.

Ipnosis guesses that neither James Pollard, whose name is on the outer cover, nor the numerous other staff and volunteers from the modalities who wrote the report, will warm to what *Ipnosis* has to say. Be assured that *Ipnosis* accepts your good will and benign intentions are not in question; however the expectation in your text of a robust response is something *Ipnosis* has taken very seriously

The document opens with a statement of aims: The aims were to:

- Improve levels of cooperation between UKCP and other bodies in the field of psychotherapy and counselling;
- Separate the regulatory functions that exist within the UKCP and its member organisations from the non-regulatory;
- Address any anomalies in the way it is structured *prior to handover of voluntary regulatory functions*. (*Ipnosis* italics)

It all sounds very reasonable—unless you think regulation will be a disastrous mistake.

> This report addresses all three of these aims within the context of preparing the profession for statutory regulation and against the criteria set out by the HPC.

Preparing *the profession* for statutory regulation. Keep in mind that these people claiming ownership of *the profession* of psychotherapy are registered, supposedly ethically sound practitioners who might be supposed, owing to the claimed benchmark quality of their training, to have a sense of how power can be abused by institutions—not least the extent to which all professions have a tendency to become a conspiracy against their clients.

Development of a Framework for the Improved Regulation of the Profession of Psychotherapy (a UKCP submission to the Department of Health, October 2005) It first appeared in *Ipnosis*, 29 May 2006

The project being reported on is to be regarded as '... work in progress ... Because for the project of making UKCP fit for regulation it will be ... necessary to encourage debate and discussion within the profession.'

Don't hold your breath. On the evidence so far it seems likely that UKCP's approach to the debate and discussion, both within its membership and in the excluded or dissenting psychopractice communities, will continue to be that of systematically ignoring to death anything that even remotely contradicts its preset course.

The report moves on to grasp the nettle of the HPC's requirements for regulation. For example, HPC criterion 4: 'The profession must have at least one established professional body which accounts for a significant proportion of that occupational group.'

There are no prizes for guessing who claims to satisfy this criterion. Interesting is the use of the word 'significant', a very loose and flexible signifier. UKCP is around a quarter of the size of the BACP but it is still, we must suppose, significant. Dissent against regulation, however, is apparently insignificant; and yet, despite no sign of an evidence-base for the harm due to psychopractice in the UK of the kind the DoH claims is essential in psychological medicine, the anecdotal evidence of practitioner harm is regarded as sufficiently significant to merit state regulation.

Perhaps aware of these potentially terminal anomalies, the report reassures us that:

> These comments are made from a UKCP perspective ... The comments are offered respectfully and in the knowledge that other organisations in the field are robust organisations capable of speaking for themselves.

Yes indeed, and *Ipnosis* is doing that right now. Gearing up its Department of Dubious Claims, the report asserts that:

> Significant progress has been made in taking forward the debate about key issues, for example over the relationship between psychotherapy and counselling and the relationship between different elements of psychoanalysis and psychoanalytic psychotherapy ... frameworks for dialogue have been developed ... which will produce results if they are utilised.

Ipnosis tends to see this kind of statement as a trance induction, which seeks to disallow discrimination in the reader while implanting a suggestion, in this case of a psychopractice unity that is manifestly missing. For instance, no one listening to the anguish in psychoanalytic circles about the fine grain of regulation, or hearing the silence in the room at a recent training conference when the BACP representative outlined why they saw no reason to insist that all counsellors in training had personal therapy, would believe that there is 'significant' unity across the psychopractice occupations regarding regulation.

One of the HPC criteria says: '... the profession must *apply* [*Ipnosis* italics] a defined body of knowledge.' Note that knowledge is something that is *applied*. The HPC falls at this hurdle as a regulator, since it clearly does not understand the facilitative nature of psychopractice. More on this below.

The report tells us that:

If there is to be a consistent process of linking titles, methods and training there needs to be a thought-through, consistent and economical framework for structuring the profession ... anomalies need to be addressed and local particularism needs to be overcome.

Hmm. Especially the local particularism of psychopractice communities, and individual practitioners who have yet to find a voice, and who refuse to be part of any project to weld psychopractice onto the state.

In another dubious claim, the report says that it: '... reviews the structure of the profession of psychotherapy, its distinct knowledge base, the relationship between the scientific approaches of psychotherapy ...'

Aha: *scientific*. Here we get to the nitty-gritty of being acceptable to the DoH, or the HPC, or some made-to-measure Mental Health Council. Science is mentioned no fewer than forty times in this document. If you are a counsellor or a psychotherapist, does that match the extent to which you see your practice as scientific?

And, as last year's example of mapping 'research' showed the 'scientific' methods so far are old paradigm 'power-over' research *on* people—not the participatory research that could be expected from a community supposedly subtly nuanced around the ethical dimensions of power.

Why is full-out participative research that parallels much (most) actual psychopractice not used? Because the findings of such research are unpredictable and might produce results that contradict the prevailing institutional agendas? Therefore, questionnaires will be what we will see—and more bean counting, and no doubt a continuing obsession with the taxonomy of roles, modes and psychotherapy schooling.

Here are two further examples of this document's spurious scientific gloss.

... counselling, psychology and psychoanalysis, and the range of *scientific* approaches within psychotherapy.

Psychotherapy is a distinct profession from counselling, and evidence demonstrates that there are a number of sub-groupings supported by a researched *scientific* base.

Finally, there is the continued mistaken presumption that *input* regulation is the way to ensure client accountability. 'Any regulatory structure will need to reflect this diversity and ensure recognition of an appropriate training route required to achieve statutory registered status.' This is contrary to research, for example from Dan Hogan (see Chapter 14) and IPN's 12-year experience, which shows why *output* accountability is essential.

When writing to the DoH, sound confident, make magnanimous gestures, and hope nobody really looks at what is going on behind the institutional front:

This report recognises the coterminous relationships of psychotherapy, psychology, psychoanalysis and counselling and makes recommendations for a regulatory structure that recognises and is responsive to these.

... and then makes a claim that suggests it has reinvented hubris:

The profession of psychotherapy is in a position to move towards statutory regulation.

What a pity then that: 'Questions remain about the Regulator, which will need to work effectively with the complexity of the profession of psychotherapy and the neighbouring professions of psychology, psychoanalysis and counselling.' There are indeed questions about the Regulator (note the capital letter), or whether there will ever be a Regulator. Here is yet another trance induction: assert the distinctness of these occupations, call them 'professions', and (for people whose political discrimination is shaky), it makes it so, makes it seem a done deal.

The report then runs through the first six of the ten HPC criteria for regulation, and recommends research on the relationship between psychotherapy, psychology, counselling and psychoanalysis to ensure that registration routes are made available. Here again is an unquestioned commitment to input regulation. Trainers train, i.e. they have ownership of input to psychopractice. Their approach to regulation is to propose regulation rooted in what they do, i.e. training, rather than ongoing quality assurance of the situation downstream of their training—which, we might suppose, is what clients actually need.

Happily, unique input registration routes will be available because:

> Each of these groupings is able to demonstrate a degree of homogeneity and a degree of *scientific* difference. [*Ipnosis* italics] ... [UKCP recommends] That statutory registration is made on the basis of there being a generic recognition of the activity of psychotherapy (psychotherapist).

Yes, but wouldn't registration/regulation by the HPC or a Mental Health Council be *state* regulation, not *statutory* regulation?

In a hint of the deep fissures in the psychopractice field, the report admits that work will need to be undertaken on: '... the relationships between psychoanalysis and psychoanalytic psychotherapy and the most appropriate location of these professional groups within the regulatory structure.' Also that research be commissioned, presumably by the DoH, '... to consider greater emphasis on research of the efficacy of the range of psychotherapies beyond those that are more naturally suited to the medical model of the randomised control trial.' And, as *Ipnosis* fancies, so as to ensure that, because science has such high status (in the DoH), '... the relationship between the scientific base of psychotherapy and ethics is taken into account in identifying the appropriate regulator.'

Further down the page the report assures the DoH that: '... training standards are reviewed to ensure that supervised clinical work forming part of the training includes work that will develop an understanding of serious psychiatric disorder.'

Oh yes: be sure you have your copy of DSM IV to hand when you go to supervision—as though 'serious psychiatric disorder' were not a highly contested notion, not least by dissident psychiatrists such as John Read and his colleagues (Routledge, 2004) who have come to see psychiatry as a scandal. Yet again, as an example of unwitting collusion with a medical model of human (mal)functioning.

After some items wondering whether it wouldn't be a good idea to research the need for personal therapy in training and the value of CPD, the report gets down and ugly: 'UKCP has expressed serious reservations concerning the appropriateness of the HPC as the regulator.' This is October 2005, but the report was being written during the middle of that year.

> It is possible that there will be a significant reorganisation of the HPC or a broader reorganisation of the regulatory structure for the health professions as a whole ... The report notes the negative response of the British Psychological Society to the consultation on the proposal to regulate 'Applied Psychology' through the HPC. The BPS had concerns that parallelled some of the concerns that have been expressed by UKCP.

The report recommends a *Mental Health and Development Council* operating within the Council for Healthcare Regulatory Excellence (CHRE)—a notion that for some, including *Ipnosis*, denotes continuing unacceptable deference to a medical model of psychopractice. And, we would want to ask, who are CHRE? How are they appointed? What is their brief?

With yet another scientific flourish, the report reminds us that: 'The purpose of the regulatory structure is to protect the public, ensure good practice, and promote the scientific development of the professions.' This scientific development does not as of this moment, *Ipnosis* reminds the reader, include adequate, or even any, research to establish an evidence-base demonstrating that there is significant harm due to psychopractice in the UK. 'Public protection' is yet another long-standing trance induction intended to disallow dissent.

And none of the many psychopractitioners I know would remotely consider their practice as scientific, even, so far as the positivist science of 'research *on* people' was concerned, actively contradicting its findings and supposed high status.

In a foggy series of sentences worthy of Cold War diplomacy, the report says that:

> ... there are organisations that have an identity derived from attaching significance to difference which are relatively minor.
> ... there are organisations which have an institutional interest in blurring distinctions that are fundamental to the field.
> ... The process therefore needs to proceed in part by the testing of the viability of models.
> ... The methodological and intellectual overlap of a number of professions does not justify a leap to the abandonment of the fundamental distinctions between the different professions.
> ... a key principle to be applied is that all those involved deserve to be treated with respect.
> ... treating with appropriate scepticism both claims to similarity and claims to distinction.
> ... within the framework of this attempt, it follows that no one individual or organisation is a prior authority.

This process or protocol, whatever it might be, is nonetheless claimed to be: '... essentially a democratic process in which individuals and organisations are staking their own claims, to be judged by the community as a whole.' And also, DoH take note, it is *scientific*: 'This is consistent with scientific method and the requirement for "evidence-based practice".'

Science is once more wheeled on stage, apparently as arbiter of what really matters around regulation; but actually this is scientism, science as decoration— see the next sentence: 'Respect is necessary but a prioritisation of evidence over the self-referential authority of an individual or a group is the starting point of the whole scientific enterprise.'

Yes, let's have Respect; let's even look into having George Galloway as a regulator—but let's also be aware that this sentence, like several *Ipnosis* has earlier pointed to, abuses science by using it as decoration. *Ipnosis* found this misuse of science strongly reminiscent of the transcendental meditation movement, which thirty years ago similarly used science as decoration to enhance its appeal to scientific illiterates.

And there is more: 'The HPC is surely right to identify the status of a profession as a science, or the status of science within a profession, as a key issue.' If you are a registrant of organisations such as, for instance, Psychosynthesis and Education Trust, Institute of Psychosynthesis, Chiron Centre for Body Psychotherapy, Centre for Transpersonal Psychology, British Psychodrama Association, Karuna, Spectrum, London Association of Primal Psychotherapists, Re-Vision, or any of the others—note what is being asserted in your name,

As though uncertain of the continuing efficacy of earlier trance-inductions, the report tastefully brings on stage one UKCP frequently used in the 1990s: 'It is likely that the regulation within the European Union will be of increasing significance to psychotherapy in the future.' Then, having rejected the HPC's legitimacy as a regulator, the report moves on to discuss its ten commandments as though they were updates from the Moses originals.

> ... the ten criteria set out by the HPC for applicant professions are useful questions to address.
> 1. Cover a discrete area of activity displaying some homogeneity.
> 2. Apply a defined body of knowledge.
> 3. Practice based on evidence of efficacy.
> 4. Have at least one established professional body which accounts for a significant proportion of that occupational group.
> 5. Operate a voluntary register.
> 6. Have defined routes of entry to the profession.
> 7. Have independently assessed entry qualifications.
> 8. Have standards in relation to conduct, performance and ethics.
> 9. Have Fitness to Practise procedures to enforce those standards.
> 10. Be committed to continuous professional development (CPD).

Note the use in item 9 (this is psychotherapy we are talking about) of the word *enforce*. If training 'standards in relation to conduct, performance and ethics' are adequate in the training organisations, why would there be any need to enforce these standards? As *Ipnosis* and Hogan (weblink page) would argue, input regulation of psychopractice cites accountability in a way that guarantees malpractice, whereas output accountability, as IPN demonstrates, is overwhelmingly likely to minimise it.

The UKCP of this report often seems to be endlessly preoccupied with taxonomy, with the minutiae of boundary disputes between its members. Is this perhaps a reflection of the inner turf wars that have been its history for decades?

Curiously, perhaps because of a lack of creativity and innovative, out-of-the-box thinking, it seems to recommend looking to a European model of what psychotherapy is, or at least point to a way of resolving these internecine disputes. Apparently the European Association of Psychotherapists (an organisation that *Ipnosis* recalls not long ago was anathema to the UKCP) has adopted as a working definition the definition of psychotherapy used in Austrian law:

> § 1. Definition of the profession of Psychotherapy
> (1) The practice of psychotherapy is the comprehensive, conscious and planned treatment of psychosocial, psychosomatic and behavioural disturbances or states of suffering with scientific psychotherapeutic methods, through an interaction between one or more persons being treated, and one or more psychotherapists, with the aim of relieving or removing symptoms, disturbed behavioural patterns and attitudes to change, and to foster the maturation, development and health of the treated person. It requires both a general and a specific training/education.

Apart from the self-referential awkwardness of having 'psychotherapists' and 'psychotherapeutic' inside a definition of psychotherapy and the medicalising presumption of 'treatment', here again—but not meriting comment—is '*scientific* psychotherapeutic methods'.

In a later scan of possible ways of defining psychotherapy we find another version, this time home-brewed: '... treatment is comprehensive conscious and planned and it is based on scientific psychotherapeutic methods.' This is a curious claim that seems to belie the facts on the ground. Is it really so, I ask again, that UKCP registrants from Psychosynthesis and Education Trust, Institute of Psychosynthesis, Chiron Centre for Body Psychotherapy, Centre for Transpersonal Psychology, British Psychodrama Association, Karuna, Spectrum, London Association of Primal Psychotherapists, Re-Vision, etc., have gravitated to giving 'treatments' based on scientific psychotherapeutic methods? Or had they not noticed?

Further preoccupation with the taxonomy of psychopractice subgroups leads us to a discussion of the acceptability of counselling, which the report claims is: '... more directly focused on solving problems than psychotherapy'.

However:

> Many counsellors have developed a practice that in intent is akin to, or even indistinguishable from, psychotherapy.

This evidently makes some in the UKCP very unhappy:

> An issue here is whether counsellors who practise as psychotherapists should not, in fact, state clearly that this is what they are doing.

UKCP's obsession with categoric exclusivity for psychotherapy, a project surely doomed to failure, makes them even more unhappy when facts on the ground contradict its obsession with tight boundaries: 'Attempts to resolve the problem of the status of counselling by the assertion that it is indistinguishable from psychotherapy is profoundly unhelpful to this process of clarification.' And we have research to prove it because it is: '... clear from IMP [Interim Mapping

Project] that there is very widespread acceptance in practice of the distinction between counselling and psychotherapy.' Even though, as *Ipnosis* knows very well, there is also a widespread *lack of distinction* between psychotherapy and counselling. But the research was designed to identify distinctions and that's what it found.

> A hypothesis worth investigating is that counselling is felt to be useful to many individuals and institutions precisely because of the nature of the intent, and is perceived to be acceptable because it is safe as a result of the limits of its intent. There is a greater risk, if delineations are too blurred, that an individual might approach a counsellor seeking limited help with a particular problem, and find that they are drawn into deeper work for which the counsellor's training may not be sufficient and for which the framework available may not offer adequate support.

UKCP then continues this patronising grinding of its institutional angst, over what seems to be perceived as the contamination of psychotherapy by counselling, with the suggestion that: 'It may emerge that some of those who currently practice as counsellors would more accurately, and therefore with greater clarity for the public, be practising, at least part of the time, as psychotherapists ... the consideration of methods and training standards is confused by attempts to simply conflate psychotherapy and counselling.'

However, let's not get too worked up about this, as one UKCP hand doesn't necessarily know what the other is doing. On page 50 of this report there is the fundamentally contradictory claim that:

> UKCP has taken the important step of recognising the links between psychotherapy and counselling. To this end it has created the Psychotherapeutic Counselling Section. It is of course open to the practitioners of other professions to seek to practise according to psychotherapeutic methods as they understand them. Some appropriate borrowing of psychotherapeutic methods by other professionals is greatly to be welcomed. The practice of these professionals in regard to their levels of training is a matter for their own professional bodies, as would be any other similar conduct. This will not be prevented by an indicative statutory regulation of the title 'psychotherapist'.

This huffy, patronising haughtiness about potential transgressions pauses the discussion on counselling, but only for the moment.

After some prolonged gathering of the virtues of psychotherapy, we come to the following remarks. Again note the genuflection in the direction of science. 'Psychotherapy training is aimed at the understanding of the whole of the problems of treating psychosocial, psychosomatic and behavioural disturbance or states of suffering within a particular scientific methodology.'

However, in this continuing, if tedious competition for territory, counselling is a poor relation:

> ... the acquisition of distinct skills which may be useful in a range of contexts and which would cumulatively equip someone to be a counsellor is not the basis of psychotherapy training.

Even though not much is agreed between the larger institutions of psychopractice within UKCP version of psychotherapy, there are settled groupings, meaning presumably the modalities.

> Each of these groupings is able to demonstrate a degree of homogeneity and a degree of scientific difference.

In this formal recommendation to the HPC, here again science is used as decoration. Take out the word 'scientific' and read the paragraph again.

As most psychopractitioners know (and welcome): 'The body of knowledge upon which psychotherapy rests is itself a series of overlapping bodies of knowledge.' But sadly, there are 'profound epistemological differences within the profession … and it is possible but difficult to … distinguish between major fault lines and minor distinctions.'

But we can still try. And even go on to launch the contradictory but entrancing claim that: 'The profession is within sight of the development of a coherent and workable framework.'

Except for the inconvenience that up to now no firm knowledge base has been established: 'One unitary alternative to this approach creates an image of the knowledge base and the consequent practice and training requirements that is too general to form a coherent basis for a profession.' Rejected—because as the report details, it would lead to lowest common denominator practice. 'A second alternative unitary approach sets training standards at a high level in relation to one or more modalities.'

But then, for reasons that are not at all clear, the report says such regulation would not work, apparently because the regulator wouldn't be able to tell whether the practitioners are dogs or horses: 'A third alternative is to recognise a range of groupings so numerous that even a reasonably well-informed observer could only be confused.'

Who is this 'reasonably well-informed observer'? Why should the multiple distinctness of psychotherapy practitioners be a problem, other than to a training organization trade association that seeks to generate and control psychopractice through creating a state-regulated monoculture?

Sadly and regretfully, the report admits:

> There are many groups that are very anxious to promote their own particular identity and accordingly wish to achieve a level of distinction that is not appropriate within the broad framework. That it is not appropriate represents a judgement, but it is precisely this kind of judgement that will have to be made if a regulatory structure is to be established.

Yes indeed, and who keeps gate for the gatekeepers? Who judges the judges?

After twenty pages in which the UKCP's five modalities set out their stalls vis à vis regulation, we come to a section of the report entitled: 'The Profession must support a practice based on evidence of efficacy.' And here once more we come to the curious brotherhood of science and psychotherapy: 'The term "scientific" appears both in the HPC requirements and in the EAP definition of psychotherapy.' In response to this observation, the report pulls three arbitrary, if pre-existing, notions about psychotherapy out of the psychopractice hat: 'There is an overlapping debate about psychotherapy as a profession, psychotherapy as a specifically health profession, and psychotherapy as a science.'

Some of us would add psychotherapy as education, psychotherapy as personal development, psychotherapy as experiential inquiry, psychotherapy as spiritual quest. But they would distract us from the UKCP's intent here, which appears to be to erect a sufficiently credible piece of window-dressing that will convince the DoH that, at least among the psychotherapy community, the UKCP are sensible, rational civilised citizens who will keep such 'wild' human matters as being born, surviving schooling, begetting children, bereavement, getting old and dying, etc. from getting in the way of the audit/surveillance culture glacier. Science has been good at that: 'At the heart of scientific method is "the radical notion that our understanding of ourselves should be based on experiment and observation, rather than merely speculating about things."' That's right; but one of the clear findings of the history of science is that institutions commonly develop science that magically turns out to support their political agendas.

UKCP's long history of fear-based trance inductions that attempt to corral psychotherapists who were havering about the value of registration, let alone regulation, does not inspire trust that they will be any more even-handed in the commissioning of new research. *Ipnosis* would argue that the evidence points to the reverse: that any UKCP-driven research may be reasonably taken to imply a scientific agenda of coercion—elegant, civilised, and reasonable, but coercion nonetheless. 'Every new science has to develop its own methodology and as it develops to some extent redefines what we understand science in practice to be.'

It is true that positivist, 'power-over' research *on* people, the science of randomised trials, is unappetising for psychopractitioners. But where are the signs that anyone in either the UKCP or the BACP knows what alternative research *with* people, action research, or cooperative inquiry [CI] is, let alone how to do it? This would be an approach to science that might match the personhood of the people who come as clients and those of us who meet them as practitioners, and might be reliably independent of the commissioning institution. That perhaps is why it doesn't happen, except in IPN, which *Ipnosis* has long seen as being structured as a large cooperative inquiry in which the outcome is continuing civic accountability in the IPN member groups.

A page or two further on, there is the beginning of a hint that science might be an obstacle to, rather than a lubricant for regulation.

The human sciences encounter an epistemological problem ...

Of the human sciences psychotherapy faces this problem most acutely.

The perception that knowledge (including 'objective knowledge') is generated intersubjectively and is subject to that intersubjectivity is fundamental to psychotherapy.

No human science is more immersed in this problem than psychotherapy because it is precisely concerned with the generation and regeneration of subjectivity.

Yes, but: the notion of psychotherapy as a human science is still presented here as entrancing, as though it were uncontested, with the intent to conflate science and psychotherapy. We must not do this blurring with counselling and psychotherapy, but it is OK with science and psychotherapy. Handily, the report, while expressing its doubts in a discreetly gentlemanly tone, sees this as sharply problematic for the regulation project: 'A major concern about the Health Professions Council is that, having developed primarily to serve professions intellectually based in the natural sciences, it will have little comprehension of these problems.' And it adds that: 'A subsidiary concern is that it might be used to support those who wish to sustain an alliance of thought with authority but masquerade as scientific.'

Yes, indeed: but set your own house in order before trying to entrance us with what Bad Others might do. Helpfully, for those practitioners outside the UKCP's exclusivity, 'an alliance of thought with authority that masquerades as scientific' is a very cogent way of expressing the danger ('concern' is a corporate euphemism) that clients are potentially exposed to by the whole regulation project.

The section continues this 'scientific' discussion with a sideways attack, presumably on one of the fractious psychoanalytic factions that have yet to sign up to the UKCP vision:

> How are we to understand the almost religious maintenance of the terms first proposed by Freud to structure the analytic experience? Was Freud really the first, and did he really remain the only theoretician of this supposed science to have introduced fundamental concepts? Were this so, it would be very unusual in the history of the sciences.

Ouch!

> Progress has been made, but more is needed, in developing a framework for promoting a scientific attitude that respects the intersubjective foundation of the profession and is consistent with its present state of development

Yes, *Ipnosis* would sign up to that, but not unless it is an attitude rooted in 'power-with', participatory research *with* people. That doesn't sound all that likely, because the coercive conflation of science and psychotherapy continues:

> For the scientific development of psychotherapy it is essential to resist four unhelpful pressures: firstly, an excessive dominance of (self-promoted) authorities over evidence; secondly, an over-commitment to positivism; thirdly, an excessive negative reaction to positivism; and fourthly, a reluctance to structure the profession in a way that recognises and supports different scientific methodologies.

'Excessive dominance of (self-promoted) authorities over evidence'? Hmmm: isn't this exactly the reason why so many of us object to UKCP's decades-long imperialism and denial of evidence that contradicts it? And why only an *excessive* dominance? Can we take this to mean that normal dominance, i.e. bullying, is OK?

REGULATING THE PSYCHOLOGICAL THERAPIES

The authors of the report are troubled that HPC criteria for regulation separate 'psychotherapy as science' and 'the ethics of psychotherapy' without any indication of the links between these two issues.

In considering a regulatory framework for psychotherapy it is essential to understand the links between science and ethics which exist in all sciences, but are unavoidable in psychotherapy.

Freud's solution was to focus on health.

The trouble is ... 'Health is to a considerable extent a social construct, especially in the field of mental health.' It is, indeed, a social construct, and 'mental health' is a related construct from which many psychopractitioners seek to disconnect themselves but which, via a 'mental health council', UKCP is happily promoting as the preferred institutional way forward.

A few more erudite quotations and a sidelong glance at Freud and Lacan lead us to the filling in the sandwich—a statement with which *Ipnosis* can at last wholeheartedly agree.

It is not good enough to say that the profession can regulate itself, but the regulatory process needs to be protected from the oversimplifications of those who, with their unquestioned positivist assumptions and materialist thinking, presume that the regulation of all professions is the same.

It cannot be relied upon that the appointment of professional experts by an institution will protect the process from the complacent, narrow and uninformed assumptions of that institution.

Yes, indeed—especially if such institutions have the kind of coercive history that has brought UKCP to its current role of 'putting together the pieces', which were not in need of its attention anyway, as Mowbray (1995) cogently argues. However, referring back to its alarm about HPC's inadequate integration of science and ethics, the writers of the report take yet another opportunity to underline the power to entrance of 'the scientific', i.e. science as decoration, when they ask ... 'that the relationship between the scientific base of psychotherapy and ethics is taken into account in identifying the appropriate regulator.'

The report goes on for another 30-odd pages, but as with mathematical proofs and other aspects of science, and indeed people, there is a point where enough is enough. *Ipnosis* hopes that in lieu of spending the best part of a day reading the UKCP document, this review will prove enough for you.

Reference

Mowbray, R (1995) *The Case Against Psychotherapy Registration: A conservation issue for the Human Potential Movement*. London: Trans Marginal Press

Background: I welcomed this presentation; it seemed one of the rare occasions when a proponent of state regulation of psychotherapy was prepared to argue the case for it publicly. I also admired the courage it took to frame the debate in religious terms: something I have long felt was appropriate but for different reasons. I guess I was one of the few people present who was familiar with Heward Wilkinson's equally courageous eight-page editorial in the *International Journal of Psychotherapy* (see Chapter 10), describing, we were invited to suppose, the constitutional uncertainties of the UKCP as potentially fascist (Wilkinson, 2000). The presentation did not, for technical reasons, include the slides (weblink page) and the title is of course an *Ipnosis* confection.

CHAPTER THIRTY

The UKCP is Our Shepherd,
We Shall Not Want …

The UKCP presentation begins with the notion that there is a visible psychotherapy and an invisible psychotherapy.

PSYCHOTHERAPY
INVISIBLE

and

PSYCHOTHERAPY
VISIBLE

It then moves on to invite us to think of psychotherapy as analogous to christianism.

> For Christians the Church Visible, fortunately, does not coincide with the Church Invisible.

> The Church Invisible is catholic and indivisible, the single and united Body of Christ.

> The Church Visible is disunited, and no one of its ecclesiastical nuclei has the power, unilaterally, to reunite it, even whilst they continue to claim to be 'the one true Church'.

We are, *Ipnosis* supposes, invited to identify the UKCP with both 'church visible' and 'church invisible'. The notion that psychopractice is disunited, and that none of its ecclesiastical nuclei—including the UKCP—has the power unilaterally to reunite it, is certainly welcome; however, UKCP does appear to be claiming to have possession of the deep, inner truth of psychotherapy, even to be 'the one true church'.

Curiously the next slide—an image from the Vatican website labelled 'The Church Visible' and evoking the papacy (weblink page)—handily reminds us of the scale of the damage that a bureaucratic institution can do to radical notions about how better to relate to each other.

The presentation moves on to declare that in its ambition for: '… a fully integrated Visible Profession, at this point UKCP, has failed … We simply don't have agreed concepts either of "personal therapeutic experience" or "external validation"!!' However, all is not lost because UKCP, like the Vatican, claims to

---

Review of a UKCP presentation by Heward Wilkinson at the *Therapeutic Training after Freud Conference*, 20 May 2006, at Roehampton University. It first appeared in *Ipnosis*, 29 May 2006

have a line of authority back to the one true church of psychotherapy: 'Continuing to represent the Invisible Unity of the Profession, UKCP has moved, with success, to a facilitative role in the field.'

It has apparently had the reshuffle of its member organisation modalities endorsed by the DoH and this joint cooperation, the presentation claims, may yet to be blessed by the emergence of a 'Mental Health Council' to replace the Health Professions Council.

A Mental Health Council? I have had the impression, down the years, that many people in the UKCP did not see themselves as even remotely engaged in the myth of 'mental health', a profoundly medicalised, pathology-driven notion. Where are their voices?

And what a bizarre rationalisation of the sleep-walking reality of psychopractice professionalisation to claim to represent the Invisible Unity of the Profession. However, just in case some sin from the christianism of the first paragraphs of the presentation had attached itself to the begetters of this remarkable conceptual contortion, the presentation goes on to: '... honour how the Independent Practitioners' Network represents the anti-regulatory impulse, that nearly all of us feel in part of ourselves. And why not? UKCP feels the same impulse;'

Really? This is surely massively disingenuous. If UKCP feels the anti-regulatory impulse, why has it been diligently promoting the regulation of psychopractice for at least a decade and a half? See for example *UKCP's Love Affair with the State* (Chapter 29). Doesn't significant doubt always constitute a 'No'? Is it 'feeling the anti-regulatory impulse' that has caused UKCP as an institution to studiously ignore to death the critique that IPN participants and others have raised of this trade association's imperialism?

This dubiously framed complimenting of IPN is followed in the UKCP presentation by a proposition that reeks of exactly the kind of compromised, bankrupt universalising that feeds *Ipnosis*'s intuition that regulation, as presently being pursued, will be a historical disaster for UK psychopractice. The significant (but denied) doubt about the value of regulation claimed for UKCP now mutates into a pair of trance inductions. '... pragmatically, the least worst policy is to achieve regulation, on a basis which maintains the spirit of the Profession'—i.e. regulation is inevitable. UKCP can (a) be trusted as the priestly celebrant of what constitutes the spirit of our psychopractice occupations, and can (b) be trusted to orchestrate for you this spirit's relations with the state.

'And, why should we as a Profession not simply be accountable in the form of Regulation?' *Ipnosis* would want to revise this to 'Of course, as a trade association driven primarily by training interests, UKCP has long been actively interested in having accountability take the form of State Regulation.' Ipnosis has no problem with accountability; the issue is accountability to and through whom?

> We represent a vast, complex, and in some cases lethal, actual and potential body of knowledge and praxis; our scope and influence is expanding into all fields of praxis; why should we be absolved from accountability?

This inflates the importance of a tiny fraction of the UK working population—7000 UKCP registrants out of a total of say 50,000 UK psychopractitioners (the NHS has 1.300,000 staff)— into being a major player on the international stage. Status for psychotherapy, in sight at last: but status of a disastrous kind. As Nick Totton remarked in the IPN presentation at the same conference, 'Psychotherapists are not just turkeys voting for Xmas; they are inventing Xmas, and writing the menu.'

The presentation moves on from this inflated assertion of representing a vast complex expansion into all fields of praxis to another conflation of spirituality and psychopolitics:

> The state already owns our souls; the question, from our side, is, upon what basis? And, if we desire influence for good in this modern age, if our souls are in their turn to own the State, a State-recognised identity is essential.

Ipnosis was strongly reminded by this paragraph of the parallel with the actual Established Anglican Church in the UK and the sense that, awarely or not, on the basis of this presentation the UKCP may believe it mirrors Anglicanism's inclusivity (while as yet lacking its Crown imprimatur).

The Anglican ministry is indeed a church divided, and its internal dynamics of compulsive hierarchical dispensation and disempowered lay members matches the unfolding psychopractice regulation situation quite well—not least, *Ipnosis* feels inclined to add, in the way that as an institution Anglicanism has ensured that the radicalism of the 'Jesus message' has too often been dissipated into dull social conformity.

In another, perhaps more acute parallel, the Anglican church was founded—and some would see it as continuing to be shaped by—the raw state power of Henry VIII, who appropriated its predecessor's assets and forced it to reflect his government's style and priorities.

'The state already owns our souls.' Here is another trance induction, the intention, or at least the effect of which, is to dislocate discrimination; it seeks to install the belief that we are powerless in the face of the state and thus eliminates the option of choice. Let us remember, this is psychotherapy speaking: psychotherapy advocating powerlessness and 'che sera, sera'. We are intended to forget, or to fail to notice, that UKCP has historically always been committed to having psychopractice regulated by the state.

Elaborating on the first suggestion, the trance induction continues, 'If our souls are in their turn to own the State, a State- recognised identity is essential'. Again this is intended to shut down, or foreclose, discrimination. The choice that a psychopractitioner might see the interests of their clients, let alone their self-interest, as much better served by NOT signing up to the audit/surveillance culture that has distorted and damaged the NHS and public education in the UK, is disallowed.

A state-recognised identity will result in the terminal contamination of working alliances—not only, *Ipnosis* would argue, by what is insisted upon, but by what is omitted; what gets sidelined, disallowed, regarded as unpredictable, outrageous, too loud, ecstatic or wild. Through UKCP and its brother organisations' regulationist fear inductions, the richly sonorous, unpredictable music of deep psychopractice already feels to some of us to have become muted; it becomes muzak, a lifestyle enhancement.

Once the institutional doubts about the value of such a psychic amputation have been successfully denied (and expiated by congratulating IPN for its dissent) the benefits of joining modernity are available to us: '... we enter the "external validation" realm of mapping "competences", "occupational standards", "earning outcomes".' There is a danger here, however, because sin is still a live notion in this presentation: 'The great sin of psychotherapy—a sin we have all committed!—is inauthenticity, the subjection to some system of technical terminology.'

Here is another bit of bankrupt universalising. Don't many people take up psychopractice as a continuing search for authenticity, i.e. as a vocation or calling? And why should psychotherapy as education, all of which is an extension of learning to ride a bicycle, have to carry this burden of sin? Is playing scales on the piano sinful?

The answer comes in the succeeding paragraphs that reveal once more the extent to which the core perspective of UKCP is founded on training: '... philosophically, psychotherapy is not merely empirical science. Its mode of engagement with temporal causal experience is an inextricable interweave of a priori and empirical.' '... how on earth can this be mapped into competences, learning outcomes, occupational standards, etc?'

In a line that entrances us into thinking that the only route to accountability is that of input, one necessarily determined by psychotherapy trainers, the UKCP presentation proclaims:

WE ALREADY DO IT IN TEACHING IT
We all teach our form or vision of psychotherapy; well, how do we do it? And how do we know we have done it? We all have answers in practice to those questions.

So that's all right, then. Because training institutions train psychopractitioners, we, the rest of the people already in practice, can and should accept the reduction of the field to competences, learning outcomes, occupational standards, and should delegate the definition of them to the handful of people from the key training institutions who actually do the ongoing negotiations with the DoH (only to be sidelined, as the DoH *Next Steps* process unfolds, by Skills for Health, a subsection of Skills for Business)—as though the taxonomy of these categories, and the processes of assessing non-compliance with them, did not involve a form of psychic imprisonment for psychopractitioners downstream of this narrowly representative leadership.

However, this unduly complicates the situation, because the UKCP—failing to recognise, through accurate problem definition, that state regulation of psychopractice is a vicious problem (one where the solution makes the situation worse)—are convinced that they have found a solution. Take, for example, emotion:

DEFINING EMOTION
How do we teach this? You all know. You all do it, experientially. And if you know, you can state the form of knowledge.

Teaching a *definition* of emotion is indeed an academic task. This overconfidently sidesteps the regulatory issue; ensuring that a psychopractitioner is emotionally competent is a horse of a different colour. *Ipnosis* would argue that because it necessitates a strong, long-term commitment to self-directed learning, there is a low probability that emotional competence can be trained for. That is not to say, (Postle, 2003), that it can't be recognised as it comes into place.

But none of this potential for psychopractice being mired and defaced by category errors counts for the UKCP. The definition of emotion (as if a definition of it had more validity for troubled clients than an each-way bet on the 4:30 at Cheltenham) is regarded as good enough.

The form it takes, for instance, in the Health Profession Council's formulations, is not rocket science!

Registrant Arts Therapists must 'know theories relevant to work with an individual'.

That's it! As regards 'work with an individual' qua individual, that's it, for the HPC!

Terrific. Unbounded enthusiasm breaks out all over NW1. Registration is a doddle; why have we been concerned about it? Accountability? Well, 'know the theories of emotion relevant to work with an individual'—that's all the HPC will ask you for. Here is yet another trance induction. It hides the permanently intractable impossibilities of the State regulatory categorisation of psychopractice behind the false promise that, on the day, it will be easy for you. Even trivial.

We are also committed, as we dialogue with the Department of Health, to mapping the relation between our specific, or our broader general, modalities, and the generic concepts which are in common to us all.

So trust us. You are in safe hands. We won't let you down. Let us get on with our task as shepherds of the flock. Keep eating the rich, green grass of your working alliances. Trust us to lead you though the Valley of the Shadow of Regulation, safe in the knowledge that neither of us has noticed that our destiny is to become mutton and woolly jumpers.

References

Postle, D (2003) *The Mind Gymasium: Letting the Heart Sing.* CD-ROM, WLR, pp. 352–379

Wilkinson, H (1999) Editorial: Psychotherapy, fascism and constitutional history. *International Journal of Psychotherapy*, 4:2,117–126

Wilkinson, H (2006) Slides for the UKCP presentation at the *Therapeutic Training after Freud Conference*, May 20 at Roehampton University (weblinks page)

Background: On finishing James Scott's book *Seeing Like a State* (Scott, 1998) I felt that I at last understood why state regulation of psychotherapy and counselling is such a vital generic concern. My long-held intuition that it will compromise the client experience was now supported by a deep international analysis of several previous, equally well-intentioned, but disastrous social interventions. The insights of Scott's text, which I outline below, were further enriched by the coincident arrival of concrete evidence from the DoH of the process that he describes.

CHAPTER THIRTY-ONE

The Regulation Journey:
From Taxonomy* to Taxidermy

Two strands of psychotherapy and counselling regulationism converged in July 2006. In mid-July the *Foster report on non medical regulation 2006* was posted on the Web. I'll come to that in a moment; but first let's look at the letter that, in common with a hundred-plus UK organisations, IPN received from Professor Louis Appleby, National Director for Mental Health.

Taxonomy

Professor Appleby wrote to outline the next steps in the DoH's *Next Steps* process of codifying and regulating psychotherapy and counselling. As was promised at the end of 2005, the accumulated know-how of psychopractice is to be subject to a formidable array of technical experts whose declared field is taxonomy, i.e. to treat the subtle, often ineffable skills of human interaction as though they were trays of butterflies to be catalogued. If this seems unduly dismissive, look at the organisations listed in this paragraph from Professor Appleby; the first three are all subsections of Skills for Business:

> Skills for Health will coordinate the production of an initial framework which will identify the scope of practice involved in psychotherapy and counselling, and will be based in the first instance on existing relevant competences held by four sector skills councils and a national training organisation, and training standards where these are known. The four sector skills councils include: Skills for Health, Skills for Justice, Skills for Care and Development, and SEMTA. ENTO is the national training organisation also involved ...

Curiously NDAH, the National Development Agency for Hubris, is not mentioned, though it would seem have an important perspective to contribute. Not least, their staff might remind us that a consequence of the taxonomy expertise of such organisations is, as James Scott outlines (see below), taxidermy: preserving outward appearances after the living organism has been removed.

Is this an exaggeration? Professor Appleby goes on:

---

* Taxonomy, the practice and science of classification ... taxonomies are frequently hierarchical in structure, frequently displaying parent–child relationships (*wikipedia*)

This article first appeared in *Ipnosis*, 13 August 2006

… all other professional bodies in the field known to us to have an interest, [will
be invited] to contribute to the population of the framework by demonstrating
to Skills for Health where your standards fit within it, and where there may be
gaps.

Therapists and counsellors, many of them brimming over with know-how about
interpersonal and group dynamics, will be invited to demonstrate to the DoH
how their standards fit into an existing taxonomy.

It may be recoverable, but this feels like an inflection point, a critical moment:
the point at which psychotherapy and counselling practitioner power came under
the thumb of the DoH. Arguably, this was already apparent at the so-called
Reference Group meeting last November, which *Ipnosis* attended.

The letter from the National Director of Mental Health also tells us about
that meeting:

> At a meeting in November 2005 of all training organisations known to BACP
> and UKCP, the Government's objective was reiterated, and agreed by the majority
> of those present, that statutory** regulation was accepted as being necessary for
> protection of the public by setting standards of practice, conduct and training
> for these professions.

Contrary to Professor Appleby's text, the meeting was declared as a presentation
of a DoH/UKCP/BACP mapping exercise. This presentation was followed by an
unannounced set of PowerPoint slides from Ros Mead, Manager of New Regulation
projects at the DoH outlining the *Next Steps* in the DoH, regulatory plan. This
appeared to be news to everyone at the meeting and there was next to no
opportunity to discuss either the mapping exercise results, or Ms Mead's
presentation. There was certainly no vote, and no show of hands on whether
those present agreed with statutory regulation as 'necessary for protection of the
public by setting standards of practice, conduct and training for these professions'.
At a conference on therapy regulation a few months later, those of us from IPN
who at this meeting had declared regulation to be 'a mistake' were congratulated
by other attendees who hadn't felt able to voice their dissent.

But back to Professor Appleby:

> The way forward proposed at that meeting was to hold a preliminary planning
> meeting of sector skills councils, qualifications authorities and others with
> expertise in competence development for these bodies to plan setting up a
> competence framework covering the practice of psychotherapists and counsellors.

The first paragraph of his letter makes clear that 'the way forward' heard at the
November 2005 Reference Group meeting was not a proposition but an
announcement. As the DoH picks up the regulation agenda—so diligently polished
for them by the UKCP and BACP and others—Professor Appleby's looseness
with language betrays the highly unethical tendency towards abusive power
relations which the DoH and their trade association collaborators have

---

** Evidently not yet up to speed in these matters, Professor Appleby doesn't seem to realise that
if the Foster Report is to be believed, what he is planning is state regulation, not statutory
regulation.).

demonstrated in recent years. These are people who aspire to install exemplary standards of ethical behaviour, but they often seem not to have brought any with them. (I would not include Ros Mead of the DoH in this critique; in her relations with IPN she has been direct, accessible and scrupulous.) Professor Appleby ends by hoping that practitioners: '... will contribute to this *exercise* [*Ipnosis* emphasis], which marks a significant step forward in ensuring safe and effective services provided to patients and clients of psychotherapists and counsellors.'

Again the language betrays the technocratic lens through which psychopractice is being viewed—as an *exercise* in fitting in—'demonstrating to Skills for Health where your standards fit within it, and where there may be gaps'. Tragically this approach to accountability is for practitioners not only an exercise in 'self mutilation', as a recent conference paper about the regulation of psychoanalysis by Chris Oakley (2005) called it, but one that, if accepted, will terminally compromise the quality of psychopractice working alliances with clients. And yet in this upside-down techno-universe of the DoH and its collaborators (free also, it sometimes seems, of much of the core knowledge that therapists might be expected to have about human relating), regulation is still claimed to be for the benefit of clients.

Mêtis and Techne

Before I come to look at the *Foster Report's* policy pointers to our regulated future, I want to mention a very helpful resource in understanding why psychopractice regulation is destined to be a disaster for clients and practitioners. In *Seeing Like A State*, James C. Scott (1998) traces the emergence of the State's need to first map, and then regulate and bring onto its books, aspects of society that had otherwise escaped the reach of its administrative and legal grasp.

In the seventeenth and eighteenth centuries—Scott gives France as an example—the definition of property rights via surveying and cadastral maps enabled the state to better enforce taxation (and conscription). Contemporary practices of inheritance and ownership were legible locally, but because of their vernacular language and diversity of incompatible measurements, tended to be invisible to the state. Through unified measurements—notably the metre, kilogram and hectare—plus uniform map scaling and standardised legal language used in its documentation and in registration of property, the state grasped previously local knowledge about who owned what, and made it global, i.e. legible to the state.

Scott shows how, from these beginnings, through the globalising of local vernacular knowledge, the infrastructure of the modern state grew, and in a sense became the state. While we benefit from many such developments, Scott lists numerous state initiatives entered into with the best of intentions that, owing to to hubris, ended in tragedy or failure. One of his contentions is that states often feel driven to colonise areas of daily life that are perceived as wild or that elude their jurisdiction. The mapping and measuring this entails generates categories of territory that can be manipulated centrally.

So far as the state believes that any reality is ultimately reducible to administrable components—a tendency strongly apparent in recent government circles—this can be very damaging. Some people would see the continuing crises in UK schooling and the NHS as examples of this. For our present psychopractice regulation context, there is an equally problematic kind of damage: a tendency for a procrustean transformation in the field being colonised, in which reality is stretched, or alters itself, to fit what the state can administer.

In *Seeing Like A State*, Scott introduces the notion of Mêtis, local practical knowledge, in contradistinction to Techne, technocratic, or scientific knowledge. Mêtis is the sort of practical ability needed to fly a kite, ride a bicycle, drive a car, fly a glider, make love, care for a baby, or sustain a working alliance with a client. Mêtis is experiential knowledge and it is almost always local. Mêtis is that subtle, intuitive perception that there is something significant being left out of a client's story. It is 'the ability and experience necessary to influence the outcome—to improve the odds in a particular instance' (p. 318), as for example in navigation, which to be successful requires responsiveness and improvisation and skilfully judged iterations of trial and error.

> ... the context of mêtis is characteristically 'situations which are transient, shifting disconcerting and ambiguous, situations that do not lend themselves to precise measurement, exact calculation or rigorous logic.' (p. 320)

> Only by grasping the potential achievement and range of mêtis is it possible to appreciate the valuable knowledge that high-modernist schemes deprive themselves of when they simply impose their plans. One reason mêtis is denigrated, particularly in the hegemonic imperium of scientific knowledge, is that its findings are practical, opportune, and contextual, rather than integrated into the general conventions of scientific discourse. (p. 323)

> Mêtis 'is the mode of reasoning most appropriate to complex material and social tasks where the uncertainties are so daunting that we must trust our experienced intuition and feel our way.' (p. 327)

> Mêtis knowledge is often so implicit and automatic that its bearer is at a loss to explain it. (p. 329)

> Mêtis, far from being rigid and monolithic, is plastic, local and divergent. It is in fact the idiosyncrasies of mêtis, its contextualness and its fragmentation that make it so permeable, so open to new ideas. Mêtis has no doctrine or centralised training; each practitioner has his or her own angle. In economic terms the market for mêtis is often one of nearly perfect competition, and local monopolies are likely to be broken from below and outside. If a new technique works it is likely to find a clientele. (p. 332)

However, despite its intrinsic value, as Scott reminds us throughout *Seeing Like A State*, mêtis is constantly being eroded or denigrated or destroyed. The diffusion of modernity over the last 200 or more years has seen progress overwhelmingly shaped and driven by the antithesis of Mêtis: Techne.

> Techne is a 'characteristic of self-contained systems of reasoning in which findings may be logically derived from the initial assumptions. To the degree that the

form of knowledge satisfies these conditions, to that degree is it impersonal, uniform and completely impervious to context'. (p. 320)

It would be a serious error to believe that the destruction of mêtis was merely the inadvertent and necessary by-product of economic progress. The destruction of mêtis and its replacement by standardised formulas legible only from the centre is virtually inscribed in the activities of both the state and large-scale bureaucratic capitalism. (p. 325)

Mêtis is exactly the kind of unpredictable, intuitively perceived, inexactly expressed and—dare we admit it—emotionally rooted know-how of psychotherapy and counselling that the technocratic sieve of the Foster Report posted on the internet in mid-July 2006, seeks to colonise and pacify. The report sets the context for the Blair government's policy for the regulation of psychotherapy and counselling, and yet fails to mention them by name.

Taxidermy

The *Foster report on non-medical regulation 2006* is a lengthy text: 72 pages with a 14-page summary (weblink page). Despite being on the list of psychopractice organisations that engaged with the 2005 DoH-funded mapping 'exercise' (I'll come back to that word), IPN was not invited to contribute to the Foster report, and only after the intervention of my MP (and very grudgingly too) were IPN participants able to make a submission.

You might think, looking at the topic and title of the *Foster Report*, 'non-medical regulation', that this is an even-handed look at the myriad forms of working with the human condition apart from medicine and how they could be regulated. Not so. Outside perhaps of hospital consultants' pay negotiations, a more concrete example of medical-model hegemony would be hard to find.

Neither 'counselling' nor 'psychotherapy' appear in the document; all the examples given are intrinsically medical, and overall the report can be seen as a primer for how the NHS might absorb/capture/accommodate any appetising technical roles that are as yet unincorporated. Examples that repeat and that indicate the narrowed vision of the Foster team are: Anaesthesia Practitioner, Emergency Care Practitioner, Endoscopy Practitioner, Medical Care Practitioner and Surgical Care Practitioner.

So that's OK, then; nothing here to concern psychotherapists and counsellors? Again, not so; on p. 46 the report endorses the DoH status quo on who should do what: 'A regulator like the Health Professions Council, dealing with a range of disparate professional groups, can deliver the functions which public protection requires.' And then, despite the omission of any discussion or context, further down the page is the announcement: 'It follows that any new profession coming into statutory regulation should be regulated by one of the existing regulatory bodies, probably the HPC.' Not only that, but:'Some aspirant groups have argued that new bodies should be set up to regulate their professions. The preceding discussion has led to the rejection of that approach.'

I can imagine that this announcement hasn't been that well received by some accrediting organisations, such as the UKCP or BACP, with large numbers of members who see themselves as outside a mental health discourse. The Foster report seems to offer clear evidence that for the DoH, 'medical' is all there is.

The downside of this is that the core knowledge of the last hundred years of psychology, however much it is contested— matters such as projection, denial, displacement, etc.—appear to be entirely beneath the DoH radar. How else can we explain the report's devotion to the notion that: 'All regulators should adopt a single definition of "good character", as one of the legal requirements for getting registration. This should be based on objective tests.' (p. 10)

Let's ask a few questions. What else does 'good character' mean, other than the application of Foster and his assistants' (socially constructed) model of human nature? And isn't this exactly the kind of issue that any capable psychopractitioner will find emerging in their working alliances, i.e. what counts as human and natural? And doesn't it sound like the headmaster of a minor public school instructing his heads of school on its hiring policy? That's what 'socially constructed' means.

Let's go on a bit further. Doesn't 'good character' imply that there is also 'bad character', implicitly creating a false dichotomy, as between 'weed' and 'cultivar'? Doesn't the use of 'objective' show that Foster, and the great and good on the list of people who signed off his report, are ignorant of, or more likely in institutional denial of, the hard-won understanding that claims of objectivity are instruments of coercion and subordination: 'power words' that are intended to enforce compliance and conformity?

If, as seems certain, this report, regardless of its omission of any mention of counselling and psychotherapy, is set to define government policy, this catalogue of ignorance reinforces what has been intuitively obvious to many people in the field over a decade: that taking part in the state regulation of psychopractice is a form of digging your own grave.

References

Oakley, C (2006) *Psychoanalysis and its Self-mutilation*. Paper given by at the College of Psychoanalysts International Conference, Psychoanalysis and State Regulation, 31 March–1 April

Scott, JC (1998) *Seeing Like a State: How Certain Schemes to Improve the Human Condition Have Failed*. London: Yale University Press

Background: I tried to avoid a sense of triumph, or vindication, in this account of the October Reference Group meeting of mainstream accrediting psychopractice organisations as they appeared to realise what the facts on the ground of state regulation actually meant. Sadness is more apt; and incredulity. Having purposefully driven the train of counselling and psychotherapy into the tunnel of state regulation they had failed to realise the light ahead of them was not the sweet dawning of official recognition, i.e. parity with psychiatry, but the locomotive of government bearing down on them.

CHAPTER THIRTY-TWO

The Penny's Dropped

'The Penny's Dropped': so read a large sign for Maestro plastic money in Liverpool Street station as *Ipnosis* travelled to the 10 October meeting of the psychotherapy and counselling Reference Group, an ad hoc collection of mainstream psychopractice organisations. As we discovered, for the organisations who have been pursuing state regulation of psychotherapy and counselling, the penny has at last dropped that it promises to be a disaster.

The meeting's core agenda: how to respond to the proposals for progressing state regulation of counselling and psychotherapy in the Foster review of non-medical healthcare professions and to Professor Appleby, National 'Mental Health Czar'—as an NHS insider described him at a recent IPN gathering.

This agenda unfolded (unravelled) something like this:
The Foster Report is appalling and inept, and regarded as 'excruciatingly embarrassing' by the DoH, but even though they find themselves between a rock and a hard place because of it, Foster will likely shape government action. The reference group organisations also regard the HPC as inept, inadequate, wholly medical in its worldview, and not 'fit for purpose' as a regulator of psychotherapy and counselling.

However:

1. State regulation of psychotherapy and counselling is INEVITABLE—fervent emphasis from the reference group chair (an *Ipnosis* rejoinder that this statement amounts to a trance induction was ignored).

2. The Foster Report says 'no other regulator than HPC'.

3. After decades of wishing for state regulation, the BPS looks to have got their wish, to be 'state-registered psychologists'. Unfortunately—panic, panic—it means being taken over by the HPC, i.e. they get their wish, but not in the form they had dreamed of.

How do they, the BPS, avoid turning from princes into frogs?
The emerging subtext of the meeting was that the BPS position regarding state regulation by the HPC (despite their having 'pulled back' in their negotiations with HPC) was 'precarious', i.e. there appears to be a high chance that regulation

This article first appeared in *Ipnosis*, 28 October 2006

by HPC will be applied, whether BPS like it or not, during the passage of the Mental Health Bill later in the year. The meeting seemed fairly obviously a panic reaction to the latter possibility, but there was a second subtext: the prospect that, having devoured the BPS, the HPC would pick off the remaining organisations one by one. So ... how should psychopractice organisations respond to the Foster review's 10 November consultation deadline for comments on the regulation process?

The BPS, aided and abetted by BACP and UKCP but not, so far as we could tell, by the major psychoanalytic organisations, sought in the meeting to orchestrate support for first, unified (but polite and respectful) opposition to HPC and Foster and all his works; and second, a proposal for an alternative approach—regulation of counselling and psychotherapy via a Psychological Professions Council [PPC].

In the characteristic fashion of the mainstream psychopractice organisations, the UKCP, BACP and BPS had devised a 'draft', running to 36 pages, detailing how the PPC would be structured; however, only the 'partnership group' had seen the text before the meeting. Oh yes—and send comments/suggestions for the draft by 23 October please: a 'stitch-up', as a prominent UK professor of psychology later described it.

The meeting's tone of determined urgency strongly suggested that the BPS knows, or is close to certain, that they are up for imminent HPC regulation. The meeting was held in the BPS's chrome-and-glass City office and Professor Cooper, the prestigious BPS president (but what does he know or care about counselling and psychotherapy?), found time to chair the first hour before leaving for a meeting. One or two people voiced the opinion that the proposal for a PPC will be ignored by the DoH, since it can be read as a way of holding onto the current status quo while paying lip service to state regulation. Others felt that unless user groups, who as someone said would provide 'a leverage point', could be 'harnessed' in their support, the PPC notion would be seen as a further example of professional protection.

From an IPN regulation watcher's perspective it was hard to contain 'I told you so' responses. To reiterate and extend Nick Totton's excellent notion—'In seeking state regulation, psychotherapists and counsellors are not just turkeys voting for Xmas; they have also written the menu'—they now feel alarmed as they see the cook turning on the oven and getting ready to pluck, stuff and cook them.

When, a day or two after the meeting, Nicola Barden, Chair of BACP, wrote to participants and organisations who had not been able to attend, outlining what had been discussed, missing from her account were the urgency of the BPS's 'precarious position', and the possible domino consequences for UKCP and BACP of BPS being summarily imprisoned in the HPC.

These quotations give the flavour of her text:

There were several points of principle around which there was general agreement.

1. The Health Professions Council (HPC) is not fit for purpose as a regulator for the psychological professions. Its processes do not offer public protection in this field. The Foster Review, which offered no change to the regulatory framework

for the psychological professions, failed to address any of the concerns raised by the field in response to the consultation.

2. A united approach by the professional bodies holds the strongest promise of effecting a change of view in the Government regarding its approach to regulating the psychological professions.

3. The involvement of user groups would be a powerful and necessary part of developing a fit-for-purpose alternative to the HPC.

4. It is helpful to present the Government with a positive alternative to the HPC, as well as a critique of it and of Foster.

... The draft PPC is very open for discussion; *the general structure of a regulatory council around which the proposal is built is fairly standard and therefore difficult to alter.* [*Ipnosis* emphasis]

... Following 25 October, when there is a meeting of the 'partnership group' that originally considered this proposal (BPS, BACP and UKCP and a number of psychology organisations outwith BPS), and following feedback from the 'reference group', it may be possible to put together a shared statement with a list of signatures. This would be circulated to participants for agreement prior to any publication.

Ipnosis feels that it can't be said too often that the claimed inevitability of state regulation of psychotherapy has been a persistent trance induction generated by the mainstream psychopractice organisations over a period of at least a decade and a half. That its advent would involve cascades of government-led coercion and domination has been predictable for the whole of that time.

The inevitability trance denies a profound confusion of ends and means; if you have signed up to be state regulated, keep in mind that 'protection of the public' by regulation in anything like the form planned, HPC or PPC, will be overwhelmingly outweighed by the damage it will do to the user's experience of psychopractice services.

Background: The politics of marginality or opposition can often be very dispiriting, and morale is often sustained only by recalling that sometimes quite a small movement of the rudder will take the ship of state, or state regulation, to a different, more benign destination. Following a 21 October 2006, AHPP–sponsored meeting in Norwich, *'Statutory Registration—Where Are We Going?'*, I was again reminded by a colleague that a much neglected issue in the way that regulation was being pursued was *mandate*. The mainstream organisations did not have a mandate to negotiate with the DoH on my behalf, on IPN's behalf, or on behalf of the mass of other psychopractitioners who fit poorly or not at all into the regulation of counselling or psychotherapy straitjacket. How could we interrupt/contradict this?

CHAPTER THIRTY-THREE

An Historic Moment?

In his July 2006 letter to over a hundred stakeholder organisations Professor Louis Appleby, Director of Mental Health UK, asked The Independent Practitioners' Network [IPN] for support for the Department of Health proposals for the regulation of counselling, psychotherapy (is psychoanalysis too hot a potato to handle?). This request was parallel to the consultation on the Foster review of the regulation of non-medical health professions that closed on 10 November 2006

How to respond? Have we arrived at an historic moment—the point when the state begins to take control of the psychological therapies? And are we prepared to silently bystand it?

There is some evidence of an historic moment. At recent meetings that *Ipnosis* has attended (see Chapter 32) there have been clear signs of considerable 'despair', and even panic, in the mainstream accrediting institutions. Have mainstream insiders heard that the government is going to announce, contrary to mainstream opposition, that the HPC will be tasked with regulating the psychologists, and possibly psychotherapy and counselling as well? Add to this that the closing date for Foster review feedback falls a few days before the Queen's Speech when such an announcement might well be made ... is it a coincidence?

Several of us in IPN who have a history of concern about state regulation of psychotherapy, counselling and psychoanalysis feel that this does indeed appear to be an historic moment: another point at which it is essential to refuse to bystand the damage to the psychopractice field for practitioners and clients that state regulation is overwhelmingly likely to entail.

We responded to Professor Appleby's request by developing the following '*Statement of opposition to state regulation of counselling psychotherapy and psychoanalysis*', and asked people who support the statement to sign up to a list of endorsees that would be distributed as widely as possible.

Sponsors:
Guy Gladstone, group and individual psychotherapist, The Open Centre London, UKAHPP, IPN
Jill Hall, Psychotherapist, IPN
Sue Hatfield, IPN
(Dr) Richard House, Senior Lecturer in Psychotherapy and Counselling, RCTE, Roehampton University, and Magdalen Medical Practice, Norwich, IPN
Grace Lindsay, counsellor and teacher, IPN
Denis Postle, Psychotherapist, IPN

This article first appeared in Ipnosis, 14 November 2006

Statement of Opposition to the State Regulation of Psychotherapy, Counselling and Psychoanalysis

There are many reasons for opposing the state regulation of the psychological therapies. Among the range of arguments are the following:

1. No reputable or systematic research exists to demonstrate that counsellors, psychotherapists and psychoanalysts abuse or exploit clients on a scale that warrants the costs (financial, political, cultural and psychological) of state regulation.

2. The medicalised framing of current regulation proposals violates the public's right to choose practitioners who do not define them as patients suffering from illnesses or disorders, and who offer a rich variety of other models for human well-being and development.

3. Given the lack of evidence that regulation will effectively protect the public, it is difficult not to conclude that training and accrediting organisations have been promoting state regulation because it enables them to market state validation as an exclusive passport into practice, in turn justifying rising training costs and ever-higher academic attainment as key criteria for acceptance into training.

4. Existing research suggests (a) that good therapeutic outcomes are not demonstrably related to levels or types of training; (b) that good outcomes are strongly correlated with the successful creation of an effective helping relationship between practitioner and client.

5. Regulation based on training falsely promises that training guarantees good practice, and reliance on this unwarranted view in turn misleads the public: the ability to achieve good results ultimately counts for more than the level of training achieved, and this can only be effectively monitored through client feedback, supervision, case seminars and ongoing peer review.

6. A centralised monoculture of psychological regulation, gridlocking therapy into standardised training, competency and ethical criteria, is intrinsically inferior to the current diverse and appropriately local ecologies of psychological service provision. This rich diversity of the psychological therapies is a precious and desirable phenomenon.

7. It is not the proper business of the state to control the provision of counselling, psychotherapy and psychoanalysis. Such control can never be apolitical. State regulation of psychological therapies will compromise practitioner neutrality, lead to risk-averse practice and erode the client's freedom of choice.

State regulation will install a terminally damaging confusion of ends and means. If the end need is for 'client protection', the damage done to services delivered to clients by means of occupations that are statutorily regulated is likely to overwhelmingly outweigh any enhancement of their interests that might ensue.

Since psychopractice is ultimately a form of conversation between consenting others, the creation, funding and enhancement of service-user education and information would be far more cost-effective and beneficial to users than state regulation, which will be ineffective in minimising abuse or exploitation.

For some or all of these reasons amongst others—all of which have been argued and evidenced at length elsewhere—we, the undersigned, are of the opinion that the government should relinquish any intention statutorily to regulate the fields of counselling, psychotherapy and psychoanalysis.

*****

The statement, plus a shorter version by Nick Totton and the full list of endorsees at 8 November, were mailed to the Foster Review consultation desk; Professor Appleby, National Director of Mental Health; Nic Greenfield, Deputy Director of Workforce; Marc Lyal, programme manager, Skills for Health (a department under the employer-led umbrella of Skills for Business); and several of the mainstream psychopractice organisations that might not have seen it.

By 29 December 2006, the response to the two statements had been very substantial, approaching 500 sign-ups from across the whole spectrum of UK psychopractice. We decided to keep the list open for a few weeks/months, so as to reach as many as possible of the practitioners who have felt disenfranchised by the mainstream accrediting bodies' pursuit of state regulation. The opposition statement and the list of signatories can be found at: <http://ipnosis.postle.net/ SRStatementOpposition.htm>

Background: As the year (2006) draws to a close, I have been touched by the hundreds of people from across the whole spectrum of UK psychopractice who accepted the *Ipnosis*-sponsored invitation to sign up to our 'statements of opposition' to the state regulation of psychotherapy, counselling and psychoanalysis, thus publicly identifying themselves with the perception that state regulation would indeed be a 'huge mistake'.

Alongside this, the majority of members of the mainstream psychopractice organisations pay their dues and keep their heads down, having, often very unhappily I suspect, delegated their civic accountability to parent-like forms of occupational governance. This apparent passivity and herdangst continues to be disappointing. Yes, engaging with the exercise of power is messy and time-consuming. No, it doesn't pay the bills. And yet this is psychopractice. Might not the disconnect between the values lived daily in the therapy rooms and what happens in the boardrooms of the mainstream accrediting organisations be worthy of more psychological attention from those represented? And if not, why not? Is it because if they stop to feel it, many practitioners know very well that something deeply unpleasant, and incongruous with their values is being done in their name, with their support? And they choose to look the other way?

CHAPTER THIRTY-FOUR

Guilt Hardens the Heart?

Responses to the consultation phase of the Foster review of non-medical healthcare professions are now with the DoH. Those that *Ipnosis* has seen express very significant doubt about the Foster review which, as *Ipnosis* readers will recall, doesn't mention the psychological therapies at all, but lays out the terms under which the Health Professions Council will regulate them as a sector of the medical universe.

If you follow Will Schutz's excellent notion that significant doubt is a 'No', only the IPN participant's response calls a spade a spade, rather than an instrument of husbandry. It gathered several hundred signatures in less than two weeks for statements saying an unequivocal 'No' to any state regulation of the psychological therapies.

Not to be outdone by such a paltry few no-sayers, three days later the BPS and its new friends BACP and UKCP posted a press release declaring that '100,000 non-regulated professionals have said "No" to the Government's proposals for their statutory regulation. Nine professional bodies ... have worked together to develop an alternative of how their members might be best regulated to give the *public protection on a par with that guaranteed with Medical Practitioners'* [*Ipnosis* emphasis].

More accurately, as I have previously reported in 'The Penny's Dropped' (Chapter 32), coming face to face with the reality of taking delivery of their wish for state regulation provoked in the BPS and its allies a very unscientific panic-and-despair mindset. The result, in August/September 2006, was a quick and nasty defensive response to the DoH—sound a fanfare for the Psychological Professions Council [PPC]—(or should that be Permission Please to Control?).

With one very eloquent exception (Litten, 2006), other responses, so far as we have been able to gain access to them, say 'no' to Foster but dress up their bitter (and entirely justified) complaints about the report's inadequacy in pleading protestations along the lines of 'please regulate us, but also please make sure it doesn't hurt'—as though there were any possibility that state regulation of the nuanced subtleties of therapy could be implemented without damage and pain.

The process of taxonomy that ends in capture begins with counting—last year's UKCP/BACP 'mapping exercise' (see Chapter 24)—and then moves on to measurement. For example, while autumn (2006) is pretty much over, the DoH partners, Skills for Health, are no doubt readying their combine harvesters to cut and thresh, i.e. measure our counselling and psychotherapy competencies. Their

This article first appeared in Ipnosis, 18 November 18 2006

website is instructive; if you go up a layer or two you'll find that Skills for Health lives under the umbrella of the skills sector development agency Skills for Business.

> At the heart of the Skills for Business network are 25 Sector Skills Councils (SSCs). Each SSC is an employer-led, independent organisation that covers a specific sector across the UK.
>
> SSCs provide employers with a unique forum to express the skills and productivity needs that are pertinent to their sector.

Isn't this, to hit the irony switch, just what the psychological therapies need: a 'skills for business', 'employer-led' take on what matters in the work we do? That's what I mean by damage and pain; keep this in mind when the competency questionnaires arrive in your mailbox.

But hold on a minute: in writing that sentence I'm assuming that you will be consulted, that you belong to a democratic organisation; but isn't it more likely that the responses to the Skills for Health task of establishing psychotherapy and counselling competencies (leaving aside psychoanalytic competencies) will never reach you?

Come on, Denis, how could 50,000+ practitioners possibly agree a set of universal competencies with the Department of Health's contractors? No, that's a task for the mainstream organisations. After all, we can trust them (even if we are outside their remit); they are people of goodwill, they are well intentioned.

And, as Rosalind Mead of the DoH demonstrates in a recent rebuke to the UKCP, the mainstream accrediting institutions continue to have a capacity for a genteel, competitive brutality: a quality that the headlong pursuit of state endorsement of therapy professionalisation somehow seems to generate.

Brutality? Isn't that too strong? In the decade and a half that I have been a regulation watcher, a number of images have formed of the professionalisation/ regulation process: 'glaciation', 'stealing the flame', 'turning the gold of therapy into lead', 'domesticating therapy's wildness', 'making a walled garden out of a meadow', 'fencing off and claiming exclusive rights to a sector of the psychopractice prairie', 'taxonomy and taxidermy'. These intuitions continue to identify and name a domineering, imperial vision and an ultimately brutal culture of control and expropriation. That this is carried through by well-intentioned, gentle and subtle people is not in doubt. What they don't seem to see is that state regulation of psychopractice and the manipulation and spin that it entails have the same kind of brutality as building a motorway through a nature reserve; as though historically we were not at a time when, in psychosocial and physical landscapes, ecological diversity matters incomparably more than any taxonomy (count and measure) culture of barcoded skills. As I have already outlined (see Chapter 31), such a culture mutates into taxidermy.

In his poem *Choice*, Robert Alter warns that 'guilt hardens the heart'. I guess that the brutality of the pursuit of regulation by the mainstream organisations and their urgent desire to be recognised by the state as the experts on the human condition, gives rise to considerable amounts of guilt, perhaps due to the (half-conscious) perception that they are selling the soul of psychotherapy and counselling. Continuing to be a regulation enthusiast does appear to require a certain hardening of the heart, so that the damage that regulation will entail drops out of sight.

State regulation of psychopractice will cause damage. Daniel Hogan reminds us of the US experience:

> In addition to not protecting the public, licensing in the US tends to have negative side-effects. Irrelevant and higher-than-necessary entry requirements restrict the number of persons able to enter the professions. It also creates problems in the geographical distribution, since it is difficult for professionals licensed in one state to work in another. This results in a significant increase in the cost of professional services. Reliance on academic degrees results in serious discrimination against minorities, women, the aged, and the poor. And finally, licensing inhibits important innovations in professional practice, training, education, and organisation of services.
>
> In fact, according to some political scientists, the pervasiveness of licensing is an indication that the US is returning to a guild society reminiscent of the Middle Ages. Like the guilds, licensed professionals have established and enforced compulsory membership, creating a monopoly. Like the guilds, licensing standards have become higher and the cost of licensure has increased. Like the guilds, periods of apprenticeships have been lengthened, the number of apprentices has been restricted and the possibility of licensure through apprenticeship or work experience has generally been eliminated. (Hogan, 1999)

Ipnosis would like to see the underlying justificatory notion of 'protecting the client' rewritten as 'protecting the client's *experience*'. If we make this fundamental shift, isn't state regulation a non-starter?

It has been a matter of great delight in recent weeks to have discovered, through the response to the *Statements of Opposition to State Regulation of Counselling, Psychotherapy and Psychoanalysis* (see Chapter 33), a community of hundreds of practitioners who appear to share enough of this perspective with *Ipnosis* to be prepared to join us in publicly refusing to bystand the harm to the client's experience that state regulation will entail.

Thank you.

References

Alter, R *Choice*, undated poster

Hogan, D (1999) *Mindfield: Therapy on the Couch*. London: Camden Press, weblink page, <http://ipnosis.org/rpt.htm>

Litten, R (ed) (2006) Response to Department of Health Consultation Foster Review of the Regulation of the Non-Medical Healthcare Professions Association of Lacanian Analysts UK

Litten, R <http://ipnosis.postle.net/pages/RogerLArticle.htm>

Skills for Business <http://www.ssda.org.uk/>

CONCLUSION

Chickens to Wed Fox and Live in Henhouse?

At the time of writing, in the last days of 2006, the psychology, counselling and psychotherapy chickens, having seen the small print in the state-regulation marriage contract, have backed away from a wedding with the DoH fox and are privately in a twitter about what living in the HPC henhouse would mean.

Each party in this social insanity seems to be afflicted by a confusion of means and ends—a failure to realise that the means proposed to achieve the aim of protecting the public—state-defined and state-maintained professional standards—will in fact lead to lower standards, and hence poorer protection for the public. This long-apparent contradiction has ensured that the practical realities of the chosen destination of psychopractice professionalisation remained out of sight or, more accurately, that they disappeared into the shadow cast by the single-minded determination to be state regulated.

A catalogue of contradictions

That the UKCP is a trade association, with pretensions to being seen as a professional body, is not any longer controversial, I feel. The latest of its many structural contortions, the conversion of its Member Organisations [MOs] into 'Colleges', gives a more professional-sounding spin to the underlying imperative of commercial survival of almost all of them. This, along with the founding of a commercial company, the Independent Complaints Organisation [ICO] to make the processing of complaints more independent, appears to be a further attempt by UKCP to configure itself in a way that the Department of Health finds acceptable, and as the College of Psychoanalysts has suggested in an appraisal of the ICO, (weblinks page) of holding onto overall control in a post regulation profession.

Several other matters seem to have fallen into the fog of institutional denial. Firstly, there is an implicit assumption, as Pokorny, quoted in Chapter 10, points out, and as is underlined by the advent of the ICO, that current trainings and ensuing professional working practice are expected to produce therapists who will generate client complaints, as though this were not some reflection on training. Secondly, might not the lessons from the litigious culture of the US, increasingly being imported here, suggest that a complaints *company* such as ICO, coupled with compulsory practitioner insurance, will very likely feed a grievance culture, i.e. it will generate complaints? Thirdly, the bodies seeking to wed the government fox do not have a mandate from the psychopractice field as a whole for the pursuit of state regulation of psychotherapy, counselling and psychoanalysis. Just as Lord Alderdice could be so blinkered that he failed to notice the BACP counselling population, so the current regimes of regulatory truth don't seem to notice the extent of psychopractice in UK daily life.

For example, on a short walk through the area where I live in west London, I collected the following catalogue of practitioners who appear to fall outside any of the legislation currently being discussed, but who offer psychopractice services: Alexander Technique, Career Counselling, Chinese Palmistry and Face Reading, Crystal Healing, Nutritional Therapy, Past Life Regression, Personal Counselling, Reflexology, Reiki, Shiatsu, Soul Contract Reading, Tarot and Psychic Consultations, Bowen Technique, Lomi Lomi Massage, Aromatherapy Massage, Flotation Therapy, Pregnancy Massage, Thai Yoga Massage and Body Consciousness Realignment. Before you write off these offerings as 'New Age' or 'quackery', and not a legitimate part of psychopractice, it may be worth remembering Ros Mead's injunction in her *Next Steps* presentation of the DoH agenda for statutory regulation: 'Roles must reflect what service users and providers need, not just what professions provide or aspire to' (Ros Mead, 2006).

The state-regulation plans of mainstream psychological therapy accrediting bodies and the DoH do not even remotely have a mandate from these practitioners. And yet in London W4 they appear to be meeting the needs of people whose human condition is in need of care.

Are the UKCP and its partners ignoring, or asleep to, this wider population of practitioners? Or, as I suspect, are they pulling up the drawbridge to exclude them? If they succeed in rigging the market as I believe, unconsciously or not, they intend, this will certainly diminish, demean and distort public perception of a wide variety of such psychopractitioners, as well as those of us who decline to take part in the regulation folly.

Anne Richardson, Senior Adviser to the DoH, in a talk about statutory regulation at a BCP sponsored conference in 1997 that I have referred to in Chapter 6, had a clear sense of the value of such non-mainstream approaches to the human condition:

> Another thing that militates against [statutory regulation] is the increasing evidence of the effectiveness of a variety of approaches which some people wouldn't call psychotherapy. Some sorts of stress management ... you might not call it psychotherapy ... some forms of psycho-educational approaches ... you might not call psychotherapy, but others would and do. And there is good evidence for the effectiveness of some of these approaches with mental illness groups. So if you were to regulate or legislate you might stop that, prevent that diversity, and that would be unwelcome. (Richardson, 1997)

Ten years later, this perspective seems to have become buried in the DoH drive to taxonomise i.e. map, measure and capture the psychopractice field. Is this, we might ask, because the DoH is primarily concerned to regulate the NHS sector of psychopractice, and that it's only really a matter of unthought-through convenience and institutional vested interest that the rest of the psychopractitioner field is also being roped into the regulatory system? Here is what Marc Lyall, Skills for Health Programme Manager, had to say in a recent interview about the DoH psychological therapies 'competency mapping exercise' (Lyall, 2006):

Would these competences just be for those working in the NHS?
No, the National Occupational Standards (NOS) ... would be applicable to all
workers who work in the Health Sector across the UK, whether NHS, private,
voluntary or independent organisations.

Several other major contradictions arise from the massive incongruence of the
DoH approach to these matters.

The NICE Guidelines (weblink page) say that in treating, say, depression,
only evidence–based treatment should be given to patients and, if you read further
in the Guidelines, cost-effective practice. The universal answer is CBT, more akin
to a very successful 'brand' than the panacea its exponents extol, and something
that many psychopractitioners would deploy with some clients, some of the time.
In the universe according to NICE, CBT is the only *evidence-based* 'treatment' for
depression and panic attacks; their guidelines list countless literature references
that support CBT, as though a shortage of such forms of 'double blind trial' validity
for other ways of working with the human condition closed discussion about
therapeutic effectiveness. The threadbare nature of the 'scientific' arguments for
the alleged superiority of CBT are set out in great detail in House and Loewenthal
(forthcoming).

Evidence-based practice appears to be a core value at the DoH, and yet in its
approach to regulating the psychopractice field the evidence it presents of harm
to clients is idiosyncratic and hearsay, from lobbying groups and letters to the
DoH; exactly the kind of evidence that the DoH/NICE Guidelines use to discard
anything other than CBT. Here is what Andy Burnham, Minister of Delivery and
Quality for the Department of Health, had to say when I asked for sight of the
DoH evidence of practitioner harm:

> Mr Postle is interested to know what evidence the Department has to suggest
> practitioners of psychotherapy and counselling may harm patients. The
> Department's view is that since a large amount of material exists in the public
> domain concerning instances of abuse by psychological practitioners against their
> clients, we must take such allegations very seriously.

Note—no attempt is made to define what this allegedly '*large* amount' actually is.

> In addition, we understand that disciplinary action has been taken by professional
> bodies against practitioners on numerous occasions where client abuse has been
> alleged.

So how many, precisely?—and if that figure isn't available, why not?

> The Department has, over the years, received a large amount of correspondence
> from individuals who have claimed to be the victims of abuse perpetrated by
> therapists.

Again, *how much* correspondence, precisely?—and if not known, then why not?

> However, because of the high costs which would be involved in investigating
> these cases further, and also because permission has not been granted by the

authors of this correspondence to disclose this information, the Department has not progressed the correspondence. Neither has this material been made available to other parties as evidence.

So how do we know how large the number actually is? And just how seriously is the DoH taking this alleged (potentially illegal) abuse, if they've not bothered to pursue it?

> We have listened to organisations such as the Prevention of Professional Abuse Network and have seen their data concerning the number of calls, and cases advocated and supported. We have also talked to organisations that have been prepared to share their information about complaints and have also looked at independent research conducted into the area. The Department therefore considers that there is a case on abuse to answer and that this will inform our proposals to introduce legislation to regulate psychotherapists.
>
> I hope this reply is helpful.
>
> Andy Burnham
> Minister of State
> Department of Health

And here is the response to a Freedom of Information inquiry made of the DoH by an IPN participant.

> Q: *Is there any statistical data, research or other evidence pertaining to the incidence and severity of harm or abuse caused to patients or clients by psychotherapists and counsellors?*
>
> A: I should inform you that the Department does have correspondence concerning individual cases where harm allegedly occurred. However, as they are not claims the Department investigated directly, they would not fall into the category of 'evidence'.

But you *could* give numbers of letters/complaints received, and over what time period.

> Further, the Department does not have permission from the authors to disclose their personal details. The Department has, however, listened to organisations such as POPAN (the Prevention of Professional Abuse Network) and has seen their data concerning the number of calls, cases advocated and supported. Departmental officials have talked to organisations that have been prepared to share their information about complaints and have also looked at independent research conducted into the area. By these means, the Department has been convinced that there is a case on abuse to answer.

As I have earlier estimated, (see Chapter 27), there are probably in excess of 20 million psychopractice contact hours annually. Holding this figure in mind, ask yourself: is the amount of practitioner abuse of which you are anecdotally aware significant? Significant enough to remotely justify the scale, form or cost, of the state regulation that is being planned? Not for me or any of the practitioners I know.

That there is abuse and harm due to ethical transgressions, incompetence and misunderstandings that occur in psychopractice is not for me an issue. But is its prevalence significant enough to justify the glaciation of UK psychopractice by state regulation, and how else might any harm be eliminated? These are questions that remain unanswered and unresearched—and ignored by policymakers and psycho-institutions alike, notwithstanding numerous challenges over the years emanating from like-minded colleagues and myself.

There is another equally harmful and deeply embedded problem: the sleep-walking buy-in by the UKCP, BACP and other organisations into an archaic and outdated culture of complaints.

Why am I so convinced this is problematic?

Fit-for-purpose quality assurance

One of the virtues of being of a certain age is that life experience accumulates across diverse boundaries, often with unexpected results. Shortly after completing a lengthy training as a facilitator, I was hired to be part of a team of people developing for the Ford Motor Company what we would now call a multimedia approach to quality assurance.

Initially I had thought I would only be directing drama enactments for this enterprise. As development started, I began to see that there was a curiously exact fit between the quality assurance that Ford was bringing to bear on its automotive production and the cooperative inquiry/experiential inquiry process with which I been had been involved in the previous five or six years. Both were iterative, implemented as cycles of action, reflection and feedback, along with validity checks.

In a nutshell, up to this point in time, the mid 80's, Ford's quality assurance was based around input quality assurance—*inspection and rejection*. The tolerances, i.e. sizes, weight, strength, texture and other qualities of automotive parts they made in house, such as gearboxes, and those that they received from suppliers, were checked and if they were found to be 'out of spec.' the item was binned, either for scrap or rework. However, the quality inspectors constantly missed faulty parts or assemblies, the result being expensive and wasteful errors—clunky gearboxes, doors that didn't close properly, and engines or transmissions that leaked oil—faults that came to light only *when buyers complained.*

Decades earlier, Far Eastern vehicle manufacturers had picked up proposals from an American production engineer, W. Edwards Deming (2000) which resolved these difficulties by shifting quality assurance from inspect and reject to scrutiny of the process of production itself, so that responsibility for quality was devolved to each individual operator, who in turn was embedded in an ongoing quality assurance process.

The programme we were developing was designed to transform Ford's scrap or rework culture into one where there was this kind of constant vigilance at every stage of production. The essential ingredients were: specifying the quality to be attained, verifying the capability of the process for delivering it, and the essential innovation: continuous monitoring of manufacturing output—so that if production of an item was seen to be drifting 'out of spec.' production was stopped until the process was corrected. So far as this output-based quality assurance process was followed, production became almost entirely error-free. The manufacture of most commonplace hi-technology items, from computers to video cameras and recorders, would be entirely impractical without such Deming-style quality assurance.

UKCP, BACP, BPS and BCP and HPC run and propose to continue with an input quality assurance system that primarily detects out-of-specification practitioner behaviour after it has become a problem, *i.e. when a client has complained about it*. Very inequitably, the client is cast in the role of 'quality inspector'. After investigation of the alleged behaviour, if serious error is proven, the practitioner is 'struck off', i.e. binned for scrap (HPC, 2006).

Is it not inevitable that such a fear-based system also inhibits practitioner/ practitioner whistle-blowing and leads to a 'defensive psychotherapy'? Yes, I'm aware that there is a long tradition, of supervision but that may often (and necessarily) be focused on the content of client work. Continuing Professional Development [CPD] is also an element in regulation plans, but how seriously do practitioners take an imposed CPD requirement—is it little more than a spin-driven chimera to give the *appearance* that accountability is being taken seriously? I believe that without long-term, output practitioner quality assurance based on long-term, face-to-face contact/disclosure with peers, supervision and CPD are insufficient to ensure that working alliances with clients will be free of contamination by the unresolved personal issues that lead to abuse or exploitation. The input-based state-regulation process administered by the HPC, which forms the basis of the Foster report recommendations on non-medical regulation, has all these damaging limitations, as does the counterproposal for a Psychological Professions Council.

The consortium of accrediting bodies who favour the PPC have hitherto been compliant with the DoH taxonomy process of mapping, counting and measuring, and generally becoming 'fit for purpose' in DoH eyes; but they couldn't stomach the prospect of actual capture, (by the HPC), i.e. State Regulation. Shortly before this text went to press, the nine organisations in this consortium (six appear to be subsections of the BPS, and there were no psychoanalysts) issued a press release, declaring that '100,000 non-regulated psychologists opposed government plans to regulate them' (weblink page). They await the government's next move. It's test of nerve for both parties.

Civic acountability and protecting the client's experience

As I recount in Chapter 25, at the close of a meeting towards the end of 2005 of the Department of Health regulation 'reference group', which included the DoH lead manager for regulation, a colleague, Richard House, asked her and the meeting to consider whether, as he put it, 'Aren't you making a huge mistake?' It is perhaps the most succinct statement about the state regulation of psychopractice I know, and as readers of this book who have reached this point will appreciate, I wholeheartedly support it.

How, I ask, having been a trainer and a member of a training organisation, can the Huge Mistake of psychopractice regulation be avoided? A better way of framing the question would be to ask 'How can practitioner/client accountability'— notice both in the same phrase—'be better implemented, in ways that protect the client's experience or that enhance it?'

Already in place to an extent, via the multiplicity of psychopractitioner sites on the internet, is an informal version of a proposal I have made for a public Full Disclosure Practitioner List (see Chapter 22). Its key element, disclosure, though problematic for psychoanalytic practitioners, I argue is the missing ingredient that brings together the accountability needs of both client and practitioner, having the potential to reduce the level of disputes between them to close to zero.

In the event that an Order in Council is enacted to enable the HPC to capture counselling, psychotherapy and psychanalysis, the DoH seem presently unlikely to support a scheme such as the Full Disclosure List, which would be in competition with state regulation—what else might be liveable?

I have long felt that a UK version of US psychotherapy licensing opt-outs could easily, with the requisite political will, provide a relevant alternative for those of us who are not prepared to allow state regulation to compromise client experience. Suppose, for instance, that UK practitioners who are opposed to state regulation lobbied the DoH for the inclusion in any Order in Council of a UK version of the Vermont State's provision for a 'Roster of Psychopractitioners Who Are Non-Certified and Non-Licensed' (weblink page). To paraphrase the Vermont legislation, the purpose of this would be:

- To ensure that consumers of psychotherapy services are provided with the information relating to the training and qualification of nonlicensed and noncertified providers of psychotherapy necessary to enable them to make informed decisions concerning their choice of providers.

- That psychotherapists who are nonlicensed and noncertified are entered on a roster and practice according to standards of professional conduct which they declare, along with the grievance/mediation procedures to which they are committed, including the sanction of removal from the list, if they fail to adhere to those standards.

Such a roster should, as Daniel Hogan proposes:

> ... promote client autonomy and responsibility. Licensing laws are not meant to ensure a high level of professional competence, only that a practitioner is not likely to harm the public. This means that licensing laws should adopt minimum requirements for entrance into a profession, and these requirements should be clearly related to minimally competent practice. In this regard, licensing laws should emphasise the regulation of output, not input ... they should be concerned with a person's actual skills, not how those skills were obtained. Since so little is known about the effective training and selection of professionals, a further purpose of licensing should be to promote a pluralistic system for the delivery of professional services ...

… Regulation through registration, in which practitioners are required to register with a government agency but are not required to meet any academic or other prerequisites, is the most desirable form of regulation … Registration allows all people to practise so long as they provide certain information to the state. Practitioners can, however, be removed from the roles if they engage in incompetent, harmful or unethical activity. Registration has the advantage of bringing all [psychopractitioners] into the fold. (Hogan, 2000)

I am wary of proposing any version of state involvement in psychopractice; however, the UK psychological trade associations may succeed in their desire to wed the HPC fox and learn to live together in the henhouse of state regulation. Were this to happen, a Vermont-style 'non-licenced, non-certified' roster, that could include the diverse range of psychopractitioners I describe earlier in the chapter, may turn out to be an essential alternative that might well have support from Human Rights and Office of Fair Trade legislation.

Best-practice accountability

I'm going to end by floating a different but related proposition aimed at cultivating protection of the clients' experience and civic accountability of practitioners: that in the event of state regulation, all licensed and certified practitioners be required to become a member of an ongoing quality assurance group, i.e. a civic accountability group, with a minimum of five and a maximum of say, seven members who, with or without facilitation, meet regularly for a considerable number of hours a year; and who are charged with getting to know each other well enough as persons and as practitioners to be able to formally 'stand by', i.e. take responsibility (alongside supervision) for holding quality assurance of each other's work. Such a group process would take time, energy, and commitment, and a level of relating skills and emotional competence (Postle, 2003) that might be supposed to be at the heart of effective psychopractice.

The groups would be tasked with defining for themselves what would count as competence criteria and, alongside this, with getting to know enough about the work and life of each of its members to be able realistically to stand by their work. As this shared responsibility came into being, the group would be in a position both to monitor any life changes that might have unhelpful effects on a member practitioner's abilities, while holding the sanction of ejection from the group for any failure to adequately address concerns that the group raised.

Through their continuous mutual scrutiny, such groups would honour accountability to clients through reducing to close to zero the likelihood of abuse occurring; at the level of mistakes or disputes, they would provide an immediate forum for client contact; and for practitioners working with deeply problematic material, such as suicidal impulses, these could be declared and processed within the group, the better for both them and the practitioner to be held. As they form, such groups would benefit from (and could be required to engage with) outside facilitation of their group process, i.e. was the level of engagement appropriate to the group task of mutual accreditation; was there sufficient awareness of, and confrontation of, collusion?

And yes, the reader might wonder: what point is there in these proposals? Aren't they too little, too late? Perhaps … but that is only the case as long as the political will is missing to embrace, and institutional vested interests prevail over, such a rigorous accountability alternative. Would they ever work? What I describe, and in the form closely resembling what I describe, is already implemented and has been running for almost a decade and a half in the form of the Independent Practitioners' Network. If you like the sound of it, sign up and take the first step towards embracing best-practice accountability.

References

Deming, WE (2000) *The New Economics for Industry, Government, Education, 2nd Edition* Cambridge, MA: MIT Press

Health Professions Council < http://www.hpcuk.org/assets/documents/1000179FHPC_In_Focus_Issue_8.pdf (p4)>

Hogan, D (1999) Protection not Control. In *Mindfield: Therapy on the Couch*. London: Camden Press

House, R and Loewenthal, D (eds) (forthcoming) *Against and For CBT*. Maidenhead: McGraw-Hill Education. Open University Press

IPN Briefing Document: <http://i-p-n.org/static/IPNBriefing07.pdf>

IPN User Guide: <http://users.i-p-n.org/ipn-documents/ipn-user-guide/>

IPN What is IPN? <http://i-p-n.org>

Litten, R (ed) (2006) Response to Department of Health Consultation Foster Review of the Regulation of the Non-Medical Healthcare Professions Association of Lacanian Analysts UK

Lyall, M (2006) Mapping Competencies Interview. In *Therapy Today*, December: 43

Mead,R (2005) Statutory regulation of Psychotherapy and Counselling. *Next Steps* Psychotherapy and counselling reference group, Powerpoint presentation DoH:14

Postle, D (2003) *Letting the Heart Sing: The Mind Gymnasium*. CD-ROM, WLR

Schutz, W (1979) *Profound Simplicity*. USA: Joy Press

POSTSCRIPT

Diagnosing Rogue Status

> UKCP remains committed to preventative legislation to inhibit therapists who
> do not meet enforced training and ethical standards, and to safeguarding the
> public against unsafe or rogue therapists.
> Lisa Wake Chair, 23 February 2007 (from an email to registrants)

On 21 February 21 2007, six weeks after the main body of this book was finalised,
the Government was due to issue its promised White Paper on regulation of the
psychological therapies. When I rang the DoH media desk to ask if it had been
posted, the voice said 'do you mean the Shipman White Paper'? 'No', I said, 'the
one that deals with psychological therapies', after a pause the voice reassured me
that the Shipman White Paper did indeed deal with the psychological therapies.

The White Paper, *Trust, Assurance and Safety— the Regulation of Health
Professionals in the 21st Century*, is a further government response to the perceived
catastrophic failures of existing medical regulation. In the document's hundred
pages, counselling and psychotherapy only merit a few paragraphs, in Section 7,
pp. 81–5. They announce that no new regulator will be created and that the
Health Profession Council's one-size-fits-all, medicalised, 'health' mode of
regulation, is set to prevail.

The quotation at the top of this page arrived from a correspondent as I was
finalising this Postscript, a handy reminder that UKCP, along with BACP and
BCP, continue to claim that state regulation of the psychological therapies is
necessary to protect clients from 'rogue' practitioners. A dubious category, but let
us take Lisa Wake seriously and play with it for a moment. Who else might be
thought to qualify? Over recent decades this emphasis on 'rogue' practitioners
has masked the existence of dysfunctional institutional behaviour in the
psychopractice field that I feel itself merits 'rogue' status, as I hope will be clear
from this book.

Ethically high standards for practitioners commonly include self-reflexivity,
i.e. sufficient awareness of blind spots to ensure they don't unwittingly impose
their worldview on others, don't misuse the power of language to entrance and
mislead, and abstain from force or coercion with clients or colleagues.

Do the above listed institutions themselves practise the ethical standards
that they might be supposed to advocate for registrants? The answer, as readers
will have divined from previous chapters, is no. Not only are they not ethically
squeaky clean, their institutional style has been characterised by the attempted
annexation of psychopractice territory, un-mandated representation, trance-
inductions, and inter-institutional bullying. While at one level well intentioned,
too much of their behaviour has seemed incongruous of their claim to embody

the highest ethical standards, qualifying them, I suggest, for 'rogue' status as institutions.

If we ask the same question of the DoH who, following a decade of lobbying, have picked up the regulatory agenda from the training/accrediting bodies, what do we find? How congruent are they with the ethical standards they promote? Do they merit the 'rogue' epithet too?

Despite its title, the entire contents of the Foster report, *The regulation of the non-medical healthcare professions*, referred to medical matters relevant only to the NHS, or people adjacent to it; neither psychotherapy nor counselling, let alone psychoanalysis, is mentioned; submissions to the cosmetic Foster consultation that overwhelmingly dismissed the HPC as an appropriate regulator for the psychological therapies field were apparently completely ignored. As I report in Chapter 32, the Foster review was held internally by the DoH to be 'appalling', 'inept', and 'excruciatingly embarrassing' and yet, as we saw above, Foster's recommendation that there will be no other regulator than the HPC for the psychological therapies has been adopted as government policy. A decision based on 'fitness to practise'?

While only the tip of an iceberg, the frequent reference to 'objective/ objectivity', fourteen times in the seventy-two pages of the Foster review, and twenty times in the hundred pages of the recent White Paper, points to a DoH culture that has become unhelpfully technocratic, and ignorant about 'meaning-making'—hermeneutics. Alongside this, and highly incongruous, the DoH argues strenuously for evidence-based 'health-care' practice, but its *Next Steps* in regulating the psychological therapies deny the need for systematic research evidence of significant harm due to psychological malpractice. Finally and more important, the February 2007 DoH White Paper seems entirely unaware that the imposition, via the HPC, of a 'mental health', 'medical', model of human functioning on the psychological therapies is massively incongruous and potentially constitutes a gross abuse of power that is likely to raise Office of Fair Trading, and even Human Rights, legislative issues.

With the caveat that I appreciate from personal contact these attempts to grasp the chimera of state regulation are being shaped by the best of *conscious* intentions, the White Paper, *Regulation of Health Professionals in the 21st Century*, arguably qualifies the DoH to join the catalogue of institutions that merit 'rogue' status.

And continued resistance.

INDEX

abuse, 245
domination and client, 111, 134
  sexual, 104
  therapeutic, 98
accountability, 46, 159–66, 191–5, 218
  best-practice, 249–50
  civic, 247–9
  to clients/peers, 47–8
  criteria for adequate client, 192–3
  criteria for practitioner, 50–1,
  government-sponsored, 165
  input vs output, 208
  new kind of, 160
  output, 205
Adaption/Innovation Theory, 70–2
adaptive creative style, 71–5 *passim*
AHPP, 22, 23, 27, 57
'Alchemists' Nightmare – Gold into Lead'
(Postle), 45–80, 98, 108, 180
Alderdice, Lord (John), 90, 92, 110, 121, 139
  acrimony with the BAC, 136–7, 141
  Psychotherapy Bill, 120, 121, 128–33
  passim, 137, 139, 141, 142
Anderson, Jill, 20
Appleby, Professor Louis, 223–5, 231, 235
Association of Humanistic Psychology
Practitioners: *see* AHPP
audit/surveillance culture, 199
authority, 105

BACP, 150, 160, 169, 170,
  Mapping Project, 173–5, 177
  name change of, 144
  see also British Association for Counselling
Barden, Nicola (BACP), 232
Bates, Yvonne, 125
BCP, 24, 58–9, 72, 77, 90, 102, 120, 150, 151, 160
  'seniority' of, 60–1
BPS, 28, 160, 207, 231–2
Breggin, Peter, 96
British Association of Behavioural and Cognitive
Psychotherapists (BABCP), 151
British Association for Counselling
  acrimony with Lord Alderdice, 136–7, 141
  see also BACP
British Association for Counselling and
Psychotherapy: *see* BACP
British Confederation of Psychotherapists: *see* BCP
British Psychological Society: *see* BPS
bullying, 110
Burnham, Andy, MP, 244–5
bystanding (Clarkson), x

Cambridge Conferences on accreditation (1991–
2), 47, 99
Case Against Psychotherapy Registration, The
(Mowbray), xv, 33, 64, 95–7
Casement, Anne, 40, 64, 93, 94, 120
CBT: *see* Cognitive Behavioural Therapy

charlatan creation, 100–1
Clarkson, Petruska, x,
  advertisement, 28
  Open Letter to the UKCP/Janet Boakes, 29,
  141–2
client benefits, 103
client disputes, 161
  see also complaints
client education, 160, 164
client empowerment, 21
client experience,
  feedback of, 159
  protecting the, xii–xviii, 115–18, 241, 247–9
client harm, 198–9
client protection, 191
client resourcefulness, 159–60
co-counselling, 22, 125–6
Cocking, Dr Graham (ISPC), 153
Cognitive Behavioural Therapy, xv, 198, 244
College of Psychoanalysts, 169, 242
competence
  defining standards of, 152
  practitioner, 161
  sustaining practitioner, 160
competencies, 177–81 *passim*
Competencies and Roles Analysis (DoH), 197
complaints, 84
  standardised procedures, 108
  UKCP procedures, 126
  see also client disputes
Complaints and Grievances in Psychotherapy
(Palmer-Barnes), 87–8, 91
confidentiality, 117, 162
Continuing Professional Development (CPD),
146, 159, 160, 247
Continuing Self and Peer Assessment and
Scrutiny (CSPA and S), 160–1
  see also self and peer assessment
Cook, Grace Lindsay, 235
Co-operative Inquiry, 49, 126, 183–8, 212, 246
  defined, 184
COSCA, 169
Coulson, Christopher, 61–2
counselling: vs psychotherapy, 209–10
creative style, 70–5
  adaptive, 71–5 *passim*
  innovative, 71–5 *passim*
  see also creativity
creativity: compromising of, 67, 195
  see also creative style
credentialling, 159

defensive practice/psychotherapy, 67, 247
defining psychotherapy, 104, 209
Deming, W. Edwards, 246
Department of Health (DoH), 172, 177, 179, 252
dissent, 95–100
  dismissed as pathology, 76
diversity, 67–70